THE EDGE OF THE SWORD

Echoes of War

THE EDGE OF
THE SWORD

ANTHONY FARRAR-HOCKLEY

BUCHAN & ENRIGHT, PUBLISHERS
LONDON

First published in 1954 by Frederick Muller Ltd.

This edition first published in 1985 by
Buchan & Enright, Publishers, Limited
53 Fleet Street, London EC4Y 1BE

British Library Cataloguing in Publication Data
Farrar-Hockley, *Sir*, Anthony
   The edge of the sword.—(Echoes of war)
   1. Korean War, 1950–1953—Prisoners and prisons
   2. Korean War—Personal naratives, British
   3. Prisoners of war—Great Britain
   I. Title   II. Series
   951.9'042'0924   DS921
   ISBN 0–907675–50–6

Printed in Great Britain by
Redwood Burn Limited, Trowbridge, Wiltshire and
bound by Pegasus Bookbinding, Melksham, Wiltshire
Cover printed by The Furnival Press, London

CONTENTS

To

My comrades,

the Officers and Men

of the 29th Independent

Infantry Brigade Group

FOREWORD

by

Major-General T. Brodie, CB, CBE, DSO

This book is the story of The Glosters in the Imjin Battle in Korea.

It is also the story of how officers and men of the Glosters, Ulster Rifles, 5th Fusiliers, 8th Hussars, Gunners, Sappers, Doctors and Padres fought, not only in the battle, but again in captivity under appalling conditions and with inhuman captors.

Captain Farrar-Hockley, then Adjutant of The Glosters, who himself was outstanding in the battle and afterwards, has written the most graphic account of a battle and of escapes from captivity I have ever read.

This is a book which ought to be read by every soldier and prospective soldier.

Here he may learn what is meant by real discipline and inspiring leadership, of the part played by Regimental traditions and the Regimental spirit in proper units, and to what heights men can rise because of them.

He, and the civilian too, may see why the British have still got something that the rest of the world envies.

I am indeed honoured to be asked to write a foreword to this book. I am prouder to have known so well all the officers and men mentioned in it.

Headquarters
1st Infantry Division
MELF. 27

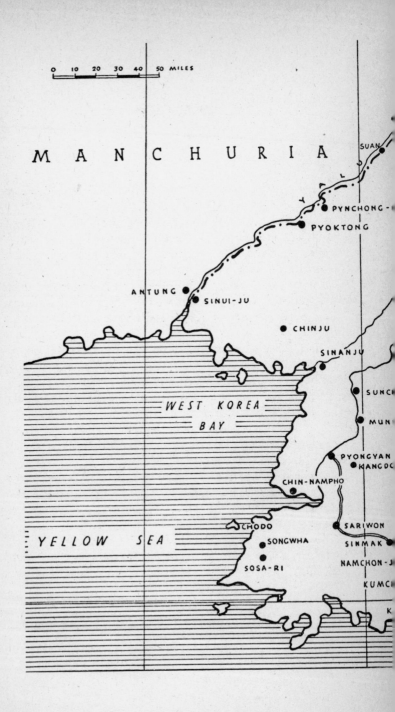

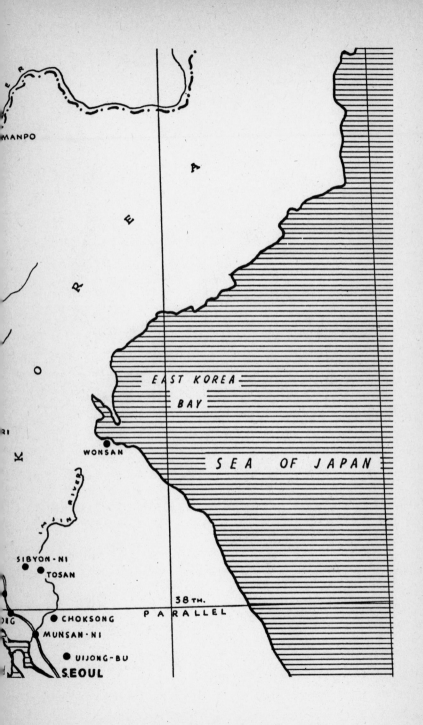

WESTERN
CROSSING

CHANGNAM-MYON

Chajipo

Chun

Changiwa-ri

Hyansong-
ni

Kwan

Chajang-ni

Tuji

Sikhyon-ni

TOKCH'ON

PART ONE
THE BATTLE OF THE IMJIN RIVER

PROLOGUE

THERE had been no movement along the entire Battalion front for days, but for an occasional old, white-robed Korean peasant, too rooted to his land to be transplanted by war.

No movement along the northern bank of the winding Imjin River, now lazy, slow, and somnolent in the dry April.

No movement upon the red Sindae feature where Terry and Alan had sought and found the enemy standing patrols, since vanished; nor yet across the Gloster Crossing among the hills, where we had searched so diligently with the tanks of the Eighth Hussars —a fruitless, two-day search across twelve miles of No-Man's Land, looking for an enemy with whom to do battle.

No movement.

And yet, of course, they had not gone. The push north across the Han River had but temporarily defeated them; for they were so many and we so few. Now they had withdrawn far, far beyond our reach, to gather for another blow; to draw fresh multitudes from China's wealthy manpower account; to fill their forward magazines and armouries; to fan their forces' fury for the fight with yet another tale of lies.

And so we waited; and as we waited, so we watched.

Forward on Castle Hill, commanding the long spurs that rose almost from the southern bank of the river, holding in part the hard dirt road that ran through the cutting along their right flank, was A Company, Pat's boys, so like the rest in that they were a mixture of both seasoned and green men; in that they knew themselves to be, assuredly, the best men in the whole Battalion. Yet different, in that they were stamped by Pat's own character, and marked by their own past record in battle and at rest.

Across the road, laying claim to some of the houses of Choksong, whose dwellings straddled it, was D Company, guarding the eastern flank of the road that led from the river: the road which crossed Gloster Crossing to wind north among the hills through countless villages and hamlets to the broken streets of Sibyon-ni. Spread forward along a feature just higher than Castle Hill, D Company patrolled forward with A Company nightly and watched by day the hills and valleys across the river bank. From this high hill, Lakri would descend to meet Pat on the neutral ground of the road before repairing to a hut in either's territory for a cup of tea and, when this needed justification, a co-ordinating conference.

At the top of the pass, the road curved west before descending again to divide in the broad valley behind Pat's defences. One fork continued to the south, entering the hills once more between high cliffs on whose western crest Spike's Pioneers secured Hill 235. And to the east, from where the gorge began, C and B Companies were disposed with their backs to the jagged crest of Kamak-San that towered above all other features within sight.

Sam's flock—Support Company—was ever a scattered one; no less around this Choksong defensive position than elsewhere. For Spike's platoon were infantry; the anti-tank platoon were jacks-of-all-trades; Theo's machine-gunners were scattered about the hills where their sturdy, reliable water-cooled Vickers might pour their fire to best advantage into an attacking force. Only Graham's mortars were concentrated; the square pits dug in between the road and the stream that ran behind C Company to turn ninety degrees by the ford, from where it ran across the valley north to Choksong. And on either side of the ford lay Battalion Headquarters.

Here stood the weathered old Command Vehicle, Haskell's pride, so like the Grand Old Duke of York; around it the signals vehicles and Guy's gunner GMC. Here was the Regimental Aid Post, where Bob dispensed medicine on all days and sherry on Sundays; where Mills provided massage for the weary. Here were the Snipers, resting perhaps from a long day immobile in a forward "hide", as they searched the hills with their telescopes or binoculars. Here were the Provost positions, their Bren gun covering the road up to Choksong. Here were Corporal Watkins, Stockley, and the cook-house helpers ready to make the next meal on their improvised ranges. Here was a tent, some said luxuriously appointed within, marked "RSM", from which might now emerge the robust figure of the Physical Training Instructor—aptly named Strong—who shared it with the owner. Forward, the Drums were dug in on either side of the road. Here, by the ford, was a sign that said "56-MAIN". This was the centre around which the 1st Battalion, The Gloucestershire Regiment, lived and fought in the area of Choksong.

But this was not all. Forward here, with the fighting element of the Battalion, was Frank's heavy mortar troop. That "independent" mortar troop! Surely, even the egregious Support Company could hardly surpass that seasoned, well-knit body of old sweats: yet not so old that they could not nip nimbly enough to the long 4.2 inch mortars that they fired so ably.

And forward, too, Guy's gunner Observation Post parties: young Bruce with A Company; Ronnie with D Company; and imminently joining Denis's Company Headquarters, Recce.

Four miles behind this line, Rear Headquarters harboured the administrative vehicles, turned back the unwanted from the rear, welcomed those weary ones who needed relief from the eternal night watches. Behind them were John, and Colour-Serjeant Fletcher, forever promising to bring socks up to the Regimental Sergeant-Major. And back in Uijong-bu were Freddie and 'B' Echelon, indenting, submitting, requesting, inviting, demanding, stealing the many things we needed daily.

Somewhere between—and a little to the east—were disposed the 25-pounder pieces of the 45th Field Regiment, including our own 70th Field Battery—Guy's Battery. Like the eyes that watched ceaselessly from A and D, B and C, in their Observation Posts, in their night Listening Posts along the river, on the peaks of the hills and in the valleys; like the ears that listened beneath the wireless and telephone head-sets along the signal nets; like the hands that waited by the mortars and machine-guns, by the surgical instruments and the dressings, the gunners were waiting.

All of us were waiting.

We waited until the 22nd of April, 1951. On that day the battle began.

CHAPTER ONE

22nd April, 1951

SHAW drove me back from Brigade Headquarters where I had been to see Boris. It was a fine mild afternoon as the jeep drove north along the road which wound among the hills. As we passed Rear Battalion Headquarters, I saw the Assistant Adjutant, Donald, and we waved to one another. I would have liked to stop but I had been away for almost three hours and it was high time I was back.

The earth and the wind smelt of April; the hillsides, as yet bearing the winter skeletons of shrub and dwarf oak, were plainly alive with new life. We reached the top of the ascent below Kamak-San, and Shaw put her into top gear as we ran on down the light slope through the gorges that led to our destination. I lit a pipe and we chatted until, rounding the last long corner, we came to the ford and the little temporary village of vehicles and holes in the ground which we called "home".

Shaw went off to do some maintenance and I walked over to the Command Vehicle. Richard, the Signal Officer, met me on the steps:

I said: "Where's Henry?"

"He's gone off with the Colonel."

"Where?"

"They're all down at the river. There's some sort of flap on. I thought you'd heard," said Richard.

Well, I hadn't heard, but I got the scout car and made off down the road towards Choksong. On the way, Yates, the driver, told me that, only an hour or two since, OPs had spotted enemy movement making south towards Gloster Crossing. It was no great push as yet: only very small parties, and very few of these—probably reconnaissance patrols. But how very odd that, after concealing

15

their hand for so long, they should alert us by sending down daylight patrols that couldn't keep themselves concealed. Was it a deliberate blunder, only a deception; or was it the real thing done by parties of rather badly trained soldiers? I thought all this over as we passed through Choksong and bumped on northwards towards the little cutting through the last low hill that barred our way to Gloster Crossing.

At the cutting, we stopped. Yates concealed the scout car in one of the many open dugouts and I made my way forward on foot. The road ran round a small bend and there, quite suddenly, one was out in the open, in full view of any enemy across the river.

Between the cutting and the river, it was flat rice paddy; flat to the edge of the river which had worn down the soil through the centuries until, now, the bed was twenty, thirty—in some places forty feet—below the top of its banks. On the very edge of the south bank lay a ruined village: a tumbled, charred wreck of a village, whose dwellings, however humble by Western standards, had nonetheless been home to their poor occupants before war had drawn two armies back and forth across the land. Among the crazy roofs, the tottering walls that remained, the 1st ROK Division had dug a network of open trenches during the defence of the river at Christmas time, 1950.

Across the rice paddy, the road ran upon a low embankment, crossed a slightly higher bund at right angles, to enter the village and form a crossroads, only to desert the houses once more as it plunged down steeply through a cutting to the very water's edge.

Originally, perhaps for generations, the road had been but a poor cart track, hardly capable of carrying tracked, much less wheeled, vehicles in wet weather. But the Sappers had widened and strengthened it, had laid steel-mesh matting upon a re-graded surface in the cutting and, by now, had set a series of marker buoys showing the course of the underwater bridge; a ford which the Koreans had built and used long before the Japanese had established their rule throughout the land.

This was Gloster Crossing.

Along the bund to the right of the road, a small group of figures were lying on their stomachs observing the opposite bank. After a second glance, I picked out the Colonel and Henry, the Intelligence Officer, and went over to them.

"What's up, Henry?"

He wriggled his way up to the edge of the bund.

"Over there," he said, pointing. "That's the fourth group we've seen—just a few men. The Colonel has got the mortars on to them."

A moment or so later there was a series of tiny flashes on the edge of the hill, over the river; a series of puffs of black smoke that disappeared swiftly in the light wind.

"That ought to tickle them a bit," said Henry.

The Colonel put his glasses down and began to look at his map. I joined him.

"This looks like the real thing," he said. "It may only be a feint—we've had all these other reports about patrol action to the east; but I don't think that it is. We'll have a fifty per cent stand-to, to-night. I think C Company had better put an ambush party on Gloster Crossing—a strong fighting patrol. They'd better come down immediately after last light. I'll brief the patrol commander myself."

I went back to the scout car and we drove back to Battalion Headquarters, where I wrote the signal about the scale of sentries and alertness, and telephoned Paul, to warn him about the ambush party. Paul said it would come from Guido's platoon; and that he and Guido would be down for the briefing.

The light was fading as Henry came up the steps into the Command Vehicle and said: "The party on Gloster Crossing is in position."

"Just let everyone know, Henry," said the Colonel.

In front of my built-in desk was the one-inch map on which were marked our positions: chinagraph symbols that formed a comprehensible if uneven pattern; symbols that translated the business of defending the approach along this country road to Seoul, the capital, from the personal to the impersonal. Yet here, in an

17

infantry battalion headquarters, in the quiet that only the passing of the stream disturbed, we knew what other watchers at higher echelons could not know in the same detail: each hill, each trench, each weapon, and, above all else, each man who would be fighting when the battle was joined.

I looked across at the Colonel. Thick rings of blue-grey smoke rose from his pipe as he sat, one hand upon his crossed knee, lost in thought. Before a battle, there must come a time when every commander reviews his strength, his dispositions, and—his prospects. And, regardless of his past successes, each ensuing combat must raise for most at least a momentary doubt, a second's fear, as to its outcome. Now, too, demands for secrecy of sentry posts, of trip flares, and of all alarum measures, must prevent, at least by night, a general tour of the force and thus withhold from its commander the special moral strength imparted by the troops' stout hearts.

As minutes passed, as hours grew upon the clock, I thought most often of those watching eyes along each section, each platoon, each company front; of all the eyes that peered into the darkness to our west and to our east, battalion flanked by battalion, Geordies, Belgians, Riflemen, Puerto Ricans, Americans, Turks, ROKs. And down by Gloster Crossing, where the river splashed against the fifty-gallon drums that marked the ford, sixteen men of 7 Platoon were watching especially as the moon rose over the broken walls of the village and lit the black waters.

A voice said, "There's someone at the Crossing, sir."

Guido looked across to the north bank and saw that four figures had entered the stream and begun to cross, moving clumsily as the current caught at their knees, their thighs, their waists, as they progressed.

The night wind seemed lifted amongst the old ROK trenches. It seemed as if a sigh stirred the men in ambush before they awoke to complete, absolute alertness; before the shock of certain, impending action was absorbed by their minds and they became accustomed to and at ease with the thought of it.

Now the first crossers were nearer the shore and had been caught up by a further three. Already, the splashing of their cold bodies, pushing across the tide might be heard above the noise of the river hurrying past the buoys and lapping upon the beach. Now their figures were more distinct, their caps and tunics moonlit, their weapons outlined. Soon they would leave the water, already receded to their knees, and step up on to the shore and then ascend the cliff, up through the cutting.

No other sounds yet break the stillness, except the river splashing round the stones, the markers, and the men. No cry of fear, no fleeing feet, no shot in panic disturbs the April midnight quiet. These men are resolute.

No cough, no careless cigarette, no clatter of a weapon clumsily handled alarms the enemy's approach. These men are trained.

The seven moonlit figures still come on; each second adds another detail to their faces, arms, accoutrements. Another twenty yards, fifteen, now ten, now five,—now——

Now!

The light machine-guns fire! The silence dies abruptly as the guns' fierce echoes sound east and west along the river between the cliffs; south to the slopes of Castle Hill where eyes and ears, alerted by the flashes, strain for more news. And north, across the river, to whatever force may be in wait along the hills that, almost yesterday, we searched so closely.

The seven men are gone, swept away, lifeless, by the fast flowing water; except for one, poor wretch, whose groans are dying away in the shallows, as the bloody water washes over him, foam-spread, and ruffled lightly from his last, faint breath.

But there are more coming, hailing, many screaming, as they run into the water, firing their weapons, splashing; careless of noise now that they see from whence the crossing is opposed. Seven, seventeen, twenty-seven, thirty, more than thirty stumbling and heaving their heavy limbs against the current's drag, panting and excited as they try to bear down by weight of numbers the ambuscade whose total strength theirs far exceeds. The echoing shots are now all theirs. A sub-machine-gun—homophonous, the 'burp' gun—is fired until its magazine is emptied, when another sends its charge of bullets to the cliff tops, and another splits the mud and wattle of the empty village walls. There is no lack of fire from the attackers, and their comrades on the northern bank provide support; heavy and light machine guns fire from bank to cliff across the water; mortars throw their streamlined bombs up into the night. Flash follows flash; the air above the unheeding river trembles with explosions.

Still there is no reply from the patrol on the hilltop. From somewhere to the south, their ears detect the sounds they have awaited; and, almost quicker than the thought, the shivering noise of shells is overhead as our artillery fire descends with all its might upon the northern bank and shores. In each succeeding sudden flare of the exploding shell is seen the last black veil of smoke from those preceding it. The mortars and machine-guns falter, quieten, die away.

But now, again, the crossing party move in shallow water. This is the moment. Again, the weapons of the ambuscade are used: light machine-gun, rifle, Sten gun, find a target each amongst the yelling figures underneath the cliffs; grenades are hurled amongst the leaders. The light of the full moon is temporarily augmented by the flares from our light mortars.

Confusion now appears amongst the enemy: of those that stand unwounded some draw back; one yelling figure waves them on from deeper water near midstream; others remain in doubt, shouting in high-pitched voices from the cover of scattered boulders in the shallows, arguing back and forth. Two wounded men, whose unsure feet are turned towards the northern bank, are swept, quite suddenly, down stream, their weakened limbs incapable of fighting with the river. The ambush party's weapons find new marks amongst the indecisive ranks now scattered below them. New flashes and explosions rise again to force decision on the enemy, whose few remaining numbers rush in panic back across the river, the last shots of the defenders cutting the stragglers down into the water, to be swept away westward through the Imjin's mouth into the Yellow Sea.

Now there is a lull. The men in ambush examine their weapons. Guido, their commander, checks the ammunition. Among the village walls, upon the cliff top, a few soft phrases are exchanged; a drink of water taken: some black smudges of burnt powder removed from a cheek or forehead. The April night seems warm to these men.

Upon the other shore, the enemy is formed again to force the crossing at all costs, the numbers of the force now ten times greater than the first small group.

Again, the tiny dark figures are illumined by the moon as they descend the northern bank. The word is passed along the ambush lines. Again, the gunners fire with terrible effect. The mortar flares burn brightly over the black water. The lull is over: battle is joined once more.

Imagine, now, the scene on Castle Hill and that long hill on its right flank where the men of D Company stand-to. Riflemen, machine-gunners, mortar and gunner Observation Posts, signallers, medical orderlies, stretcher-bearers wait now, alert and ready; those under cover smoking; those outside scanning the moonlit slopes that lead to their positions, searching vainly the black pools of shadow that mark re-entrants, folds, depressions in the ground. Often those eyes are drawn towards the river and the crossing from whence the short fierce engagements are apparent, marked by light and sound.

Behind, a little to the south, and east, the other members of the Battalion Group are wakened, too, and ready. Long since, the medium and heavy mortars have been firing and the valley mouth, wherein the Main Headquarters stands, has echoed to the noise of their discharge. The Regimental Aid Post staff is up, the dressings and the instruments laid out. Drivers and drummers, snipers and signallers perform their duty or stand by. The cook-house has brewed up a special tea container. Guy listens to the signal traffic of the Field Regiment on his wireless and then comes into the Command Vehicle, where the air is thick with tobacco smoke. Sergeant Lucas, the 'G' clerk, brings in more coffee which he has brewed up. Richard brings in another message from Guido.

"They're still trying to cross in hordes, sir," he says to the

21

Colonel who has just come in. "In another five minutes, he reckons they'll be out of ammunition."

The Colonel looks across to Guy and then to me.

"Tell them to start withdrawing in three minutes," he says. "Guy, I'm going to ask you for one last concentration, and then start dropping them short of Gloster Crossing as soon as the patrol is back at the first cutting south of the river."

By Gloster Crossing there is another lull: a fourth attempt to cross has just been repulsed. The smell of mould and decay from the village and the cold river smell are mingling with the acrid fumes of burnt explosive. Guido's ammunition is down to less than three rounds per rifle, to less than half a magazine for the Sten machine-carbines and the Brens. With the numbers against them, this will not hold another attack. But the task is nearly done as Guido looks at his watch. The second hand moves upwards, the minute hand closes on its next division. One after another, sixteen shadows slip south out of the village. Already some of them have formed a little covering party at the bund while their comrades go past, when they, in turn, slip softly back under cover of just such another party at the first cutting. Noiseless, as shadows are, they slip back across the unsown rice paddy. Calmly, as they have fought, they withdraw. Back to their slit trenches to continue the fight from there. Behind them, the body of the enemy remains unharmed—but, already he has a bloody nose.

In the quiet darkness upon Castle Hill, the word is passed: the word that began on the lips of a signaller who had heard it from the receiver of a field telephone. And now the news is sent along a fresh series of telephone lines from the company headquarters to the platoon positions, where, whispered from a dugout, it is passed from slit trench to slit trench, man to man, lip to ear. So the word ascends the steep hillside to the very earthworks upon the ancient castle foundations, where John's platoon stand watch. Yet it arrives too late, in this most forward position, to be the latest news; for as it is passed from company to platoon headquarters it meets a newer, more vital piece of news coming the other way.

22

"Listen, Jack: the patrol from C Company has come back and confirm a large number of enemy north of the Crossing."

There is a murmur at the far end of the telephone as this piece of news is passed to the proper quarter. Then:

"Well, I've some news for you, whacker. The officer says to tell the Company Commander the enemy isn't only on the north bank of the river: they're coming up our path now and they'll be knocking on the front door any minute!"

The signaller at A Company Headquarters hears the sound of an explosion in his receiver as he turns to pass this news to Pat.

The overture concluded, the curtain has risen on the first act.

The stage is almost in darkness: only the outlines of the hills appear at first in the moonlight. Yet we know where the defenders lie. Here and there appears a dull reflection of light from gunmetal; an occasional movement may be perceived in the gloom.

The attackers enter: hundreds of Chinese soldiers clad in cotton khaki suits; plain, cheap, cotton caps; rubber-soled canvas shoes upon their feet; their shoulders, chests, and backs criss-crossed with cotton bandoliers of ammunition: upon their hips, grenades—rough stick grenades so like the Boche "potato masher", but inferior. Brown eyes, dark eyes beneath the long peaks of their caps peer forward to the back of whatsoever "comrade" they are meant to follow. Those in the forefront of the battle wear steel helmets that are reminiscent of the Japanese. Their weapons—rifles, carbines, "burp" guns, and Tommy guns that we supplied to Chiang Kai-Shek—are ready in their hands. Behind, on mule or pony limbers, are drawn their guns and ammunition. Between the two lines, on sweating backs, or slung between two men upon stout bamboo poles, their mortars and machine-guns travel forward. No Oxford carriers, no jeeps and trailers, no gun prime-movers here; but if they lack these aids to war, they do not lack what we do most: men. The hundreds grow to thousands on the river banks as, padding through the night, they close with us: eight hundred Glosters stand astride the road to Seoul—the road the Chinese mean to clear at any cost.

Originally, the Chinese plan had been a simple, silent night assault straight through the front of our positions. D on their left and A on their right once removed by overwhelming, fierce assault, they reckoned on a swift withdrawal by our frightened remnant. Following this, they planned, at best, to cut this off and thus destroy at once the whole left wing of the UN 3rd Division; and at worst, to open speedily the way to Seoul .

Speed in their plan was all-important: time was against them. Irrespective of our weakness and their corresponding strength in men, they could not force a battle, once our own command, appreciating where the main threat lay, disposed our few reserves to counter it. Our skills, and our equipments, were superior to theirs, once opportunity was given us to meet them in the open. And, too, once they deployed completely, their system of communication was so poor that they could not manœuvre speedily, either to exploit our weakness as it became apparent, or to gather their strength against a counter-attack from us.

Thus, their aim was to break into, to destroy, and pass beyond our forces holding the approach to Seoul before we knew from whence the main thrust would come. And it was feasible, so thinly held were those approaches, with such gaps between the flanks of one unit and another.

Each of those units was thus forced to fight a lone battle, to resist stubbornly until the enemy's intention was clear, when the field might be arranged again to meet the new requirement.

Already their time schedule for the battle had been disrupted. The check by Guido's ambush at the Crossing had put them back for many precious hours of darkness; precious since the daylight might bring aircraft to restore, at least in part, the balance which their numbers now disturbed.

The second crossing point, unknown to us, lay west of Gloster Crossing on an unmarked, ancient underwater bridge that brought them straight across on to a sand spit, thrown up by the river waters on a hairpin bend. These were the attackers who crept forward on to Castle Hill to meet A Company in a mighty clash of arms. At that same moment, the assault force fording at Gloster Crossing should have attacked D Company. But they were still reforming from the blows the ambush party had inflicted.

Now, therefore, with silence once again restored after the noisy struggle at the Crossing, a party of about three hundred Chinese riflemen crept up the slopes towards the Castle Site, whilst others slipped across the terraced paddy fields to take the western flank and rear defences of A Company.

CHAPTER TWO

23rd April, 1951.

BELOW John's trenches on the Castle Site, a tin can holding stones is rattling; another sounds close by. The watchers, listeners all, respond without a sound to this first warning. The barbed wire rattles, barb scrapes barb and locks; the tin cans sound again. A whispered word and all safety catches are released. Here and there, the split pins of grenades are eased across the cast-iron shoulders.

A faint, incomprehensible sound is heard in the night; the air is ruffled lightly; an object falls near, by a slit trench, smoking. Less than two seconds pass in which the occupants regard it, understand its nature, duck and take cover as it explodes. This is the first grenade: the first of many.

Echoing now, the hill is lit with flame that flickers from above and below. Mortars begin to sound down near the Imjin and the call is taken up by those that lie to the south behind C Company. Slowly, like a fire, the flames spread east and west around Castle Hill; and east again across the village of Choksong, as the enemy from Gloster Crossing, tardily launched at last, meets and is repulsed by D Company.

Now, almost hand to hand, the Chinese and British soldiers meet. Figures leap up from the attacking force, run forward to new cover and resume their fire upon the men of the defence who, coolly

25

enough, return their fire, as targets come to view, as the attackers close with them. Occasionally an individual climax may be reached in an encounter between two men when, only a few feet apart, each waits to catch the other unawares, sees a target, fires, and leaps across to follow his advantage.

And now, to the defenders' aid, the carefully planned defensive fire is summoned. The Vickers guns cut across the cliffs and slopes by which the Chinese forces climb to the attack. Long bursts of fire—ten, twenty, thirty, forty rounds—are fired and fired again: the water in the cooling jackets warms, the ground is littered with spent cases. The mortars and the gunners drop their high explosive in amongst the crowded ranks that press on to the hill slopes from the river crossings.

Such are the enemy's losses that now and then there is a brief respite for the defence as the attackers are withdrawn for reinforcement. The weight of defensive fire is so great that the enemy has realized he must concentrate his strength in one main thrust up to each hilltop. As the night wanes, fresh hundreds are committed to this task, and the tired defenders, much depleted, face yet one more assault.

Mike commands D Company—Lakri is fuming in Japan, moving heaven and earth to get a plane to bring him back from leave. Victors of their first encounters, D Company are sadly weakened by the ceaseless blows rained on them. One of Mike's platoons has been withdrawn right to the hilltop and they form a close defensive ring about the high ridge line which constitutes the vital ground of the position. Ever and again by weight of small-arms fire, by sorties, and as a result of many concentrations fired by mortars and guns, the assault waves are forced back. But still they reappear. For every casualty suffered by the enemy, two, three, four more Chinese will appear to take his place. Yet D Company is holding its ground.

From Castle Hill, the news is grave. John's platoon, now decimated, has been withdrawn by Pat before they are over-run completely. Their officer dead, so many others of their comrades dead or wounded, they go back to Phil's platoon position where they wait for dawn.

The Castle Site, the highest point of our defences forward, is taken after six hours fighting.

The dawn breaks. A pale, April sun is rising in the sky. Take any group of trenches here upon these two main hill positions looking north across the river. See, here, the weapon pits in which the defenders stand: unshaven, wind-burned faces streaked with black powder, filthy with sweat and dust from their exertions, look towards their enemy with eyes red from fatigue and sleeplessness; grim faces, yet not too grim that they refuse to smile when someone cracks a joke about the sunrise. Here, round the weapons smeared with burnt cordite, lie the few pathetic remnants of the wounded, since removed: cap comforters; a boot; some cigarettes half-soaked with blood; a photograph of two small girls; two keys; a broken pencil stub. The men lounge quietly in their positions, waiting for the brief respite to end.

"They're coming back, Ted."

A shot is fired, a scattered burst follows it. The sergeant calls an order to the mortar group. Already they can hear the shouting and see, here and there, the figures moving out from behind cover as their machine-guns pour fire from the newly occupied Castle Site. Bullets fly back and forth; overhead, almost lazily, grenades are being exchanged on either side; man meets man; hand meets hand. This tiny corner of the battle that is raging along the whole front, blazes up and up into extreme heat, reaches a climax and dies away to nothingness—another little lull, another breathing space.

Phil is called to the telephone at this moment; Pat's voice sounds in his ear.

"Phil, at the present rate of casualties we can't hold on unless we get the Castle Site back. Their machine-guns up there completely dominate your platoon and most of Terry's. We shall never stop their advance until we hold that ground again."

Phil looks over the edge of the trench at the Castle Site, two hundred yards away, as Pat continues talking, giving him the instructions for the counter attack. They talk for a minute or so;

27

there is not much more to be said when an instruction is given to assault with a handful of tired men across open ground. Everyone knows it is vital: everyone knows it is appallingly dangerous. The only details to be fixed are the arrangements for supporting fire; and, though A Company's Gunners are dead, Ronnie will support them from D Company's hill. Behind, the machine-gunners will ensure that they are not engaged from the open, eastern flank. Phil gathers his tiny assault party together.

It is time; they rise from the ground and move forward up to the barbed wire that once protected the rear of John's platoon. Already two men are hit and Papworth, the Medical Corporal, is attending to them. They are through the wire safely—safely!—when the machine-gun in the bunker begins to fire. Phil is badly wounded: he drops to the ground. They drag him back through the wire somehow and seek what little cover there is as it creeps across their front. The machine-gun stops, content now it has driven them back; waiting for a better target when they move into the open again.

"It's all right, sir," says someone to Phil. "The Medical Corporal's been sent for. He'll be here any minute."

Phil raises himself from the ground, rests on a friendly shoulder, then climbs by a great effort on to one knee.

"We must take the Castle Site," he says; and gets up to take it.

The others beg him to wait until his wounds are tended. One man places a hand on his side.

"Just wait until Papworth has seen you, sir——"

But Phil has gone: gone to the wire, gone through the wire, gone towards the bunker. The others come out behind him, their eyes all on him. And suddenly it seems as if, for a few breathless moments, the whole of the remainder of that field of battle is still and silent, watching amazed, the lone figure that runs so painfully forward to the bunker holding the approach to the Castle Site: one tiny figure, throwing grenades, firing a pistol, set to take Castle Hill.

Perhaps he will make it—in spite of his wounds, in spite of the

28

odds—perhaps this act of supreme gallantry may, by its sheer audacity, succeed. But the machine-gun in the bunker fires directly into him: he staggers, falls, is dead instantly; the grenade he threw a second before his death explodes after it in the mouth of the bunker. The machine-gun does not fire on three of Phil's platoon who run forward to pick him up; it does not fire again through the battle: it is destroyed; the muzzle blown away, the crew dead.

Before dawn, the Battalion Command Post had moved up the hill to the ridge between Guido's platoon and Paul's company head-quarters. From here, in a bunker constructed under R.S.M. Hobbs's supervision some days before, the Colonel could overlook the battle on the two hill positions north of us. The desperate nature of the struggle was manifest before the morning sun rose. By night, the calls for fire support, each fresh report from A or D Company Headquarters, and the Gunner wireless links had made it all too clear that this attack was in strength. If this was feinting, it was a costly, realistic feint!

Just after dawn, Walters, at his wireless, said that Pat wanted me on the set. I sat down on the reverse slope of the hill behind the bunker and spoke into the handset. Pat replied:

"I'm afraid we've lost Castle Site. I am mounting a counter-attack now but I want to know whether to expect to stay here indefinitely or not. If I am to stay on, I must be re-inforced as my numbers are getting very low."

I told him to wait and went back into the bunker. The Colonel was standing in the Observation Post at the far end. I told him what Pat had said and asked what he intended to do. He looked through his glasses at D Company's hill and then said:

"I'll talk to him myself."

We both went back to the wireless set. I stood watching the Colonel as he spoke to Pat, the distant crackle of rifle and light-machine-gun fire in my ears, and the long tack-tack-tack of the Vickers mingling with the hollow boom of the mortars firing from just below us. The Colonel had stopped talking; from the headset came the buzz of Pat's voice. Then the Colonel replied. He said:

"You will stay there at all costs until further notice."

29

At all costs.

Pat knew what that order meant, and I knew—and the Colonel knew. As he got up I saw that he was pale and that his hand shook a little as he relit his pipe.

I watched the Colonel go back to the bunker as I put on the head-set to speak to Pat again. The next half-hour would tell how the day would go for us.

There were two questions in the Colonel's mind as he stood at the open end of the bunker, viewing the action fought by his two forward companies: would the Chinese continue to press their attack in daylight with the threat of intervention by our aircraft; and, secondly, how long would it be before the Chinese discovered that both our flanks were completely open—that the ROKs were two and a half miles to the west, the Fifth Fusiliers two to the east—and encircle us? Yet, whatever the answer to these questions, his orders were to hold the road between Choksong and Solma-ri. Very well, the Battalion would hold it. And the Battalion would remain disposed as at present just as long as each sub-unit retained its integrity; for our present disposition was unquestionably well-suited to fighting an action designed to hold the road firmly.

I began talking to Pat again, discussing the prospect of reinforcements, and telling him that his ammunition replacement was already going forward in Oxford carriers under Henry's supervision. We spoke only very briefly and he ended by saying:

"Don't worry about us; we'll be all right."

I said: "Good luck."

I did not speak to Pat again; he was killed a quarter of an hour later.

There were no planes that day; there were targets and more elsewhere. The Gunner Colonel spoke to me twice, and I knew from his voice how desperately he wanted to help us. So the Chinese were pushed unceasingly over the Gloster and Western Crossings. The guns and mortars fired all day but the Rifles and Fusiliers—to say nothing of the brave Belgians—needed support too. There were so many of them. Really, for a force reputedly

30

bent on "imperialist aggression" we must have seemed pathetically thin on the ground to the Chinese Commissars.

At about half past eight it became apparent that the positions of A and D Companies had become untenable; little by little they were being swamped by a tide of men. Each minute was widening the gaps between the little fighting groups—as yet still organized platoons and companies. The time had come when the advantage of holding the ground forward would be outweighed by the loss of much or all of two rifle-company groups. The order to withdraw was given over the wireless.

Watching from the Command Post, I saw the men withdrawing, step by step, down the reverse hill slopes: D Company and A Company leaving the ground they had fought for so well, that had cost the enemy such a price.

I went down the hill a little later and there, by the ford, the survivors of the night battle were coming in: a long, straggling line of men; for all were heavily laden with arms and ammunition. To me they looked cheerful, though tired—but something more than that: they looked surprised. I think, above all, it was a surprise to many of them that they had been withdrawn—grave though they had known their position to be, and dangerous their surroundings. Unquestionably, it was difficult for them to understand that, in holding their ground for so long, they had made a priceless contribution to the battle: but a soldier engaged in a fight that may be to the death has no time for the appreciation of such things. He is, to say the least, otherwise engaged.

Just north of the ford, along the roadsides, around the cook-house and the Regimental Aid Post, they rested now, as Watkins issued tea as fast as he could make it, and all the bread, bacon and sausages he had to hand. Comrade passed mess tin to comrade, who drank and passed in turn to his next neighbour. Men lay back, without removing their haversacks, their heads resting in the ditches, smoking, talking quietly, resting. Yes, it had been a long night.

The Colonel came down the hill. He had just moved B Company back fifteen hundred yards to the very base of Kamak-San to conform with A and D Companies' withdrawal. He had now to fit

31

the latter two into the revised defence disposition. With Mike and Jumbo he looked over the map and pointed out their new positions on the ground. Jumbo was to take the much-reduced A Company to man the key ridge to the west which Spike's Pioneers now held. Behind, looked down upon by this long feature—marked Hill 235—was a small, square, almost flat-topped hill, where Mike would deploy D Company. As Mike and Jumbo went outside again, Henry was marking the map afresh. The old, blue lines that circled Castle Hill, Choksong, the hill D Company had held, soon vanished from the shiny talc. Now two new rings marked their positions; the symbols were completed by the moving chinagraph. The operations map was fitted back into its place and Henry soon descended to correct his own in the Intelligence Office. I put out my hand to the telephone to tell the remainder of the Battalion how our new line stood, taking it from its rest without looking down. For I was looking at the tiny group of marks upon the talc; and as I looked I realized that this was what the Chinese would attack next—to-night!

When I recall that day, it rises in my memory as a series of incidents, clear in themselves, but joined by a very hazy thread of continuity.

I remember Colour-Sergeant Buxcey organising his Korean porters with mighty loads for the first of many ascents to their new positions. Nine, I think, he made. Nine times up the hill; and so, poor devils, nine times down a path at once precipitous and rough. On coming down, one wished for the easier journey of the upward climb; and upwards, sweating, breathless, weary, one envied those who went the opposite way.

When Buxcey's anxious face has left my mind, I can see Bob working at the Regimental Aid Post, one hand still wet with blood as he turns round, pausing for a moment to clean himself before he begins to minister to yet another wounded man. The ambulance cars are filled; the jeep that Bounden drives has been out time and again with the stretchers on its racks. Baxter, Brisland, Mills, the whole staff of the RAP, is hard at work with dressings, drugs, instruments. This is the reckoning they pay for basking in the sun down by the stream when times are quiet. It is a price they pay willingly and to the full.

I remember watching the slow, wind-tossed descent of a helicopter that came down for some casualties to whom the winding, bumpy road back south would have meant certain death. I saw Bob and the Padre standing back as the plane lifted, their hair blown wildly by the slipstream from the rotors as she lifted into the sky.

Shaw and Mr. Evans, the Chief Clerk, went off to Seoul in my jeep. I watched them until they disappeared round the road-bend down by Graham's mortar pits. Richard was down by the ford, and Carl, the Counter-Mortar Officer.

"I'm sending my vehicles back, except for my jeep," said Carl. "I've decided I'll stay with you to make up your number of Forward Observation Officers. I've seen the Colonel."

The lumbering half-tracks disappeared along the road and Carl settled down to chat to Guy on Gunner matters. I wondered what the Gunner Colonel was going to say on finding that his radar specialist had stayed with us. And I thanked God that the latter was a real Gunner as well as a boffin.

We were certainly going to discover that he had not forgotten how to shoot.

Donald, the Assistant Adjutant, came into the Command Vehicle. We had various things to discuss—welfare cases—two men had to go from the Battalion on a Field Hygiene course—there were messages from Freddie, who had thought of them as he rode back to B Echelon after his visit earlier in the day. Afterwards, we had some coffee and over it I told him that he had better stay forward to reinforce A Company, just for the time being. He went off happily to climb the slopes to Jumbo's Hill, as pleased as Punch that he could take command of a platoon—if only for the forthcoming engagement—before he was packed back to Rear H.Q. and his Assistant Adjutancy.

Jumbo had come forward that morning to find Pat and two of his platoon commanders, John and Philip, dead; only Terry left to lead fifty-seven fit men out of the original body nearly one hundred strong. The arrival of Donald would give him two platoon commanders. I put the phone back after telling him the news, and walked out on to the grass to get some sleep.

That morning the Padre said a funeral service for Pat, whose body had been sent back from Company Headquarters on the ammunition-laden Oxford Carrier which Henry had driven through a hail of fire descending on the pass to Choksong. Pat's body was the only one to which we could pay our last respects—but we did not forget the others. Three of us stood by while the solemn words were quietly said; then we saluted and walked away, each busy with his own thoughts.

Pat lay at rest beside the soft-voiced stream, quiet in the morning sunlight, the noise of last night's battle gone forever in the wind.

"The Second-in-Command is here, sir," said Judkins, my batman. "And are you going to have anything to eat?"

I opened my eyes to blue sky and huge white clouds. It was afternoon; I had slept for two hours. Judkins stood on the grass by the edge of my blanket, a mug and plate in one hand, a knife, fork, and spoon in the other.

I hated getting up; and I was a fool to refuse the hot stew Watkins had cooked. How little one learns by experience! I asked Judkins for some tea and had a cigarette with Digby, the Second-in-Command. He had come forward from Rear H.Q. some time before but had been unwilling to awaken me.

"The Colonel has told me to go back in view of this attack on Rear H.Q.," he said. We settled a point or two before he got into his jeep and drove off with Bainbridge at the wheel, for all the world as if he was on his way to a dinner party. They were going to a party all right. Four hours before a sizeable force, which had circled us, had attacked Rear H.Q. The road was cut, and the route forward that might bring us relief or reinforcement was— at that very moment—closing.

It is dark, the moon obscured by cloud. Night is the time for their attack. Although we have had no planes during the day, our

34

Gunners have inflicted too much damage to permit them to press their advance. Released from concern about our troops, hitherto so closely engaged on the hills forward, the Gunners delivered concentration after concentration on the almost endless series of targets before them before the enemy called a halt and went to ground.

But now it is dark. Already their stealthy infantry will have left the little holes in which they have kept hidden from the sun and our observers.

We sit in a battle Command Post. Walters is there at his wireless: nearby sit Richard, Henry, and Guy. Frank is laying a line from the Mortar Troop Headquarters where Sergeant-Major Askew keeps his solitary vigil; somewhere about is Smythe, the Signal Sergeant; Lucas, the Operations Clerk, is making yet another cup of coffee; the Colonel is sitting with his head against the earthen wall, taking advantage of the quiet to doze. I sit by Walters and, in the glow of red light from the wireless, see that his eyelids are drooping, heavy with an unsatisfied need for sleep. My eyes are heavy, too. How marvellous, what luxury, to find oneself suddenly in a bed with nothing to wake up for until, say, breakfast on a silver tray, in thirty hours' time. Well, why ask a bed? A blanket on that grass outside. . . .

Frank is talking to me, and I realize that I have been dropping off into a doze. It is better that I get up and walk about outside for a little. Richard follows me as Frank departs for his Headquarters, a hundred yards away. We hear the stream rushing over the little waterfall; the light wind cools our cheeks, hot from the close atmosphere of the dug-out. The radiance of the moon is widening in the sky above us. Beneath our feet, the old year's grass rustles as we stroll up and down, talking.

Suddenly, Richard pauses in mid-sentence. We both look up, quickly, to the eastern end of C Company's ridge. The battle has started.

In the Command Post dug-out, the telephone is ringing.

In the original Battalion defensive layout, Denis's Company—B Company—were on the far right flank, holding the approaches to

35

the great Kamak-San feature—itself too vast for us to hold—at the same time constituting the right rear base of the Battalion. Unlike C Company, they had never been absolutely in reserve, inasmuch as there had been nothing except the river between them and the enemy; although, of course, to their northwest, A and D Companies had been in closer proximity to an often evanescent foe. Now, with both A and D Companies withdrawn, their prospect of a major engagement became a certainty.

Whilst the battle had raged around Choksong village for the possession of A and D Companies' hills, B Company had been little more than spectators. A few Chinese patrols had bumped them during the hours of darkness, but they had held their fire, except at one post where a complete patrol of fifteen men was destroyed by an LMG of Geoff's platoon. Thus the Chinese did not know B Company's positions on the morning of the 23rd; for all they knew, their contact on the previous night might well have been with one of our patrols, instead of with a position in our main defences. Thus, expecting to renew the attack that night, they had sent a further series of patrols forward towards B Company during the morning; and these patrols were all in strength, designed to produce, at all costs, reaction from us.

Denis was determined not to reveal his positions unless absolutely compelled to; but, faced with a number of strong armed parties along his front, he realized that, sooner or later he would be forced to engage them. In these circumstances, he made up his mind to do so by sortie, by which means the enemy could not be certain either of the main position or—equally important—the strength of the force from which they had sprung.

Sergeant Petherick took out a force in this connection, expecting to engage, at most, twenty men: he returned after meeting two hundred. Backwards and forwards, all among the battle knolls that lay below the peak of Kamak-San, engagements flared up and died, only to be renewed elsewhere.

The daylight waned, the evening shadows deepened, merged and grew into one, to form the darkness of another night.

Below great Kamak-San, Denis's Company prepared themselves for what they knew the darkness would bring forth.

36

To the west, that night, the 1st ROK Division was to repulse, with great tenacity, a strong and vigorous attack by two divisions attempting to open up the road that ran from Munsan-Ni to Seoul —a part of the western highway that ran up from the south to the border on the Yalu River. Eastwards, the Fifth Fusiliers would fight desperately against attacks across the river in great strength; and beyond, the Belgians and the Rifles, Puerto Ricans, Turks, Americans would be engaged in increasing intensity.

Here, near Choksong, lay the centre of the attack upon the western sector; here ran the road which was, historically, the main route of invasion from the north.

Already one full day behind their time-plan for the advance, the Chinese now prepared to end the resistance once and for all, and surge along the road to Seoul through Uijong-bu, catching, perhaps, the whole left flank of the UN 3rd Division unawares.

Their problem now was, at what point should they attack? Last night's experience made it plain that one vast, human wave would never serve to overwhelm the sturdy wall of the defence. Further, the British left flank, on Hill 235, would not be easy to attack. They could not know of Jumbo's dangerous weakness on the ridge.

Then, too, attack upon the west might leave us time and opportunity to make a second withdrawal, on to Kamak-San, from which we should not easily be dislodged. The choice fell, therefore, upon the approaches to Kamak-San, and thus upon B Company and part of C, whose right flank lay across the western spur leading to the final, jagged crest.

I run into the dugout: Walters has answered the telephone, which he hands to me. Denis says:

"Well, we've started. They're attacking Beverly's platoon now— about a hundred and fifty, I should think."

My torch is on the map; and I examine the exact location of the attack as the Colonel begins to talk to Denis. Nearby, I hear the heavier sound of shells exploding above the noisy small-arms fire and mortars. Recce is shooting along B Company's front.

Paul is on the other telephone; his news from C Company is the

37

same: parties of enemy attempting to infiltrate, while others assault our positions in great strength, trying again to engulf us. Jack's platoon and David's are engaged; Guido's platoon is under machine-gun fire from D Company's former position.

It is ten minutes to twelve: the battle is warming.

Here they come again: a screaming mob of cotton-suited soldiers, their yellow faces gleaming in the light of the trip flares they have sprung and the mortar flares drifting slowly down beneath their parachutes.

An hour after midnight, the whole of B and C Companies are engaged; the guns, the mortars, the machine-guns once again deliver their supporting fire with all their might.

In character, the battle much resembles that of the previous night: wave after wave of men armed with grenades and burp-guns storm the positions under cover of mortar and machine-gun fire, are halted, engaged in a short desperate struggle, and driven back. A lull follows. Both sides reorganize. The attack recommences. The character of the battle is the same, too, in that these ceaseless blows, delivered in such strength, inevitably reduce our numbers speedily. Their casualties are high—much higher than ours; but in this battle of attrition they can afford them; we cannot.

It is in the nature of the ground that the battle differs; and the Chinese have made the mistake of attacking obliquely across our front—perhaps because they did not really know where B Company lay. Thus for the first two hours, much of the weight of their attack was spent fruitlessly. Only after great loss have they redirected their line of assault. Old Kamak-San looks down upon a ring of intermittent flame across his northern base. Last night the flames were further off. Now they are nearer; growing nearer, hour by hour.

It is three o'clock. In the Command Post we are drinking coffee and talking. The telephone is quiet for the moment but the noise of the battle reaches us clearly. As I sit talking to Richard, I wonder if he realizes how gravely we are situated: a vast body of the enemy

38

pushing south; our flanks open; the road cut behind us. It is a great comfort to reflect that, though they can take Kamak-San without firing a shot—they have only to travel round our unguarded flanks, after all—it will do them no good. We hold the road; and we shall continue to hold it.

The telephone is ringing again: Paul is speaking:

"I'm afraid they've overrun my top position," he says, "and they're reinforcing hard. They're simply pouring chaps in up above us. Let me know what the Colonel wants me to do, will you?"

This is, immediately, disaster. The enemy has forced his way up on to Paul's highest defensive post by overwhelming his men with their numbers. The result of this is that the Chinese now command most of C Company's ground, have forced a wedge between C and B Company, and dominate the valley in which the mortars lie—heavy and medium—and the entire Headquarters. If we are not quick, we may be caught by the enemy who has only to fire over open sights straight down into us.

Already, however, the Colonel, who is listening, has made up his mind.

"Pack the Headquarters up," he says, "and get every one out of the valley up between D Company and the Anti-Tank Platoon position. I'm going to withdraw C Company in ten minutes; and I shall move B over to join us after first light."

He picks up the telephone and starts to speak to Paul as I give Richard and Henry their instructions. They need but a few words: speed is the requirement here. Foolishly, I forget Frank has laid a line to the Command Post, and waste precious time going to his Headquarters. He is not there. I give a message to Sergeant-Major Askew and go on: Graham's mortars are warned—Sam's Head-quarters—the Regimental Aid Post—the Regimental Sergeant-Major. Before I return to the Command Post, the first party of signallers is moving up the gorge towards D Company's hill.

Back at the Command Post I burn those papers that must *not* be taken. Lucas and I pick up Jennings, the Rear Link Wireless commander: together we smash the fixed radio-equipment. Again, I go around the area. Overhead, along the ridge C Company is holding, there is a sudden ominous quiet. I wonder if they are already mounting a machine-gun at the head of the valley; if they are already descending to the stream, crossing by the mortar pits which I am now approaching. It is no good wondering: I shall know soon enough what they are doing. The mortar pits stand silent, strangely deserted after the bustle of the earlier part of the night. Turning back along the road, I see a mug of steaming tea standing on a box at the entrance to Sam's HQ. The RAP has gone, too; Bob's jeep is in wild disorder; packages, web equipment, an old coffee tin are scattered across the seats, flung there in haste after he had removed the other contents. Everyone has gone.

Not quite everyone. There is a murmur of voices from the signals office; a metallic rasping catches my ear. As I step down from the bank on the edge of the road, two signallers appear. They have come back for spare batteries, quite unaware that the sands in the hour-glass are fast running out. Indeed, I cannot be sure if there is even one grain left to fall: the Chinese have held the head of the valley for nearly forty minutes.

Together, we cross the road, traverse the low, flat ground, and enter the gorge.

CHAPTER THREE

24th April, 1951

I T seemed a long morning: there were many incidents.

The dry stream bed which ran down the hillside and through the gorge divided half way from the top. We had taken the left fork as we ascended.

The steep, rough, trackless hillside was crowded with men: weary, breathless men who laboured upwards carrying weapons, wireless sets, ammunition—a few water cans—on backs and shoulders; other men whose muscles cracked with the weight of the stretchers they carried; men who lay, white-faced, pain-racked upon the stretchers; more wounded men, walking with difficulty, aided by comrades up the difficult ascent. A long sweating snake of soldiers moving up into the darkness.

At the top was a saddle, connecting a knoll with D Company's new position. Beyond the knoll, a ridge ran towards Kamak-San, parallel to the road on which the Main Headquarters had been established. The occupation of this area began.

On the northern slope of the saddle, just below the crest, we set up Battalion Headquarters; Bob and his medical staff, with all the wounded, were disposed in a small re-entrant where the saddle joined D Company's hill. A section of machine-guns took on the defence of the high point of the knoll: to their right, a composite body of signallers, drivers, and police, guarded the slopes leading up from Solma-Ri to the south; and at the other end of the saddle, thickening up the defences behind D Company, Frank and his Mortar-Gunners took on an infantry role just above the Drums. When Guido arrived with the remnant of C Company, they settled into the last gap in the defences on the northern slope of the knoll.

A grey, overcast dawn broke. We were all very dirty from our scramble up the hillside, all unshaven, all tired. Our hunger merely brought into the forefront of our minds the recollection that there was, literally, no food, except a little for the wounded. Weapons, ammunition, dressings, water, wireless sets and batteries had been carried up in obvious preference to rations; of these essentials, there were not enough for a sustained engagement.

A little after seven o'clock, the sun broke through the overcast. The grey clouds thinned and, by eight, a pleasant warmth began to pervade our cold, tired limbs.

I lay by the Rear Link wireless set and dozed with the crackle of voices in my ears, undisturbed by them. Jennings and Miles, on duty by the set, were talking nearby, taking alternative pulls at a cigarette: some question of the advantage of British Compo Rations over the American C6 seemed to be involved. From somewhere above me came the sound of several grenade explosions. I forced myself to wake up, rise, and investigate.

Above me stood a group of machine-gunners and mortar-men;

41

near by two signallers. They were all watching the Colonel. Armed with rifle and grenades he was completing the rout of a group of Chinese who had crept forward along the ridge—somehow unnoticed—in order to secure the knoll. Supporting him were two of the police and a driver.

It was already over. Two Chinese soldiers lay dead about forty yards away and, a minute or so later, the Colonel was walking back, slinging the rifle over his shoulder as he came along towards me, filling his pipe.

"What was all that about, sir?" I asked.

He looked at me for a moment over the match that lit the pipe.

"Oh, just shooing away some Chinese," he said.

For the remainder of the morning we were left in comparative peace. The whole weight of their effort was now directed upon B Company, who throughout the night had fought off a series of attacks and held their ground. Now, with the dawn, weakened by their many casualties, their ammunition running low and isolated from the remainder of the Battalion, they faced a further onslaught. As with A and D Companies on the previous morning, the enemy was determined to end resistance in that area as soon after first light as possible. Reinforced with men who had crossed the river throughout the night, they flung themselves upon B Company and began their destruction, piecemeal. For this was the only means by which B Company could be overcome.

We read so often in histories, sometimes in news reports, that one or another company of such-and-such a Battalion was "cut up", "cut to pieces", "destroyed". What does this mean exactly? How is this done to a hundred odd men, organized and armed to fight a semi-independent battle, with all the means to hand of calling down artillery fire to support them?

In Korea, in the battle of The Imjin River, it was done like this. The whole Company front is engaged by fire—fire from heavy machine-guns from ranges in excess of two thousand yards, machine-guns well-concealed in hollows or behind crests which take our artillery from other, more vital tasks if they are to be engaged. There is fire from mortars and from light machine-guns at a closer range. Meanwhile, the enemy assault groups feel their way forward to the very edge of our defences; and, finding the line of our resistance, creep round our flanks to meet each other in the rear. To the defenders, these circumstances do not constitute disaster. Holding their fire for sure targets; exploiting their advantage of positions carefully sited for just such attacks as these, they are undaunted. Again and again, they see the shells from their artillery burst amongst the crowded ranks of the enemy. Their own small arms pile up another dreadful score of casualties. Each enemy assault is beaten off without great difficulty. For hours, this repetition of attack and repulse continues, the night wanes, the dawn begins to break. Little by little, a terrible fact becomes apparent to the men of the defence. This is not a battle in which courage, tactical, and technical superiority will be the means to victory: it is a battle of attrition. Irrespective of the number of casualties they inflict, there is an unending flow of replacements for each man. Moreover, in spite of their tremendous losses, the numerical strength of the enemy is not merely constant but increasing.

Now the courage they have shown throughout the long hours of the battle during the night is surely surpassed. It is no longer a question of personal bravery in the heat of the battle. This courage is now the force which makes them determined to continue an action which, for them, is almost certainly hopelessly lost. What else should they do? Why, they might run away—a number might well escape in the confusion that abounds upon a battle-field like this. They could surrender, throw their arms down, call for quarter. Surely, they might say, we have fought well; the end is the same, at all events; for us the battle is over.

But they do not. In spite of the prospect, they continue fighting with their customary skill. Being the men they are, no other course is open to them.

Thwarted, the enemy changes his tactics. Attacks continue all round; but now great numbers concentrate on one small segment of the circle. The fire directed on to Geoff's platoon is intensified. Sergeant Robinson, who has controlled the fire of a light-machine-gun group throughout the night from an exposed position, falls. His arm and shoulder shattered by a burst of fire, he nonetheless remains at duty, giving the crew their orders in this new engagement till he loses consciousness. Robson, a light-machine-gun Number One, keeps firing though his leg is badly wounded, till he too becomes unconscious with another wound. One by one, the strength of the platoon is reduced, the little fighting groups split up. Regardless of the fire which pours down in support from the remainder of the Company, the Chinese now rush in upon the few survivors—and the ground is lost.

On the long hill behind Geoff's last position, two weak platoons and the company headquarters prepare for the next blow.

From the knoll, looking across the valley we had so recently occupied, we saw the end draw near. As the sun rose in the eastern sky, the massing figures of the enemy were silhouetted on the ridge which led to the top of the hill. Below them, reinforcements were scrambling up the steep hillside. Now, at last, we could give B Company positive assistance.

Sergeant Sykes and his machine-gun section opened fire from the left of the knoll. Carl brought concentration after concentration of artillery fire down upon the northern end of the ridge, and on the reinforcements climbing up. If this support did not absolutely relieve Denis, it delayed the final assault which must overwhelm B Company.

Withdrawal to the main body during the final hours of darkness would have been quite impossible for B Company. It would have meant a long trek across hills and valleys infested with enemy, without support either from artillery or from our own Vickers machine-guns. They would have been scattered and lost within the first hour. But now, in full daylight, with additional support that we could render, there was a chance that they might break out and join us. Group by group, under cover of fire from every weapon that we could muster, and with superb assistance from our Gunners, B Company began to evacuate their hill. At last, a part of Arthur's platoon remained with less than half of Company Headquarters—no more than twenty men, in all. The Chinese on the northern slope were now thirty yards away, sniping from the cover of scattered rocks to supplement the fire of their machine-guns from

44

the hilltop to the east, and the mortars firing from the valley. The defence replied with their last rounds from the shallow trenches so painfully scooped out of the loose rock, waiting for the word to go. Suddenly, on the signal, they rose to dash in a body down the slope to the rear. The Chinese, harassed by Carl's artillery fire and the long bursts from the Vickers, could not recover quickly enough to prevent them going. And the line of attackers at the foot of the reverse slope could not resist the force of that determined rush. Before they could open fire, Denis's party had broken through and entered the pinewoods. The branches closed behind them, concealing them from the pursuit that followed.

Jennings came up to the knoll from the Rear-Link wireless.

"The Brigade-Major wants you, sir."

I put on the head-set and called Ken up: he had cheering news. The Filipino Battalion was being sent up during the afternoon to reinforce us. To-morrow, we would be relieved by a combined force of armour and infantry in brigade strength. To-morrow night we should be out into reserve with a chance to take in reinforcements and to re-equip. Already, the Filipinos were moving up along the hills on either side of the road from the south; while in the valley between, the Centurion tanks of the 8th Hussars were shooting them forward. Ken's voice sounded cheerful in the headphones. I closed by telling him that I would take a drink off him on Thursday night.

From the area of the knoll came the sound of excited voices. Henry began to run up the slope from the saddle.

"It's someone from B Company," said Richard. We wriggled forward on our stomachs and found a convenient gap in the broken rocks. Far below us, around the hairpin bend to the south, a group of men had run out on to the road below Kamak-San. They were not Chinese: at least two of them had fair hair.

I said: "It's Denis!"

Our binoculars followed them across the road. They began the long ascent of the re-entrant that led up to our saddle.

"There's Sergeant-Major Morton," Henry called, "and Denis, and Dawson."

45

They had come into full view round a rock face.

"I can see Corporal Wellington, I think," said Richard. "I wonder how many signallers he's got with him."

He stopped suddenly as a party of Chinese came running round the rock-face in obvious pursuit of the men from B Company. The sound of firing came to us faintly, and I saw that several of the Chinese had stopped to fire burp-guns at what appeared to be a party of wounded with Sergeant-Major Morton.

It was going to be touch and go. Whilst a mixed party of mortar-men, signallers, police, and drivers was assembled to make a sortie to their aid, Sam got one of Sergeant Hoper's Vickers across. They began to fire down into the re-entrant; with relief we saw that the pursuit had stopped.

Henry was still distributing grenades to the relief party when I joined him. "It's all right," I said. "The Vickers has fixed them. Denis's party will be up here in ten minutes."

I think he had been looking forward to a chance to even up a part of the score against the Chinese, for he looked very disappointed.

"We'd better just make sure," he said: and then Allum, the signaller, came tumbling down the slope.

"You'd better come up quick, sir," he said. "There's another party of Chinks just come round the end of the ridge and they're going to head B Company off. Walker's got the Bren on them."

We hurried up the slope anxiously, the Colonel with us. He had heard the news from Sergeant Smythe.

"Where's Walker?" I said to Allum. "I thought you said he was here with a Bren?"

"He was, sir," said Allum. "He was right by this rock when——"

"There he goes," said Henry, pointing: "down the hill."

It seemed that Walker had decided to meet this threat on his own. Alone, entirely without orders, he was running down the hill with the gun on his hip, firing as he went. I think it was more his fierce determination than the bullets he fired that deterred the Chinese. To a man, they ran back round the end of the ridge.

It was so like Walker: he was an independent type.

We were twenty men stronger: twenty men, and a few rifles and

46

Stens without any ammunition in them, and Denis's pistol which contained four rounds: all that was left to us of B Company. Setting aside our personal delight at their survival, the addition of their numbers was invaluable. The Colonel combined B Company with C: they made a strong platoon. We now began to take steps to remedy a few of our immediate needs.

The valley where the Main Headquarters had once stood was now deserted. Every attempt by the Chinese to penetrate the dugouts, tents, and vehicles that still remained had been thwarted; for our positions commanded the valley almost as much as theirs. Here and there, by the road and stream, the bodies of bolder Chinese, anxious, perhaps, for loot, provided a warning to any of their fellows who hoped to venture forward. But so acute were our shortages, we now decided that we must attempt what they had failed to achieve. We needed, first, ammunition; second—almost equal in importance—batteries for the wireless sets; third, a little food. Mr. Hobbs began to assemble a party of men from Support Company and Headquarters, together with some of the native porters with whom he would descend to the valley through the gorge. Guy made up a small party of gunners to pick up batteries for his own sets from the GMC.

The machine-guns waited on either side of the knoll. The northern and eastern slopes rising from the valley disappeared as the shells, bursting in a shower of phosphorous sparks, released their white smoke swiftly. The moment had come.

Hidden just above the gorge, Mr. Hobbs and his party rushed down the last few hundred yards of the stream bed into the valley; with them, the little Gunner party. By the ford, they all split. The signallers and the gunners ran towards the area of the Command Post, disappeared into vehicles and dugouts, reappeared with batteries and, in one case, a reserve wireless left undestroyed when we had evacuated the valley in the early morning. The group with Mr. Hobbs were loading ammunition with all speed on to their backs. Beyond them, Sergeant-Major Strong selected rations from our forward dump.

Carl thickened up the smoke with another concentration; a few Chinese emerged from the screen along the road to the north, but were destroyed by one of Guido's light machine-guns. Now the expeditionary force was coming back, staggering with their huge loads. I marvelled at the strength of our South Korean porters. The wooden frames upon their backs—shaped like an 'A', and so called "A-frames"—were heaped from waist to head with wooden boxes, crates, and jerricans. From the GMC came Guy, an unmistakable figure, his cap at a rakish angle on his head. They began the ascent through the gorge as Carl produced more shells—but this time, high explosive.

It was almost as good as Christmas after their return. The slopes below the knoll and behind the saddle were littered with boxes. As I went from dump to dump, I felt like the man who opens his presents to exclaim delightedly: "Just what I wanted!"

Without losing a single man, Mr. Hobbs's party had brought back sufficient to relieve our immediate necessities.

We checked our newly-delivered goods and examined the relative requirements of each element in the force. The ammunition was collected by parties of porters from each company and Frank's Mortar Troop. The magazines of rifles, Brens, and Sten machine-carbines were refilled. Grenades were issued. The Vickers machine-gun sections added a belt or two to their dwindling stocks. There had been no need for ammunition for the medium and heavy mortars; for although they had carried up the barrels to deny them to the enemy, the base plates remained in their pits in the valley. As far as the Battalion was concerned, our defence would be continued with small arms, aided by the support of our guns.

The Colonel now considered what policy we should adopt concerning our vehicles, equipment and stores that remained below. If the Filipinos should manage to arrive before darkness, there was every prospect that we could go down again to collect what we needed, and to send our drivers back with vehicles no longer required, under the protection of the 8th Hussars tanks. Yet we could not bring ourselves to believe that they were going to reach us; the Chinese were so numerous that it seemed incredible that they would manage to break their way through the numbers that were already miles to the south. However, no good purpose could be served either by showing a long face to the remainder of the Battalion, or by under-estimating the ability of the force attempting to get through. For the moment the Colonel merely wished to know whether or not to bring artillery fire down upon our Headquarters site to effect its destruction. We called Brigade Headquarters on the Rear-Link set.

It seemed that, by coincidence, Ken had been about to call us. Throughout the morning and the early afternoon, he had reported the progress of the Filipino Force. The last news had been encouraging: they had reached a point four miles south of us where, meeting strong resistance, they had been in process of mounting a full-scale attack. The outcome of this was now reported to us: the attack had failed. The Chinese had reinforced the area from Kamak-San. The 8th Hussars had lost some tanks in a road block constructed in one of the gorges, and could get no further forward that day.

That was that.

The Brigadier had just come back to Brigade Main Headquarters from a visit to the Fifth Fusiliers and The Rifles, each of whom were fighting a bitter action against enormous odds. The Belgians had been withdrawn intact across the river but with heavy casualties. It appeared that the Chinese were exerting strong pressure in an attempt to force the parallel road to the east of us; and that if they could not have both roads, they would have one or the other. Since leaving the other Battalions, he had spoken to both the Divisional Commander and the Corps Commander. There was no alternative but to hold on.

The Colonel looked down at his map as the Brigadier spoke. There was a slight pause after the latter finished speaking. Then the Colonel put his map on top of the wireless.

"I understand the position quite clearly," he said. "What I must make clear to you is the fact that my command is no longer an effective fighting force. If it is required that we shall stay here, in spite of this, we shall continue to hold. But I wish to make known the nature of my position."

These were grave words for a Battalion Commander to speak; they were spoken in a grave moment. We had less than four hundred effective men—and many wounded. Our magazine was low and ten or twelve hours fighting on a moderate scale would

49

certainly empty it altogether. Many of our weapons had been damaged or smashed completely beyond repair by enemy fire—we were especially short of Bren light machine-guns. Our wireless batteries, thanks to the expedition, might last another twelve or fifteen hours if used sparingly. We could not hope for a further supply of any of these before mid-morning to-morrow, at the earliest.

Yet, the Colonel was not asking obliquely that we might be permitted to withdraw while there was still time; that the outcome of the battle might be risked in order that we might be spared. He was not that sort of a man. He was a man who believed in facing realities; he was facing them now.

I heard the Brigadier's voice in the head-phones again. I could tell by his voice that he did not like committing us to such a desperate task. He said he realized how things stood with us, but the job had to be done; and we were the only ones who could do it. No one else could hope to get through that day. Knowing him, we were at least content with the absolute necessity of what we were to do. And, to-morrow, they still planned to send forward the regimental combat team of infantry and armour—perhaps by ten o'clock.

But to-morrow was another day.

The Colonel had gone up to Hill 235 to make a reconnaissance of the positions held now by A Company and the Assault Pioneer Platoon. He had decided to concentrate the whole force on that long thin ridge for the night. It was a difficult piece of ground to attack, since the southern approach was precipitous and the northern side extremely steep. Only the ends of the feature, north-west and south-east, favoured attack in strength, and these we could expect to hold through the night without losing ground.

We packed our few pieces of equipment and gathered together our scant arms and ammunition. Two observation planes had just completed an attempt to free-drop wireless batteries, Brens, and ammunition with but little success. To-morrow, the Fairchild Packets would bring us more supplies which they would drop by parachute. Meantime, we would make the best use of what we had got.

50

At dusk, when the Chinese could no longer see our movements, we began the march up through D Company's position to the ridge whose highest point was 235. It was a slow march, for the track was narrow and winding, often steep. The wounded, now increased in number by the few B Company had managed to bring in, and those who had sustained injury in the skirmishes during the morning, were carried by shifts of men in order to avoid returning to the knoll or saddle for a second journey with equipment. At length, the last man crossed the saddle connecting D Company's hill to our night position and the business of settling-in began.

Taking up a strange position by night is never a pleasant or easy task for a soldier. To do so with one pick and shovel among twenty men in an area at least a half of which is solid rock, is apt to aggravate the business. In spite of this, there were no complaints; spirits were high as the defence works were constructed, even where the construction involved digging away sharp stones with bayonets and bare hands. There was no frantic, panic-stricken excavation of trenches: everyone worked steadily throughout the night. Later, a pitifully small ration was issued from the stocks brought up by Mr. Hobbs, the Provost Sergeant, Peglar, and Sergeant-Major Strong. The sections each drew lots to see which portion of the rations they should have: tinned rich fruit cake or bully beef; tinned peaches or tinned salmon; half a loaf of bread or a tin of unsweetened milk. Much of the food was put away until later. Men wanted water rather than food; the heat of the day and the loss of sweat in the march up to the night position had made them thirsty, and there was no water to quench their thirst. We had rationed out a quarter of a pint per man earlier, and sent the remainder to Bob for the wounded, who now lay just south of the ridge crest in a hollow. There were some vacant stretchers there: some of the men had died.

At last there was silence: no sound of battle disturbed the night, the noise of picks and shovels in the rocky earth nearby had ceased. The signallers had dug their trenches for the night. For an hour or so, the world pretended to be at peace.

Below me, in a slit trench dug some days before by Spike's

pioneers, the Colonel slept. Behind, in the adjacent trench, slept Guy and Lucas. Biting on the stem of my empty pipe, I began to reflect on the day's events and the coming battle. Gradually, all my thoughts drifted, and I began to connect my present situation with all the things I had done or seen throughout my life as an Infantry soldier. And I remembered, suddenly, the words of a very famous general whose lecture I had attended.

"The Infantry," he said, "are the cutting edge of the battle."

If the Eighth Army in Korea was a sword, I knew full well what part of that sword we helped to form: the edge of the sword. Half-sitting and half-lying by the slit-trench parapet on that sharp ridge, the stars shining down on me through the white clouds, it seemed to me that it was not a bad description of our job: the cutting edge of the sword.

I was not to remain in fantasy for long. Nearby, two signallers had been awakened for their watch; and they had something far more real to think about. A voice that surely came from Bristol was declaring: "I don't care what you say about your fancy London beers, Jack. As far as I'm concerned, there's no beer in the world like George's Home Brewed."

CHAPTER FOUR

25th April, 1951

THE bugles wakened me.

Some time before, the Colonel had risen and insisted that I get some sleep. He had taken my place by the parapet, and I had taken his. Now, sitting up to throw off the effects of the deep sleep into which I had fallen, I heard the bugles again: not the pleasant familiar note of our own bugles, but something akin to that of a cavalry trumpet. They were playing a call which, if not exactly familiar to me, was nonetheless plain in its meaning. It was after ten o'clock: the attack had begun.

I came out on to the ridge as the first crack-crack of small-arms fire sounded to the south-east: Denis's company was evidently engaged. Almost immediately afterwards, the sound of an exploding grenade came from the area A Company were holding. No wonder the bugles were sounding. The noise of battle grew around us. Soon, the coloured lights of tracer rounds were flying over us from somewhere to the west. From the knoll and saddle we had held the day before, the bugles started another call. The Colonel decided to take a stroll round and departed for Denis's headquarters. Reports began to come in; Guy called up his Regiment and told them to stand by. They replied acidly that they had not yet stood down; there had been other calls during the night, even if we had not heard them. Ronnie began to shoot on to D Company's previous position, as a machine-gun opened fire from there. The temperature of the battle began to warm.

The tactics of the enemy were unchanged: they seemed incapable of learning by experience. Coughs, rustling, even chatter alerted our defence as their soldiers crept forward to attack. The first rush thrown back, a short pause ensued until the next assault began. The pattern was the same. And, as before, they made no effort to concentrate on one particular sector in the early stages; that would come later—much later—after they had sustained many casualties and been forced to call forward substantial reinforcements. On the south-eastern end of the ridge, Denis's Company and Frank's Mortar Troop were engaged by frequent assaults and a good deal of machine-gun fire that was uncomfortable in view of the shallowness of their trenches, most of which had been driven down only a few feet on to solid rock. In the north-west, A Company were mainly engaged in fighting for a small feature a little forward of Point 235; a mound, covered with trees and scrub. Here, Donald had forgotten that he was the Assistant Adjutant and was commanding seventeen men—in name, a platoon—who were hanging on by little more than the skin of their teeth.

I called up Ken and told him how the battle was progressing. He sounded very tired, and I knew that he had had no proper sleep since the first action began. I was just about to leave the set when the GSO 3 came on for me. He wanted to tell me that the air transport sorties would be flown sometime after nine o'clock: had we any means of marking a Dropping Zone? I felt like saying: tell them to aim for a high rock with a lot of Chinese round it, but forbore; he was doing his best. We agreed on smoke markers to save further discussion. In addition to the news about the supply drop was another cheering item: we had a promise of substantial offensive air support once daylight came. How I had wished during the past two days for a squadron—even a flight—of F 80s. Whatever happened to-day, we should give a really good account of ourselves.

The Colonel had come back by this time. We discussed the question of air support from the fighters with Guy; he had already been informed about it over the Gunner wireless net. But there was a pressing problem in this connection. Our wireless batteries were getting very low—they were certainly not going to last as long as we had hoped. We agreed to continue the practice of keeping only one of the Gunner sets open and, as an additional measure, to close the Rear-Link set again, except when we wished to pass a message. If Brigade Headquarters wanted to reach us, they could ask us to open up through the Gunners' set.

When Guy had gone over to see Ronnie and Carl, the Colonel told me that he had visited D Company. Mike seemed to be quite happy that they could continue holding their present positions. They had inflicted such casualties on the enemy that they had drawn off for rather longer than usual after the last attack; and Sergeant Murphy, with his Vickers section nearby, seemed quite secure. Young Bob, the Assistant Machine-Gun Officer, was down with them now. What really concerned him was that Donald was having a very hard time on the little feature forward of A Company's main position. He was quite certain that seventeen men were not enough to hold it. If it was going to be held securely, Jumbo would have to reinforce them as soon as he could, perhaps from his reserve platoon. Terry's platoon on the high ground of Point 235, behind Donald's feature, was in a good position to cover any party going forward along the right flank—the distance between them was less than fifty yards. A decision would have to be taken as soon as it was daylight.

It was almost daylight already. In half an hour, at the very most, we should be able to see our enemies clearly. As the light grew, I realized that the position in which our slit trench was situated was just at the top of a small path that led up the steep slope from the valley to the west. I reminded the Colonel that we had a bag of eighteen grenades with us. We put them to hand just behind the parapet.

"It seems to me," said the Colonel, "that we are going to find a job for ourselves as riflemen before very much longer."

I was to remember those words a little later on.

The bugles were sounding again.

"It'll be a long time before I want to hear a cavalry trumpet playing, after this," said the Colonel.

"It would serve them right, sir," I said, "if we confused them by playing our own bugles. I wonder which direction they'd go if they heard 'Defaulters' played?"

I was half joking, but the Colonel took me seriously.

"Have we got a bugle up here?" he asked. It appeared that we had; for when I called down the slope to the east, the Drum-Major's voice replied through the bare, scattered trees:

"Got one in my haversack, sir."

"Well, play it, Drum-Major."

But it was no good telling the Drum-Major just to "play". He was an experienced man and, in barrack routine, he knew exactly what should be played and when. On special occasions, he expected to receive instructions from the Adjutant, quite rightly; and this was undoubtedly a special occasion.

"It's getting on towards daylight," I called back to him, "play Reveille—the Long and the Short. And play 'Fire Call'—in fact, play all the calls of the day as far as 'Retreat', but don't play that!"

A little way below us in the darkness, I heard a few preliminary "peeps" as the Drum-Major warmed his instrument up. This was followed by the sound of stones being dislodged as he climbed from his slit-trench to sound the calls; for I have said that the Drum-Major was a man who knew how things should be done, and the idea of playing his bugle under cover in a slit-trench was beyond him. I could just see his tall, lean figure, topped by a cap comforter—almost a shadow in the darkness. Then he began to play. He played each 'Reveille' twice, he played 'Defaulters', 'Cookhouse', 'Officers Dress for Dinner', all the 'Orderly NCO' calls, and a dozen or more besides. He always played a bugle well; that day he was not below form. The sweet notes of our own bugle, which now echoed through the valley below him, died away. For a moment, there was silence—the last note had coincided with a lull in the action. Then the noise of battle began again—but with a difference: there was no sound of a Chinese bugle. There are not many Drum-Majors in the British Army who can claim to have silenced the enemy's battle calls with a short bugle recital.

It is morning. Beyond Hill 235, a sudden rush has driven back Donald's little group. They withdraw under heavy mortar fire which intensifies as they reach the top of Point 235. The air is black with mortar smoke; it seems as if a huge, dark screen has been dropped across the top of the hill. Men come staggering back from Terry's position; eleven men, wounded, come reeling back, their senses bemused by shock and injury. The face of one man has been laid open by a splinter of metal; another's arm is hanging limply by his side, the bone smashed. Sergeant Pugh has been wounded in the shoulder, but he has refused to go back and is helping to re-organize the position. Two men are carrying Terry back; he is quite unconscious from a wound in the top of his head. They lay him down in a slit trench and one of the medical orderlies begins to bandage his head. Donald is coming down the hill. He is wounded in the shoulder and there is a gash upon his forehead. His face is pale and drawn; it is plain that he is about to faint.

Now there are two of us to lead A Company: Jumbo and me—there is nothing for me to do at Battalion Headquarters just now. Here we are, the two of us, and the gallant little body of A Company that has had two such nights of battle as I have never seen before. We have been pushed off the little feature, which is not so serious; and we have been pushed off Point 235—which is. So we must go back to it. And we must go back now before they have time to invest it in real strength; for if they secure the height absolutely, the flood gates will have been opened and the waters will pour in upon the Battalion position, no matter how well the bottom gate is held by Frank and Denis. And D Company, further down the slope, will be washed away with Support Company and Battalion Headquarters.

I look round the small body of men in the trenches. Some of them are young men, hardly more than boys; some of them men in their late thirties; most of them are somewhere in between. I see that it is a good lot of faces to be in a tight corner with; reliable faces; the faces of old friends. After a minute or so, we are all able to manage a smile: even young Fish with a half dozen pieces of metal inside his fair head. When I see that smile, I know we are ready to go.

Clayden has come up from Support Company to give a hand: he takes the left flank. Sergeant Tuggey is on the right. In the centre, with me, are Masters and Middleton; Guilding is there, too. I pick three or four more and we are ready to go. We all start running forward.

The top is thirty yards away. The scarred, red earth flies beneath our feet, our weapons are firing, we are on them, they go back, the hill is ours: it is as easy as that. We jump into the trenches that they occupied so recently and turn our attention to securing what we have regained. Half right, the scrub and trees of the small feature are alive with enemy: we may have to make a sortie to clear that. To our front, the hill drops away in a long, gentle slope down to the valley below Castle Hill. There is good cover here for the enemy: dwarf oaks and a group of pine trees are on either side of the track running north. We shall have to maintain a careful watch on this approach. Nearer, for the first twenty yards along the track from my trench, the ground has been cleared—perhaps long ago by Spike's Pioneers. Two felled trees lie across the track, at right angles to it. Left, the side of the ridge drops steeply to the western valley; Clayden must see that we are not surprised from this direction. Only the extreme right flank is secure. Here Tom's Platoon of D Company are ready and waiting to give us fire support with their Brens. There can be no doubt as to what they can do:

57

there are six dead Chinese on the right flank, caught by Tom's lads as they ran back after our assault on the hill.

Clayden moves a little way over the edge of the ridge, towards the western valley. He can see the whole way down the slope from here very nicely, and he remains within voice range. Tuggey moves up further on the right flank so that he can engage the whole of the small feature. Middleton and two of the others move to different trenches. Everyone now has an arc to watch and to shoot in; the arcs overlap; our front is covered with potential fire. It is time for a smoke break.

It is a quarter to eight. By the sound of chattering below the edge of the hill directly ahead of me, the enemy are about to make a third attempt to retake Point 235. Someone is giving a pep talk to their soldiers; I hope he is off form this morning. Sergeant-Major Gallagher has just left me after bringing forward more ammunition. All in all, we are not too badly placed, for the moment. We can hold out for some time if they keep to the present battle tempo. Now Ronnie has come doubling over the crest of the hill. He can spare me some artillery fire if I need it just now. He has just finished a shoot for Denis. I accept his offer enthusiastically. They are going to come straight up the track at any minute; but we can deal with that party. The area I want sorted out is the small feature.

"Well," says Ronnie, "it'll mean dropping 'em a bit short. Are you prepared to accept 'unders'?"

We certainly are. For the sake of neutralizing that wretched feature, we'll accept as many "unders" as he likes. Ronnie goes back to his wireless set; I can see that his sense of propriety as a Gunner prevents him from being quite satisfied. Obviously, the Gun Position thinks the same way for, a minute or so later, I get a hail from Jumbo.

"The Gunners say that you'll have to be prepared to accept several 'unders'."

Good Heavens! Recce dropped lots of "unders" on himself yesterday. What are they so worried about, to-day?

They will have to get a move on with the shoot; the Chinese are

58

coming. Yellow faces appear among the pine trees and the dwarf oaks. A machine-gun is firing thirty yards away from that damned small mound: it has killed a man to my right. At any minute they will rush forward from their cover.

Ah! there is a whistling in the air. We all duck into our trenches. The sky darkens; the whole ground is shaken with the noise of explosions. The Gunners are doing us proud. I lie on the bottom of my slit trench, covered with earth blown in from the bursting shells. A peculiar black and orange beetle is crawling up the wall of the trench. He seems quite unaffected by the disturbance outside.

Another minute passes and it is quiet. I kneel up to shake off the loose earth. What a wonderful view; not a Chinese in sight; and the small feature is simply pitted with shell craters. Marvellous chaps, these Gunners!

Someone is throwing grenades; and they are throwing them at us. Here comes another one: a small, dark object against the background of blue sky, its wooden handle turning over and over as it begins the descent on to our positions. It falls near Master's slit-trench; he ducks for a moment as it explodes. We begin to scan our immediate front closely for the source of this annoyance.

From the direction of their flight, it would seem that all the grenades have come from a single point somewhere along the track that runs away from us down the north-western end of the feature. Yet this ground is entirely open immediately in front of us. Unless they are standing up—which would seem unlikely—they must have prodigious strength to throw from the cover some way down the track. Surely it cannot be from there. We continue to watch. Another grenade rises suddenly into the air. Ah, the trees —the felled trees: one or two very small men must have remained behind after the last attack upon our positions and concealed themselves by pressing their bodies right up against the trunks. It is from there, less than fifteen yards away, that they have been throwing their grenades at us. Three of us draw the pins from our Mills grenades, three arms draw back for the throw, three arms come up and over. We take cover as the grenades drop to the ground just beyond the tree trunk where we suspect the enemy lies. There is a flash, two more follow in quick succession; the three explosions blend into one mighty roar. From behind the tree trunk, two figures appear; two little cotton-clad men in their teacup-shaped steel helmets garnished with scraps of scrub and dwarf oak branches. One of them is unable to run; already he has fallen back, his life-blood pouring through the back of his jacket. The other is unin-jured by the grenades and runs desperately for the cover further back along the track. Ten yards from the tree trunk which concealed him, he is spun round by a burst of fire from a Sten machine-carbine and flung, lifeless, to the ground. The incident is over. Looking at my watch, I see that what seemed an hour's action took but three minutes of the morning.

The sun is rising high in the sky, and we are still on the hill. Apart from the small feature, half right—Donald's mound—we have not lost a foot of ground in spite of their repeated assaults on our positions. In A Company's area alone, we have had six counter-attacks upon Hill 235 since we threw them back just after dawn. It is certain that they will soon muster for a seventh attempt. Their voices, calling out to one another, are heard plainly from below the brow of the hill to our front; a sure sign of an impending attack.

The Colonel doubles across the slope behind me and drops into my trench.

"We've got some air support, at last," he says. "From what the air observer says they're massing to attack your positions now. Let me know where you want the air strike and I'll call them down."

We do not need glasses to survey this ground: it is a close battle. I show him the main points from which I believe they will mount their attack and agree on a means of marking our own positions. In two minutes we have said all that needs to be said. As he is going back to Battalion Headquarters, I say:

"How have things been with you?"

He does not tell me that they have been under the most intense heavy machine-gun fire for the last fifty minutes; he does not admit to strolling about under fire along the whole front in order to visit and inspire the companies; he does not say that he has made another sortie to repel a group of would-be infiltrators. He puffs at his pipe for a moment, regards the smoke difting up into the air, and taps some ash back into the pipe bowl.

"Not bad, really," he says. "Have you a match to spare?"

We are going to need that air strike quickly. We are engaged in a fire-fight with two machine-guns on the mound; another is firing indirectly from behind the brow of the hill right in front of us. Several parties have tried to rush forward to draw our fire and they have been too large to be permitted to come nearer than thirty yards. At any moment, something in excess of a hundred Chinese soldiers, armed with rifles and machine-carbines will come out of the scrub to our front and rush upon us. We are familiar with their tactics.

This time, however, there is a difference in the circumstances under which we await them: our ammunition is practically exhausted. The solution to our problem may lie in the grenade on the edge of my trench—a grenade which will release a great cloud of violet coloured smoke when I throw it forward. But there is only one of these grenades. I must judge the moment carefully or we shall be under the fire of our own aircraft as well as that from the Chinese.

High above us, their silver wings shining in the sunlight, the F 80s are circling before making their run-in. The flight-leader is already turning to begin the air strike. I unscrew the black bakelite cap of the grenade, half unwind the tape, and throw it up into the air with all my might. It lands beyond the tree trunks on the path and bursts. Released, the violet smoke seems to hang for a moment in a dense cloud, then spreads across the ridge, obscuring the mound, the track, and the dwarf oaks from our view.

This is an anxious moment. If I have thrown the grenade too soon, the smoke that marks the forward edge of our positions will have dispersed before the aircraft reach us, and the chances are that they will release their terrible load as much on us as upon the Chinese. If the Chinese are ready to attack instantly, are sufficiently well-controlled to seize their opportunity, they will rise under cover of the smoke and rush us in such strength that our few

61

weapons will be unable to destroy them before we are overwhelmed. Twenty—maybe thirty—seconds will show what turn in events the smoke grenade will bring.

There is a shout from the rear; a distant whine grows to a deafening high-pitched scream; a great, tumbling wave of air descends on the position, forcing the red dust up all around us in a choking cloud; one's mind retains an impression of a silver object that appeared and, in the same instant that it was perceived, disappeared. The F 80s are making their strike!

In passing, they have dispersed the violet marker smoke except for a single tentacle that hangs in the air just to the left of the track. Our eyes do not linger upon this. Forward, where the dwarf oaks and pines stood, there is a raging mass of flame, still rising, still spreading, from the napalm tanks the planes have dropped. There will be no attack from this direction for a time; and the men who lay in readiness beneath the cover of the oaks will never rise to make their charge. The aircraft make a second run. This time we are less concerned with watching for the enemy and see, in the brief moment that they pass over us, that they fly across the mound half-right. As they reach us, they release two aluminium tanks and these descend upon the rear approaches to the mound. They are napalm tanks; ignited, the jellied gasoline bursts out and up into a great sheet of yellow flame, consuming everything that it envelops. Now it is the turn of the mound itself. On the third run, the 80s drop their tanks early, before they reach us, and the tanks drop on to the very area from which the enemy machine-guns were firing. They are firing no longer.

In all, the air-strike involved seven runs; for, after they had dropped their napalm, they returned to distribute their rockets and machine-gun fire amongst the mortar crews, the reserve assault waves, and a heavy machine-gun firing down into Tom's position from the east. I watched them climb back to the white clouds as they returned to base to refuel and re-arm. As the shapes receded, I saw three more coming towards us from the south-east, flying at about ten thousand feet. They were transport aircraft and they had our supplies aboard. It was nine thirty; in half an hour we might begin to look for the relief column; in the meantime we were about to receive a supply drop. On our own front, the enemy had received a setback which would take them at least an hour to overcome—in fact, the time it would take to bring forward more reinforcements from, say, the area of Castle Hill. Things were really looking up! I followed the flight of the transports as they flew over us, expecting them to circle preparatory to a run-in.

They began to turn before they reached the Imjin, altering course towards the west. All at once, I realized that they were flying out of sight, had disappeared, indeed, in a direction that would take them out to sea. I was pondering over this when I got a hail from Sergeant-Major Gallagher.

"You're wanted at Battalion Headquarters, sir," he called. I told Sergeant Tuggey to take charge and ran back across the hilltop. On the reverse slope, the Sergeant-Major was busy trying to repair a Bren by removing parts from two others, also damaged. The wounded had long since been removed to the Regimental Aid Post.

"You'd better watch that ridge as you go back, sir," said the Sergeant-Major. "There's a machine-gun firing from the west—somewhere across the valley, I should think."

He was still warning me as a burst of tracer shot across the ridge from the west. It was a long burst and, while it lasted, separated A Company from Battalion Headquarters. Once it ceased, it was time to go. I dashed back along the ridge like a quarter-miler, only stopping when I reached the Rear-Link wireless set. The whole Headquarters had moved from the position I had left earlier that morning, principally because of the machine-gun firing from the west. It was this weapon that had killed Richard as he walked across to the wireless set where Dawe and Allum kept watch. He was killed instantly, of course, for the round entered his forehead. As I passed the spot where he lay, I could hardly believe that he was really dead; it was impossible that someone as full of life and fun as he was could be cut down as suddenly as that.

The Colonel was sitting by himself below the Rear-Link set, looking at his map. He stood up as I approached, looking so completely calm that I had no idea of the importance of his news. I

63

might have known that he would not have called me back to discuss some commonplace.

"You know that armoured/infantry column that's coming up from 3 Div to relieve us," he said.

"Yes, sir."

"Well, it isn't coming."

I said, "Right, sir." There did not seem to be much else to say.

The Colonel continued with all the news he had to that moment. It appeared that the Chinese were now pressing so hard to the east that the relief column intended for us would be required to cover the withdrawal of the Division through Uijongbu, below which the new defence line was being established. Our commitment was at an end; in a short time, under cover of the guns, we should commence to fight our way south.

Mike, called back from D Company Headquarters, joined us; and Bob, the Doctor; the Gunners came over; Sam appeared from Support Company Headquarters across the way, where he lodged with Spike; Guido came doubling up from the south-east to represent Denis; and last of all, Henry climbed up from the Drums position, which he had been visiting. The Colonel explained the position and gave us our orders for the withdrawal from the main feature. We should move south-west towards the right flank of the 1st ROK Division, where tanks had come forward to assist them. The Colonel took us to the edge of the ridge and pointed out the route we should take: at least there would be cover once we reached the end of the valley. We were to start at ten o'clock. When he had finished, he paused for a moment before turning to Bob.

"Bob," he said, eventually. "I'm afraid we shall have to leave the wounded behind."

Bob paused, too—just for a moment—before he replied.

"Very well, sir," he said; "I quite understand the position."

We went back to our respective places of duty to make preparations for the withdrawal.

A Company were to be the first to withdraw. We distributed our remaining ammunition amongst those fit to bear arms and made the walking wounded as comfortable as possible. Each rifleman had three rounds; each Bren, one and a half magazines:

64

each Sten, a half magazine. There were seven Mills grenades left and four white-phosphorus smoke. With this armament, we were going to fight our way back across at least four miles of hill country. We destroyed everything that might be of the smallest use to the enemy and then sat back to await the time when we should move.

We were so thirsty. The few rations distributed during the previous night remained almost untouched; only the tins of fruit and milk had been opened. Sitting there, on the forward slope of Hill 235, we thought of all the water that was flowing, at that very moment, down the Imjin River to be wasted in the sea! In front of us, the blackened surface of the hill still smoked from the napalm fires; the mound lay bare and deserted—no longer a menace, now that its cover was destroyed. One by one, the minutes ticked away towards ten o'clock.

At three minutes to ten, I gave the sign to Jumbo to set off with the main body of A Company. Although there was no sign of the enemy, we knew that we were under observation and wished, of course, to keep from him, as long as possible, the news that we were leaving our position. At ten, exactly, the small party that remained got out of their trenches under cover of white-phosphorus smoke and withdrew across the hilltop. The job was over; a new task was begun.

Back on the ridge, I saw that Jumbo was waiting with the main body just above Support Company Headquarters, where a section of the machine-guns was established to cover Hill 235. A Company moved off, and I rejoined Battalion Headquarters; for A Company were now so weak that one officer could command them without difficulty. I reached the Colonel just as he finished talking on the Rear-Link wireless, and I saw that his face was grave.

"Let Sam know," he said, "that I have just been told by the Brigadier that the guns are unable to support us—the gun lines are under attack themselves. Our orders are quite simple: every man to make his own way back."

He began talking to the other companies on the wireless, as I ran over to Sam's Headquarters. All was bustle now. Above Spike's positions, the machine-gun section were destroying their heavy gear as I went back to the ridge. Nearby, I met Bob returning to the Regimental Aid Post from a talk with the Colonel. The signallers had already destroyed their sets, and Henry was stamping on the ashes of the codebook he had just burnt. We were all ready to move. In small groups, the Headquarters split up and ran over the ridge. When they had gone, I, too, came up on to the ridge crest and prepared to descend the other side. Bob was standing alone by the path that led to the steep slopes below us.

"Come on, Bob," I said. "We're about the last to go—you ought to have gone before this. The Colonel will be off in a minute and that will be the lot."

He looked at me for a moment before saying:

"I can't go. I must stay with the wounded."

For a few seconds I did not comprehend his meaning: we were all making our way out—there seemed a very fair chance that some of us would make it; to stay here was to stay certainly for capture, possibly for death, when the Chinese launched their final assault on the position. And then I realized that he had weighed all this— weighed it all and made a deliberate choice: he would place his own life in the utmost jeopardy in order to remain with the wounded at the time when they would need him most. Somewhere, the words appear, "Greater love hath no man than this. . . ." I knew now exactly what those words meant. Too moved to speak again, I clapped my hand upon his shoulder and went on.

By now, the greater portion of the Battalion who had descended from my end of the ridge had reached the valley floor. Scrambling, slipping, jumping from rock to rock, I caught up the rear of Support Company and Battalion Headquarters. Of D Company, there was no sign. We turned towards the saddle at the head of the valley, south-west of us. Once over this, we should find cover to conceal our movements from the enemy; cover through which we might move towards the tanks, who had come forward to assist the 1st ROK Division to withdraw to the new defence line. Even now, I could see figures clambering up to the top of the saddle; some were already over the top. We hurried on along the stony path, careless of anything but speed. If we were to escape capture, we must reach the saddle. There was no hope of concealment on the bare slopes on either side of us; for what little cover there had been was burning from the napalm attacks made earlier in the day. A little way from the saddle, the main valley divided and we took the right branch. The way narrowed, forcing us to march in single file in places. A stream, which rose at the head of this branch, wove in and out across the path, and the surface became slippery with mud from our boots as we crossed a succession of fords. Nearer the foot of the saddle, where a patch of dead bushes formed a transparent arch over the stream, I saw that one of the Gunner officers was lying, face down, the back of his battledress blouse soaked in blood. I glanced at him in passing, and thought I recognized Frank.

All the way up the valley I had heard machine-gun fire sounding and resounding among the hills; but none had been directed at us. Only now, as we drew near to the saddle, as the walls of the valley seemed to close right in upon us in this dark and cheerless spot—now almost a ravine—did we feel the breath of the enemy's fire. From the hills on either side, from the hills to our rear, light and heavy machine-guns fired towards us. Yet they did not hit us. There can be no doubt that, had they wished to, they could have mown us down like grass before a scythe. Exposed entirely to their weapons, we moved along the path under the very muzzles. The message that they conveyed was quite plain: we are up here; you are down there; you are exposed; we are concealed and you are in our sights. As we moved on, the fire from three machine-guns came down again, this time a good deal lower—unmistakably lower. I knew there was but one course open to me if the men with me were to remain alive for more than five minutes. Feeling as if I was betraying everything that I loved and believed in, I raised my voice and called:

"Stop!"

They stopped and looked towards me, their faces expectant. I shall never know what order they anticipated. Then I said:

"Put down your arms!"

A few seconds later, just at the foot of the saddle, I heard Sam say the same thing to those with whom he had moved. The words rang in my ears like an echo, a shameful echo. After all that we had done, after all the effort we had exerted in fulfilling our task, this was the end: surrender to the enemy!

67

PART TWO
UNEASY LEISURE

CHAPTER ONE

IT was difficult to realize that we were captives. For a few minutes we stood about on the narrow valley path, held there by weapons and men at least two hundred yards away. I still had some tobacco and, removing my pouch from a pocket sweat-soaked after my recent exertions, I filled and lit my pipe. Hardly a word was said between any one of us; the position was now clear to all as we awaited the next move—a move that lay with the enemy. Perhaps one man asked another for a match to light his cigarette; perhaps another whispered a question to a comrade—but there was nothing more than this. The whole valley had fallen silent; and so had we.

We did not have to wait very long. Sam had just strolled down to join me when we heard a shout from the main valley. Running towards us were three men; three Chinese soldiers. These were the men who were to put the seal on our capture. As they drew closer, we examined them with curiosity; for this was our first chance to look at the enemy dispassionately—except for the prisoners that we had taken earlier in the year. Now we were the prisoners; and they were the very soldiers against whom we had just been fighting. They approached us, obviously very excited and very pleased with themselves.

They were all short men by our standards, but two of them were stocky, and of these two, one had an exceptionally pock-marked face. They wore the ragged yellow-khaki cotton uniforms we were accustomed to seeing them in—though the pock-marked man had apparently tried to patch his, with material of a different colour. They all carried burp-guns and kept their spare magazines in cheap web and leather belts strapped round their waists. None had a badge of any sort, but I noticed that the leader—one of the stocky pair—had a mark in the centre of his cap above the peak, which had quite obviously been made by a badge. The cloth of his cap had faded a good deal except where this badge had been, but at that point showed clearly the outline of a five-pointed star.

They were not unfriendly; that is to say, they did not maltreat us, though they would not let us carry those of the walking wounded who were too exhausted to go farther. It never occurred to us, of course, that they *would* maltreat us—much less, kill us. After all, this was the mid-twentieth century, and we had every right to expect to be treated as human beings by troops of a nation constantly proclaiming its humanitarianism. They were really quite incapable of controlling us; they certainly had not the first idea how to organize us; and there were many arguments between themselves as to whether we should be allowed to drink from the mountain stream, whether we should be permitted to smoke or not, and so on. Had it not been for the fact that those infernal machine-guns still covered us, we would have disarmed them and sent them on their way—if only because they so exasperated us with their manifest indecision as to what to do. Eventually, by sign-language, Sam determined that they had decided to move us back down the valley. So back down the valley we went. We were certainly not going to spend the rest of the day sitting under the machine-guns in that dark little ravine.

The main valley was filled with sunlight. But for our circumstances, it would have been rather pleasant to stroll along the track, chatting. As it was, exhausted, hungry, captive, it merely eased our situation that the weather was so fine! We drew near to the foot of the slope, which we had descended originally in our withdrawal from the ridge, and found another group of prisoners awaiting us, under a very much stronger guard. Guy was there—beginning his second spell in captivity—the Drum-Major, Sergeant Peglar—as many as fifty others; so many of us had been caught, it seemed. We could only hope that the others had all got away. We stayed there for some time, and I decided to re-open with Sam the topic which I had broached at the point of capture: escape! The night would surely bring a good opportunity, and we must be ready for it. Originally, before I realized that Sam was only just ahead of us, I had discussed the prospect with Crompton, the

72

Intelligence Sergeant, and Lucas. They were game to come with me if we could only keep together; and I now told Sam that I felt confident that the four of us could make it together. We began to discuss ways and means, while Peglar discreetly assembled one or two items of gear that we should find useful.

The guards began to move amongst us, removing the few cameras in our possession, but they missed my binoculars. After they had passed, we began to close up again to resume our conference but, at that moment, there was a good deal of shouting from above us and we looked up to see Henry being led down the hill between three guards. He explained, on joining us, that he had been discovered hiding under a bush, awaiting darkness. From him we got the news that the whole ridge had been invested by the Chinese in considerable strength, and that they were searching the general area for others who had had the same idea as himself. He had seen Bob, the Padre, and Brisland marched down the hill from the Regimental Aid Post and was certain that they had not been allowed to continue to care for the wounded who were still on their stretchers above us. This was bad news; we resolved to take this matter up with our captors as soon as we could find some reasonably responsible person —if necessary, by drawing pictures to explain ourselves.

Henry joined our escape conference. When we had a minute to ourselves, I asked him what Chinese casualties he had seen on the upper slopes.

He said: "Only one small group—that party which tried to rush Sergeant Clayden on your left. Otherwise, the rocks prevented me from seeing; I had my back to a boulder."

We decided to count the dead lying on the slope immediately above us. There were many scattered groups, most of which had been killed by artillery fire during the early part of the morning. We agreed to count independently, and then to compare our figures. Henry made it two hundred and seventeen, I had counted two hundred and sixteen. If this was the toll on one hill slope in one morning, I could not estimate what casualties they must have lost throughout the battle area over the whole period.

It was obvious that many others would want to try to escape as soon as possible. We began to pass out as much information as possible concerning our exact location, and the best direction to take for the journey back to our own lines, the approximate distance they must expect to travel, and the like. Just then, the guards entered our ranks once more and took Henry out, leading him back up the hill. We protested that he should remain with us, but, though they smiled and made re-assuring signs, they continued to lead him away. Short of attempting to overpower them as a quick way of committing suicide—there was nothing more that we could do. We were learning the first lesson of captivity.

The chatter of our remaining guards seemed particularly animated and one of them began to hail. We soon saw that this was provoked by the appearance of another Chinese along the track that came from Choksong village. He was rather better dressed than the other soldiers—his suit was certainly new—and his head was not cropped, like theirs. His personal armament was a small pistol in a brown leather holster. He was obviously a man of authority.

Sam wasted no time in raising the question of the wounded on the top of the hill and those by the saddle at the head of the valley, where we had been taken. The Chinese officer spoke no English and we, of course, no Chinese; so the negotiations took rather a long time. Eventually, he seemed to understand and a number of us went back up the valley to pick up all the wounded we could find. If we achieved success in this particular, however, we failed utterly in our attempts to persuade him to let us bring the wounded down from Hill 235. He would not let a single man go up the slope.

By the foot of the saddle, we found three men of Support Company lying beside the stream, and one of A Company. Carl was near them, looking leaner and paler than usual from a wound in the left shoulder—it was he I had mistakenly identified as Frank earlier. The man from A Company had a bad wound in his thigh; we had to carry him back. The remainder followed slowly, supported on either side by fit men. The guards kept us going and, when we arrived back at the point where the others were waiting below Hill 235, they joined in behind us as we continued on along the path in the direction of Choksong.

We reached the end of the ridge—the point where the north-

74

western slope actually joined the valley bottom—and I saw that the Chinese were bringing their dead down from above. They were apparently not bothering with those burnt by napalm; for all the dead laid out by the track were casualties from artillery or small-arms fire and must have been killed in the earlier attempts to take the hill. I did not count the bodies—they were on the other side of the track and a number of our own men screened them from me. What I could see plainly was a party of about sixty Chinese washing in the stream at the point where it left the valley and entered the great open bowl bounded on the north by Castle Hill. There was a waterfall here; stripped to the waist, the soldiers were washing their backs with tiny towels. On the bank, two or three men were undoing a pile of long, thin canvas bags—they looked almost like elongated liver sausages. All of them pointed excitedly at us, and shouted questions to the guards, who, to demonstrate their authority, gave one or two men a push to hurry them up.

The march continued for an hour. Our pace was slow because of the wounded, and we resisted the attempts of the guards to hurry us. It was quite evident that they were getting worried about another air attack. One or more of them would always be looking up at the sky, and once, when some aircraft were sighted in the far distance, they stopped us whilst they hid under the eaves of a nearby Korean hut. After we had been marching for about three-quarters of an hour, I realized that we were approaching the road that we had used between Battalion Headquarters and Castle Hill before the battle. Sure enough, five minutes later we were on it, walking back towards Battalion Headquarters' original position by the ford.

"There's another crowd of prisoners down there, sir," said Sergeant Peglar. "Look, down there, on the side of the road."

About three hundred yards away, on the eastern side of the road, we saw another large party. We began to strain our eyes to identify them. After a few paces, I could recognize Bob, the Padre, Sergeant Brisland, Baker, the Support Company Sergeant-Major, and two of the snipers. In spite of the efforts of the guards to keep us separated, we surged in amongst them, shaking hands, congratulating each other on escaping alive, and commiserating with one another on being made prisoner. In his haversack, Bob had a stale loaf of bread—part of the ration issued up on the ridge. He now shared this between nine of us as he recounted what had happened after our departure. Munching, suddenly conscious of our hunger, we sat listening by the roadside. For twenty minutes or so, there had been no sign of the Chinese. Then, with great caution, a group had come over the top of Hill 235 and, seeing the ridge deserted, had rushed forward. At this point, Bob, who had discarded his pistol, came forward with the Red Cross flag which accompanied the Regimental Aid Post. Apparently, the soldiers in the lead had either not been informed of the significance or were careless of this sign, for they opened fire on him. It was only due to their appalling lack of skill in musketry that he was still alive. Then an officer or senior non-commissioned officer came running forward and told them to stop shooting—perhaps because Bob was plainly unarmed and showed no sign of resistance. The soldiers obeyed, with one exception: one man with a burp-gun kept firing, and he stopped only after the Chinese officer had shot him. Bob felt that this was an encouraging sign. Coming forward, he showed them his Red Cross armband, surgical dressings, and other minor pieces of medical equipment. They seemed to understand that he was, at least, some sort of medical attendant. They did not harm the wounded, many of whom were unconscious and thus unaware that they were prisoners. Yet when Bob, and the Padre—who had volunteered to remain with the unmarried members of the Regimental Aid Post—attempted to organize the evacuation of the wounded from the hill, the Chinese stopped them.

Bob was prevented from giving even a drink of water to a patient; nor were any of the others allowed to attend the injured. Shortly afterwards, Bob's party were doubled down the steep hill track to join the group of prisoners who had been caught on the eastern side of the ridge. With the latter were about four men who had been walking wounded, but whose condition had so worsened through exhaustion and lack of treatment that they had become stretcher cases. Amongst them was Sergeant Hoper of the Machine Guns, Donald, and Fish of A Company. We felt some concern about Walker, the signaller, whose gallant charge down the hill on the 24th had brought the remnant of B Company in safely. He had a bullet through the lung, and needed constant attention. Yet, grave though his condition was, I felt somehow that it was going to take more than this to kill Walker.

After half an hour, we were marched back towards the ford and the original Headquarters and Mortar area. A series of exceptionally irritating incidents occurred, relieved, now and again, by a few which permitted us to laugh at our captors.

The whole Headquarters area had been broken into by the enemy soldiers in search of loot. Letters, handkerchiefs, articles of under-clothing, photographs, and newspapers were scattered over a wide area. Medical stores, which Bob was denied at the point of the pistol, had been smashed or thrown away by the Regimental Aid Post tents and vehicles; we were not even allowed to pick up the spare stretchers that we needed for the wounded with us, but managed to steal three, in spite of our captors. We marched back and forth along the road from one point to another whilst our captors argued over where we should go. The second time we returned to the ford, my anger was abated by the sight of a little Chinese who, having eaten a tin of peaches attacked another, a tin of solid fuel! The lid prised off, he dug a spoon that he had found into the waxy contents, and then conveyed a pile of it into his mouth. For a moment, there was no reaction. Then he turned a ghastly colour and uttered a terrible croak as he dropped writhing to the ground and began to vomit. This incident kept me fairly cheerful for the rest of the day.

Finally, we were marched back past Graham's mortar pits, round the hairpin bend, southwards through Solma-Ri, and up the side of the hill into a small re-entrant. In this location after much argument, some of us were searched. Peglar passed a compass to me that he had managed to retain, and I hid this. The search over, we were marched north again across the ford and herded into a dry stream-bed just north of C Company's original hill.

The Chinese were now so worried about attack from the air that they hid us and themselves throughout most of the afternoon. Lying under cover, I began to appreciate to the full that I really was a captive, subject to the instructions of the enemy, controlled by his Government. I think that I only fully realized this when we reached the Headquarters area where, with all the familiar things about me, I found myself unable to come and go as I pleased. From this moment on, the consequences of captivity became real and apparent. The sensation of living in a half-dream vanished, except for my first moments of wakefulness after sleep.

Just before we moved in the late afternoon, a Chinese came into the stream bed and asked, in very broken English, for drivers to come forward to drive our vehicles for them. We decided that this was an excellent opportunity to wreck those that remained, and sent off twelve men under Ronnie to put this into effect. A few minutes later, we were ordered to our feet and began the march north. The route lay along the familiar road to Choksong village, between the hills D and A Company had held. All along the road, we met enemy reserves moving up for the night; hundreds upon hundreds of soldiers, each carrying a pine branch in his hands. As soon as an aircraft was spotted, they would halt, raise their branches like banners, and give as good an imitation of pine saplings as they knew how.

Choksong village contained pile upon pile of their dead; with these were dead mules and a few ponies. The air-strike of the day before had been terribly effective in inflicting casualties. Unfortunately, the Chinese commanders were not worried about the price they had to pay for an objective; their pockets were full enough to pay whatever was asked—and more. Along the roadside, scraped out of the banks of the rice paddy, were little holes in which hundreds more Chinese were curled up, sleeping; others were sheltering in the houses nearby. Once we were spotted by a party of soldiers wheeling bicycles past us, their trousers rolled up to their knees, their heads covered with coloured base-ball caps. The bicycles were marked, "Hercules. Made in England."

We marched on down towards the river, turning west along the bank into a small village. Here we waited for darkness to fall. The wounded on stretchers were put into two empty houses, while the remainder of us were crowded into four ragged lines on a track that led to the river. We sat or lay upon the packed earth and stones, filthy, unshaven and tired. There was no food for anyone;

there was no medical attention for the wounded, though Bob did what he could for them, in spite of the fact that two of the guards had just taken his portable medical kit from him. After forty minutes, a Chinese appeared with two tin cans, the contents of which was steaming.

"Rice!" cried a voice, and in a second almost everyone was up, looking for some form of container.

It was not rice; it was boiled water; but it was not ungratefully received. Mess tins, mugs, old tin cans, almost any article that would hold water were found. Those without discovered someone who would share and so all were served. Yet I noticed that, even though the spirit of comradeship remained strong and, outwardly, relationships remained as before, there was a difference in the way that the majority—officers and men—behaved. I studied this for quite some time before I realized what it was: they were suffering from a form of mental shock and were still living in a world that was only half real—as I had been that morning.

I had another conference with Sam and we considered our previous plan in the light of experience gained since the former discussion. He had managed to get a certain amount done for the prisoner-of-war column to date and he felt that he must stay with them to render this service as long as he was permitted to do so. If the Chinese removed him from the rest, he would be ready to escape. The same applied to Bob. There was another consideration: a new set of guards had now taken charge of our column, who were not only more vigilant, but far stronger in numbers. As I was a strong swimmer, it seemed to us that I had better try to make my escape alone whilst crossing the Imjin that night; for we had no doubt that it was the intention of the Chinese to get us back over the river as soon as possible. The others—all parties concerned—should make their attempts as opportunity afforded, until such time as it became possible to institute a system of priorities. This was agreed between us as we sat by Donald's stretcher, ostensibly taking him the water he was sipping from the Padre's mess tin. As we left the building to go back to the others, my mind was settled: I was definitely going to make my escape that night.

Our guards waited for full darkness. The night was cloudy, and the

79

moon had not yet risen; I hoped that we should not be delayed in our trip to the river crossing, whichever one we were to use. Eventually, after much confusion, we were formed up on the road, and set off, carrying the stretchers with us. It was tiring work. The road itself was narrow and crowded; many of the men were too exhausted either to carry the wounded for more than a few hundred yards, or to carry them at all. Of those really fit, quite a number were helping the walking wounded. The poor visibility alone made changing the stretcher shifts difficult; obstructed by the guards, and hampered by lack of space and men, it was often a nightmare. With frequent halts, the column proceeded along the road that ran east and parallel with the river, until we reached the road junction below Choksong, where it turned north through the last cutting. Only then could I be reasonably sure that our crossing was Gloster Crossing.

As we drew near to the road junction, we became aware of a growing din. This cacophony was compounded of the shouts of mule drivers, the chant of coolies padding along, bearing ammunition on either end of a bamboo pole, the wheezing engine of an occasional ramshackle truck, and the cries of those who had become separated. There was absolutely no traffic control. Two streams of human beings, animals and vehicles, flowed along the narrow track to the river in opposite directions. Soon we were part of one stream, when I observed that the one going south was three times the size of ours. Sweating and stumbling we progressed down the rough track to the crossing, the stretchers jolting on our shoulders. It is to the credit of the wounded that they did not cry out during this rough passage.

At last we reached the bund, and began the descent to the river through the village where Guido's ambush party had lain. The Chinese wanted to push on, but Sam insisted that as many as were able to should remove their boots and socks, knowing that a long night march in wet footgear would bring blisters at a time when we could least afford them. This short halt provided me with my opportunity. I handed over my stretcher to the Padre but did not rejoin the forward part of the column. As we reached the river shore, I gave Crompton and Clayden a warning to be ready. The guard with us was dodging back and forth between my stretcher and the next, watching both sides of each pair of stretchers. We entered the water together, his right arm actually touching my left side. We could feel the rising water and the pressure of the current. Now we were ankle deep—now up to our knees—now to our thighs. The guard moved off, between Clayden and Crompton at the rear of the forward stretcher and the Padre and Guy at the head of the one next to me. I gave the signal: Clayden and Crompton dropped back and closed the gap between stretchers. At this instant, I sank into the black waters of the river.

When I surfaced about thirty yards downstream, I half-expected to hear the sound of shots and the cries of the guards coming after me. There was plenty to hear but nothing of alarm or pursuit. Turning from the uproar of the crowded crossing, I went on downstream. The water was very cold but not deep just here. Indeed, in places, I was actually crawling along the bottom of the river. For seven hours I continued in this way, sometimes swimming, sometimes crawling; and all the time the chill was extending through my body. It was impossible to leave the river during the first few hours because I could hear their sentries on the banks. Afterwards, I was fearful lest there might be sentries that I could not hear. The cold had almost made me decide to take the risk when, rounding the spit of sand that pointed, like a finger, into the river below Castle Hill, I found myself in really deep water in the middle of a strong current. Twice before, that night, I had got out of my depth completely for short periods, and had been forced to swim in to the bank. But now I was beginning to feel the fatigue of the long battle; the exhilaration of escape had faded; my limbs were stiff with cold; my clothes were saturated and my boots were filled with water. I began to sink: I realized that I was drowning.

I was filled with panic. Being a strong swimmer from childhood, I had never before experienced such terrors. As I came to the surface for a moment, I looked up to see a single bright star shining from the cloudy sky. For some reason, this brought me to my senses. I drew off my beret which was filled with water, tore the binoculars from their hiding place beneath my arm and, free of these extra weights, turned over on to my back, pushing my head almost under water. Clumsily, with much splashing at first, but heedless of discovery in this moment of crisis, I began to swim towards the south bank where I knew I should find shallow water.

It was a difficult task. The current tended to keep me in midstream so that my course towards the shore was oblique. It was too dark to distinguish progress; I could not be absolutely certain that I was making any progress at all. My arms and legs protesting more and more over the work to which I was putting them, I struggled on, pausing every two hundred strokes to put a foot down to see if I had reached a standing point. On my fourth attempt, when my legs were almost too stiff to move, I felt sand under my boots. Slowly, like a very old man, I began to wade to dry land.

The beach was deserted; there were no footprints in the sand that I could see. I walked on up to the river bank, my teeth chattering with the cold, looking for somewhere to rest and recover my strength. After a while, I was able to increase my pace, and was just ridding myself of the numbness caused by the cold, when I stumbled against a dead mule. I sank to the ground, and listened carefully before going on. There was no sound of voices or movement; so I decided to explore.

The mule was at the edge of a hollow; into this I descended. There were other mules there—and men, too—the remains of an artillery troop which had received attention from our air force during the battle. They were all very dead. I saw nothing worth taking except an old mule blanket, which was a most valuable find. Clutching this like a conspirator, I crept away into the night, found a hole in the river bank and, wrapped in my newly acquired covering, dropped into a sound sleep.

I did not wake up until twenty minutes past eight on the following morning. I should not have awakened then, but for the fact that I heard footsteps coming towards me; and I think the events of the past few days had sharpened the alarm system in my brain. The footsteps grew louder. The hole that gave me shelter was in the river bank itself and, here, the bank was broad enough to permit a cart to move along it. I lay back in my shelter, hoping that whoever was passing that way would do so on the far side, and so miss me.

The next moment, two pairs of feet came into view, marching in single file. Looking a little higher I saw the faces of two Chinese soldiers. They carried rifles.

They did not see me instantly: I lay still and looked as dead as I could. Then the rear man stopped, said something to the other, and pointed to me. The front man stopped also, and turned his head. I did not move; I had stopped breathing; my jaw hung open, conveying, I hoped, that *rigor mortis* had set in! Whatever they thought, they could not have considered me dangerous. After a few moments, the leading man grunted, and went along the bank; a second or so later his companion followed. It was only after they had completely disappeared from view that I breathed again.

Emerging from the hole in the bank, I made a swift reconnaissance. There was no one in sight. I should have to take a chance on that particular part of the river bank being under observation. What I could not risk was the return of a party of Chinese, after the two passers-by had reported my presence—dead or alive. I looked round for a place to conceal myself. The whole area of the south bank was open; there was absolutely no cover, apart from hollows and re-entrants, which might well be used by the Chinese themselves for reinforcements or stores. The north bank rose steeply across the river, but was split, here and there, by re-entrants in which scrub and pine abounded. There was only one course open to me: I must cross the river before nightfall.

I hurried down to the beach, and began to look for the most suitable crossing place. I needed, first, a point where I could enter the water without leaving footprints. Secondly, in view of the current, I wanted to be sure that there was a re-entrant into the northern cliffs at a suitable distance—certainly one that I should not overshoot. I found a patch of shingle that would take me to the water's edge and, about four hundred yards down-stream, a small V-shaped re-entrant that looked ideal. Reluctantly, I waded into the chill water and began to swim across.

It did not take me very long; I swam strongly after my night's rest, and I was spurred, too, by fear of discovery. My clothing soaked again, I climbed up the re-entrant from the water, selected

83

a hiding place, and stripped off my outer garments. There was a cold wind that morning, but my hiding place sheltered me from this. Whenever the sun appeared from behind the clouds, its warmth came through a hole in the cover above me and helped to keep my spirits up, in addition to drying my clothes. In this way, I spent the hours of daylight, resting, and preparing for the journey back to our own lines.

Looking at my damp maps, I saw that I had about seventeen thousand yards to go to the nearest suitable point on the new defence line. My quickest route lay back over the western spur of Castle Hill, up the valley in which I had been captured, and over the saddle which we had hoped to climb. The alternative was to float down the Imjin River to the confluence of the Han and Imjin rivers and thence across to the Kimpo peninsula and safety. Frankly, with the memory of the previous night's experience in the water, I was not anxious to take this course. It was not merely that I feared the possibility of drowning through cramp or fatigue in a river that would grow ever deeper as I neared the sea—though I *was* afraid of that. What dissuaded me most was my knowledge of the powerful tidal races at the mouth of the two rivers and the extreme unlikelihood of my having the strength to overcome these single-handed, even if I had a boat. In spite of these difficulties, I could see that the river-route offered a speedy way out if luck went with me. I decided to chance it if I could find a boat or, better, some buoyant object on which I could ride down on the current, and yet remain concealed. During the afternoon I began to look about and, after an hour's fruitless search, I remembered that, several weeks before, I had noticed a large, empty, fifty-gallon fuel drum on the sand spit in the river. If it was still there, I might be able to roll it into the water and climb on to the rear-end, using my legs as a rudder. In the shadow of the pines along the clifftops, I walked up-stream towards the sand spit. Once round the last bend I found it easily; it was lying just as I had remembered it, no more than thirty yards from the water. I sat down to wait for dusk, when I planned to cross back to the south bank.

Watching the river as it came round the sand-spit, I was struck by the way in which the waters began to tumble at a certain point

84

between the two banks. Examining the banks themselves, I saw a mass of footprints on either side, though it was too far for me to see in which direction they led. What became perfectly plain, however, was that there must be a second under-water bridge here, the one, almost certainly, by which the Chinese had crossed to attack Castle Hill on the night of the 22nd. Such a bridge would save me a second swim and thus permit me to make my journey in dry boots, should I decide finally on the land route back. In the twilight, I made my way down a steep path to the northern shore and stripped, making a bundle of my clothing inside my smock. I now followed the foot and hoof-prints to the edge of the water, and began to cross.

The water was up to my waist before I was half-way across, but, knowing myself to be taller than the average Chinese, I persevered. Holding my clothes bundle high above my head, I went slowly on. To my relief, after rising an inch or two more, the water stayed at a constant level until, as I neared the wide sand beach on the south side, it began to recede again. Two minutes later I was dressing myself under the cover of the river bank.

About half-past eleven that night, I reached the western spur of Castle Hill, with the river behind me. The fifty-gallon drum had proved to have a huge hole in its side, and I lacked confidence in my ability to survive another eight- or ten-hour river trip without it— even if only partly clothed. I had chosen the land route.

The clouds had dispersed and the whole heaven was bright with stars. I had made my way with great caution for the first part of my journey since, while I was still on the river bank, I had heard once more the distant clamour from Gloster Crossing. I felt sure that there were units still quartered in the Choksong area.

The approach to Castle Hill had taken me across an old stream-bed, in which I had found what I took to be the remainder of the battery whose annihilated troop had supplied me with a blanket for my night's rest. They, too, had been destroyed by an air strike. Now, as I moved across the western spur, I found more bodies on all sides—bodies that had lain there since Castle Hill had fallen, part of the huge losses inflicted on the enemy by A Company. I was glad to descend into the broad valley on the far side.

It took me four hours to reach the point of my capture. There were vehicles on the roads I had to cross, and the hillsides in the valley were still burning from the napalm, illuminating the whole area. At last, however, I began to climb the saddle which I had failed to reach two mornings before and, finally, I stood on top of it, the first phase of my journey over. There was no path down the other side but I could see that a passage had been forced through the underbrush and trees in a dozen places—probably by our own men less than forty-eight hours earlier. I selected one of those openings near me and began the downward climb.

When God made the world, he invented, for some excellent reason unknown to me, a bush which puts out long, thin tendrils, covered with tiny thorns. The sole purpose of this bush seems to be to impede and exasperate such passers-by as are unwary enough to come within range of it. I swear that the other side of that saddle was covered with those bushes. No sooner had I released myself from one set of thorns than another bush had me in its grasp, and I descended, cursing, sweating, and growing progressively angrier, as my clothing, flesh, and hair became entangled. To add to my difficulties, a part of the slope was covered with loose shale, and my attempts to move silently were thwarted at almost every step. By good fortune, however, there were no sentries at the bottom of the saddle and I broke out on to a path without entering an ambush.

I knew from the map that the course of the re-entrant, at the head of which I now stood, led directly along my route. I decided to follow the path down this into the valley, as dawn would break in less than an hour and before full daylight I must be in the hills on the far side. Apart from a few turns, here and there, round a rock-face, the path was reasonably straight. I made good progress, moving in bounds of about forty yards, pausing at the end of each to listen as I crouched by the side of the path. This policy served me well. I had been travelling for less than half an hour and was expecting to see the valley at any moment when, listening at the end of a bound, I heard voices quite close by. They seemed to come from the end of the re-entrant—perhaps at the very point where it opened into the valley. I moved on very slowly.

A hundred yards further on, rice paddy began, and the path

swung to the right to run along the base of the hill. Looking down, I could just see the end of the re-entrant and the valley beyond. Between this and my position, a large body of the enemy were digging weapon pits in the paddy banks and on the hill slopes on either side as far as I could see.

I had to make up my mind quickly. Either I must pass through the line of troops ahead of me, or I would have to make a detour round their flanks. If I took the former course, I had to chance finding others in the valley and on the hills beyond it. The alternative risk was that their flanks might extend for several miles in either direction—might even be unbroken as far as the Uijong-bu road to the east, or the Munsan-ni road on the west. I decided that my original intention to cross the valley before daylight must be adhered to if I was not to lose valuable time: I began to move down the re-entrant.

I discovered that the diggers were Chinese. They were laughing and joking a great deal amongst themselves in between spells of work, and seemed very confident that they were secure; I saw only two sentries. Wriggling along on my stomach, crawling on hands and knees, sometimes running for short distances under cover of a bank higher than the others, I moved obliquely across the floor of the re-entrant, wending my way between them. Once, I thought I had been seen by a soldier who threw down his pick and came towards me, looking directly at me. He was only drawing aside to urinate, however, and I moved on with a thudding heart as soon as he had gone back to work. The darkness was already waning when I reached the far side of the re-entrant a short way from the valley. There was no cover through which I could move—the rice paddy continued into the valley. I began to climb the hill on my left, crawling through the scrub.

At the top of the hill I came across open ground; in the centre was a set of large stone burial tablets. After listening carefully, I ran across this towards a group of young pines. Standing there, I could see the valley below me in the first light of dawn. It was going to be a race against the daylight. I ran on down the hill.

The whole valley was given over to rice cultivation. I kept running across the tiny, flat fields, jumping the few irrigation ditches that lay across my path. Suddenly the ground sloped away, and I recalled that a stream flowed along the valley's length. This was it. It seemed fairly deep, but I felt sure that somewhere near there would be a crossing point for the villagers. I turned right, deciding to search no more than a couple of hundred yards before fording. I walked along the river path, peering down at the water for a line of stepping stones. After about two minutes I found what I was looking for—and more.

Overlooking the crossing was a sentry with a burp-gun.

Other than surrender on the spot, there was only one thing I could do. I descended the bank a few yards away from him and put my foot on the first stepping stone. He called something to me that sounded less like a challenge than a remark. I mumbled something back—as incomprehensible to me as it must have been to him—hawked and spat in the way of the Orient for the sake of effect, and crossed the stream, taking my time. I expected a burst from the burp-gun at any moment—but nothing happened. I did not dare speed up until I was well over the top of the other bank.

As soon as possible, I left the path and began to ascend the hill ahead of me; a high hill that was heavily wooded on the upper slopes. Pausing for a moment to check my bearings, I heard the jingling of harness; and a few seconds later, voices came from a small pinewood a short distance away. I hurried away to the east, and struck a track leading up to the top of the hill. I was about to cross it when a voice challenged me; the opening and closing of a rifle bolt followed almost immediately. I gave a complaining mumble—the sort of mumble that I hoped would say, "Good Heavens, one can't move an inch on this hill without being challenged!"—and followed it with another spitting sequence. This time it only half-worked. The sentry did not fire but he did ask another question, which I felt would not be satisfied by more mumbling. Taking a chance, I dodged round a bush on to the path and ran as fast as I could go. Soon I was nearing the hilltop—and none too soon: it was daybreak. I could see the valley clearly now through the trees and, not more than two hundred feet below, a team of mules pulling a mountain gun into position. Here was the explanation for the jingling I had heard. Although there were no signs of pursuit, I felt very exposed in spite of the cover of the trees, and climbed on to the top of the hill.

The huge feature which I had ascended was roughly triangular in shape, and bore three peaks, the highest of which now lay beyond me to the south-west. Like the others, it was well wooded and contained much closer cover in the form of evergreen bushes. It lay sufficiently near to my route to form an ideal observation post from which I could study the ground and the dispositions of the enemy. I left my own hill-top and crossed the saddle towards it. Right in the centre, half-sitting in a slit trench was a dead Chinese, still wearing his steel helmet, his rifle smashed by fire. He had not been dead for more than a day or so—I hoped that he had been killed only yesterday, as this could mean that many of our men had reached the safety of our own lines in this very area. But his position on the saddle was right in the open—it must have been dug during a night attack—and I could not risk a closer examination in what was now full daylight. I hurried on.

As I had expected, the next hill-top gave me a splendid view of the country for several miles along the valleys on either side, and upwards of ten miles across the hills. There was all the cover I needed in which to rest after my night's journey; only the weather seemed against me. The clear night had given way to a cloudy dawn. It began to drizzle; the drizzle turned to a steady, light rain. Unable to sleep, I sat up to watch for the enemy, hoping to get some clear idea of the direction and extent of his line in this area; the battle line had undoubtedly changed considerably since our last information forty-eight hours ago.

My route back now lay almost due south. The feature on which I sat extended in that direction, as did the valley I overlooked. The former was trackless in the direction I wished to follow; the latter was cultivated up to and including the lower hill slopes, with one quite large village in the centre, and a few scattered hamlets along the hillside, as well as on a road running south beside a small river. There were Chinese in the village. Careless of their movement, now that the low clouds hid them from aircraft, they ran about from house to house, and even cooked in an open-fronted barn. I saw nothing in the hamlets but Korean peasants, who did not move beyond their garden fences or borders throughout the morning. The only people on the roads were a few bent old men, their clothing protected from the rain by rice sacks. As the rain continued to keep the enemy indoors, a fresh plan—perhaps provoked by my successful bluff at dawn—came into my mind; a plan which became more and more attractive, as I saw the clouds descend lower and lower until they threatened to obscure my view of the valley completely. At a quarter to one in the afternoon, I made up my mind.

I left my cover and began the journey downhill through a pine-wood. By one o'clock, I had reached the edge of the cultivated area on the hillside about a mile south of the big village. Here, in a hollow, I had seen a sort of lean-to shelter, made of rice sacks set on a wooden frame. Running out of the woods, I took the biggest rice sack I could find, doubling back into my cover immediately afterwards. Under the pine trees, I cut open one side of the sack, threw it over my shoulders and continued my walk parallel with the cultivated ground, until I reached the spot where the road rose temporarily from the valley into a cutting on the hillside. With great reluctance, I removed my smock and hid it here; concealed my watch, pen, pipes, cigarette lighter and handkerchief about my clothing; darkened my face with earth—and stepped out on to the road, the sack about my shoulders.

All was quiet. I did not hasten, trying to give the impression of age. Leaving the head of the valley, and coming into strange country through a cutting, I found part of a thin branch of a tree which I picked up to use as a walking stick. As I took it from the roadside, I spotted a telephone cable running along the ditch. It looked exactly like the line used by the Americans and I thought that it might have been left by the 1st ROK Division. I decided to keep my eye on it. Watching the cable that disappeared occasionally into the trees beside the cutting, I eventually came to a sign in white on a black background. It said:

"3783", and an arrow pointed straight on.

Now, the use of figures to denote units is general amongst British forces: it is a means of maintaining security. I tried to remember if the ROKs had the same custom, but could not recall whether they did or not. One thing I could not believe was that the Chinese would employ such a symbol; the figures were Arabic and I felt sure that they had figure characters of their own. I began to wonder if I was in No Man's Land; if I had just come through the Chinese front line; if the Chinese in the village behind were merely troops who formed the extension of that line; if. . . . I almost convinced myself that I was through their lines. Only two points prevented me from hurrying on: first, I had seen a mountain gun right amongst what I was calling their most forward positions; second, why were they not in occupation of that dominant feature? I realized that I had been indulging in wishful thinking: the cable and sign were left-overs from the withdrawal a day or so before. The speed with which our troops had fallen back accounted for their overlooking the signs, and being unable to wind in their telephone line. All this went through my mind as I plodded on down the Korean country road.

I passed through a deserted village where the road forked: still no sign of the enemy. Taking the right fork, I shuffled into the front room of a house where I checked my position on my map. It was now only eighteen hundred yards from the new defence line which we reportedly planned to hold at all costs, and I was over two thousand yards south of the outpost line held at the time of our capture. Squatting in the corner of that room, my back against the mud and wattle wall, I decided that I could not risk delay at this point. At any time the village or the hills round might be occupied in strength by the Chinese; I must go on. Pulling my sack up on my shoulders I set out on what I hoped was the last stage of my journey.

Every yard seemed a mile; I felt that the whole area was filled with observers. The road wound between low, tree-covered hills, partly shrouded in mist. The only sounds were the sound of my own boots on the road and the light pattering of the rain. Otherwise there was a complete, unnatural silence. The village vanished behind a bend in the road; a few rice fields ran up a tiny re-entrant to my right. I tried not to hurry my steps.

"Hi!"

Someone had called me from the hill to my right: I felt like saying:

"Who—me?"

A figure came running down from the trees, the bushes rustling loudly as he passed through them. I saw that it was a Chinese; in his hand he carried a long-barrelled pistol that looked like a Mauser. It was pointing in my direction. I decided that the time had come to try the biggest hoax of all; for above me I saw two yellow faces looking down along the barrel of a light machine-gun.

He ran up to me, motioning me to raise my hands. I did so. Satisfied that I had no weapons in them he ran his hands over me, turned me round and raised the rice sack over my shoulders. I had screwed up my eyes in an effort to distort their roundness and now, in a shaking voice that was not entirely feigned, I pointed up the road and said almost the only words I knew in Korean:

"Comupsom-nida"—which is, "Thank you."

I could not tell whether he was impressed or not. He circled round me twice, evidently not sure what to make of me. Then, to my amazement, he seemed satisfied and waved me on. I did not look back, but kept going until I had turned the next bend in the road, where I paused, ostensibly to wipe the rain from my face. It was, in fact, sweat.

I could not believe my good fortune at first. When I was able to realize that I had got past, I felt that I was experiencing a tremendous run of luck. Relating this incident to my journey as a whole, it seemed to me that at last I really had passed through the Chinese forward lines. This theory was supported by the position of their mountain-gun. The other area was obviously a reserve defence-line which, though dug, was unmanned on such a day as this, the troops remaining in shelter below. I had now much less than a thousand yards to go to our defence-line, and so must be in No Man's Land quite certainly. Yet, in spite of my growing conviction that I really was through the enemy lines, I maintained my gait, and held on to my rice sack as before; a patrol might be following me.

The distance to my destination decreased steadily: eight hundred yards—seven hundred—six hundred—the road ran now up a slight incline towards yet another small cutting. In the centre of this, a pit had been dug in the road—presumably to cover our with-drawal. I skirted it and walked out through the far side of the cut-ting. Facing me at a distance of about fifteen feet, as I came round the bend, was a beetle-browed young man in a navy blue serge uniform which I knew, at once, to belong to the North Korean Army. He was in the process of unwrapping an automatic pistol from a piece of red silk, as I appeared, and, before I could excuse myself, he was pointing it at my chest. I knew beyond a shadow of a doubt that I was recaptured!

CHAPTER TWO

I HAD played my luck too long and it had run out. I could not hope to convince this man that I was a Korean; it would only make matters worse if I did. When I tried to confuse him, he picked up a large, sharp stone and threw it at me with considerable accuracy; when I failed to obey his instructions to walk back down the road, he threw more. All the time, he kept his pistol pointed at me steadily, but remained sufficiently far away to avoid assault. Eventually, I got tired of being stoned and so, with a heavy heart, I began to walk back along the road. He would not even permit me the shelter of the rice sack but kicked it into the ditch; so I was both wet and miserable.

Just before we reached the bend in the road where I had been challenged by the Chinese, we turned off towards the east along a narrow path. As we came to junctions or forks along it, he would indicate the new direction to me with a grunt and a nod of his head. At the third turning, the telephone cable reappeared and by it I saw, with horror, a sign:

"3783."

It had never occurred to me that this was the sign of a North Korean unit! We were to follow it for the next two hours.

Our immediate destination was, apparently, a Korean village, considerably north and east of the road down which I had walked. I decided that it must lie midway between this road and our own original Battalion supply route. I did not deem it politic to take my map out just then to make a check. Here, in the centre of the village, we met another group of officers outside the school on which someone had fixed a large, new, red star, and a heavily varnished picture of Kim Il Sung, the President of North Korea. My captor was a Second Lieutenant—the North Koreans wear badges of rank, unlike the Chinese. He was warmly congratulated on his work by the others we met, all senior to him. They crowded round me, and regarded me rather as one might a hare that some friend has got with a chance shot on the road. I felt the analogy keenly.

After a few minutes chatter with a Korean civilian, who had evidently taken over the village leadership, they slung their leather map-cases over their shoulders and left the village at the opposite end to that of our entry. Two officers now guarded me with drawn pistols as we marched, but my Second Lieutenant kept on coming back to ensure that they had not lost me and were keeping me subdued. For good measure, he landed a couple of hearty kicks on the side of my leg as I passed.

By nightfall, it became apparent that we were lost. Every few minutes the party would stop, whilst one of the two Majors with us would inquire from a civilian household which route we should take, and once he attempted to get information in this respect out of a passing Chinese. I was now thoroughly wet and cold, to say nothing of my depression at being recaptured just when everything had seemed set so fair. However, as we marched, I consoled myself with the thought that we were still south of the Imjin River and that to-morrow—maybe even to-night—there might be another chance to escape. But I was not sorry when our journey ended. The Majors were fed up with the rain, it seemed: they turned a family out of the next house they came to and began to make preparations for the night.

There were fires under the floors, which was a blessing, and the one girl with my party—a civilian camp-follower, by her clothes —began to cook a meal. Soon a borrowed tray was set with large bowls of rice and soup. As it disappeared into their quarters, I became very much aware that I had not had a meal for over three days. Later, the shorter of the two Majors came over to me and, with much secrecy, gave me a small brown-paper parcel. Unwrapping it, after he had left me, I found it contained a ball of cold rice—perhaps a picnic dinner he had forgotten. I admit that I ate it with relish.

The next morning was bright and sunny. As there had been no opportunity to escape during the night, I began to look about me as soon as we set out towards our real destination. The "3783" signs appeared at intervals along the route, so I was reasonably sure that we had not lost our way altogether during the night march. What I was anxious to do was to spot some recognizable landmark by which I could fix my position. Unfortunately, just before starting that morning, it had occurred to them that I ought to be searched thoroughly. I had lost almost everything: maps, compass, watch, knife, pipes, tobacco, lighter, and pen. But this was not a major setback. I knew the general direction of our line, and once I could find a landmark, I should be well prepared.

Early on an argument took place between us about carrying their gear. I refused to carry loads, particularly as I had been given no breakfast. But when they told me to pick up a rice sack I changed my mind, hoping that I might get an opportunity to steal a few handfuls during the march.

There was another incident which served to cool our relationship. At mid-morning, we came to an area below a hill where a large group of North Korean soldiers had gathered, talking excitedly. We also stopped to examine the spot. To my horror, I saw that they were looking at the bodies of three American soldiers who had been shot through the back of the head. Their hands were still fastened behind their backs with thin telephone cable—assault cable, in military parlance—and they had been shot but recently. A great argument began about me, almost immediately, and I quickly realized that, if it was a question of a straight vote, I should join those poor GIs. I think it was the little Major who saved me. He spoke for about five minutes with great heat, and his words must have been powerful ones. With obvious reluctance, the crowd

95

began to disperse and one man, who had cocked his pistol meaningly while standing by my side, walked sulkily away.

At noon we stopped to eat. On this occasion, I was given a portion of the food by the girl, on the instructions of the Major I had come to regard as my benefactor. The officers then slept for an hour, whilst the five non-commissioned officers with the party took it in turns to mount a double guard on me, as they had done throughout the previous night. At two, as I saw by my watch on the wrist of one of the captains, we started out again, beginning the ascent of a long, steep path up the side of a mountain. After almost an hour's climb, we reached a pass between the two highest points. This was our immediate destination; the personnel of "3783" crowded the entire area about us.

I was removed from the curious crowd of ragged male and female soldiers and ordered to sit down by two officers, one of whom was a Colonel. To my surprise, the other, a senior Captain, spoke some English; but the questions were not at all what I had expected:

"Why have you come to Korea?"

I did not answer. He began to supply the answers, reading with difficulty from a small pamphlet he suddenly produced, showing General MacArthur, caricatured as an octopus, feeding Korean women and children into his mouth with four tentacles, and bags of US dollars into it with the others. There was a great deal about American stockbrokers and the gallant fight of the North Koreans to defend their country from this menace. When he had finished, he asked:

"You have understood this?"

"I have nothing to say," I replied.

"Too many Englishman," he said, pointing down the track. "Go."

Feeling that this was rather an ominous statement, I left him and was taken in charge by a warrant officer and two soldiers, who doubled me down the far side of the pass. I was still mulling over what the captain had meant when the answer was provided for me. Mid-way along the column we were overtaking, I found Privates Fox and Graham of my Battalion. What the North Korean had meant to say was:

"Two more Englishmen."

Here they were.

Graham was a Reservist, a dour north-countryman who was fast growing a magnificent red beard. One of Spike's Assault Pioneers, he had been caught independently of the main body, having got over the saddle at the end of our valley. Fox was a young volunteer in D Company, originating from Liverpool but living in the Isle of Man. He, too, was growing a beard—a fair one that was beginning to curl most elegantly. The story that he had to tell made it clear to me why we had seen nothing of D Company during the attempt to break out. Mike had seen the fate of those leaving the ridge by our route and had decided to try another way. D Company, Young Bob, and Sergeant Murphy's machine-gun section made off almost due west, remaining unengaged until they reached a valley, where the 1st ROK Division was fighting a withdrawal action, aided by an armoured force of the 1st Cavalry Division. Their course to this valley had not been entirely for-tuitous for, about midway between the tanks and Hill 235, they had been sighted by an alert and courageous Air Observation Pilot. Circling and pointing, he had led them to the tanks. Within sight of escape, their good fortune partly deserted them. First, they came under heavy fire from the Chinese on the hills, as they moved down the valley: Tom and a good many others of D Company were killed or wounded. Then our own tanks, seeing a group of many figures appearing from the east, were temporarily confused and added their fire to that of the Chinese. Disregarding the fire directed to him, the "spotter" pilot made several runs down the valley towards the tanks, making signs to them that Mike's force was friendly. At length, his meaning became clear to them, and they covered the remainder of Mike's party up to and through their positions. Fox estimated that about thirty men had reached the tanks uninjured out of the whole force. The remainder of D Company were either killed, wounded or, in a few cases such as his own, captured. Prevented by fire from reaching the tanks, he had slipped into the hills, only to be caught at dusk, while quenching a thirst unsatisfied since the third day of the battle.

We shook hands warmly, and told our stories to one another, as

97

we continued the march in a direction that was generally south-east—approximately towards Uijong-bu, I thought. I explained this to my companions and began to discuss escape, a prospect which they viewed with enthusiasm. My sack of rice had been removed at the pass, so that we had no food between us and, as the Koreans had been giving them very little food, it seemed unlikely that we should get an opportunity to save up. However, it was a fine, warm day; the three of us were together; we were all set to escape the moment a good opportunity presented itself, and—we were marching in the right direction. Morale was high.

The march continued throughout the afternoon, ending in a valley containing a long, scattered village. Outside a house about half-way down the valley, the column halted and dispersed; we were taken to a Korean house on the low, western slope which was already under occupation by twelve Chinese soldiers. Here we shared a room with three of our Korean porters, one of whom had established himself as the leader and was taking every opportunity to ingratiate himself with our captors. He was a dangerous element in our midst: an informer, a thief, and very lousy. We kicked him over to the other side of the room, which kept him at a distance of six feet. He remained there, glowering and mumbling to himself or at his fellow porters throughout the day, only leaving his corner to spring upon the infrequent meals of boiled rice that were brought to us.

We lived in that house under close guard for five days. Graham had sufficient of a pack of cards to play three-card Brag, and we played endlessly. He was also a master at getting tobacco out of those Chinese soldiers who came to stare at the curious foreign prisoners. On one memorable occasion, he obtained enough to roll us a cigarette each with some left over to put by for a communal one that evening—if we could get a light for it. During the third night, a Puerto Rican, named Morales, was brought in to join us. He had one special virtue in Graham's eyes: he did not smoke the tobacco scrounged for him.

Each evening, our artillery carried out a harassing fire programme up and down the valley. We were always delighted to see this fire, not only because it frightened the North Koreans, who were very objectionable at every opportunity, but because it made us realize how close we were to our friends. On the evening of the fifth day, we were taken out of our prison in the middle of this fire, and hurried away from the valley the moment it lifted from our particular area. At first, I was afraid that we were going back to the north, but we soon took a path that led south-west. From the stars, it seemed to me that we must be travelling parallel with the front, which, from the information Morales had, now ran obliquely towards its lower end above Seoul, the capital. In the distance we could see a searchlight beam, and I could not help wondering if it had been put up as a guide for men trying to get back through the lines. We kept alert for any opportunity to escape. The path was crowded with men, animals, and small carts going in both directions. I was always hoping for a complete block in the traffic, when we might manage to slip away in the press and confusion.

We marched for about eight hours, halting frequently when the path became exceptionally crowded. Finally, we reached a motor road and turned due west along it. The Chinese were digging in four American "Long Tom" howitzers here, and this caused another protracted halt: they would not let the party pass. Finally, just before dawn, we reached a village north of the road, where we were billeted under a concrete bridge for the night. Sandwiched between fifteen North Korean soldiers, we went to sleep with the smell of garlic in our nostrils.

The next night we left the bridge and set off again—this time to the north-west. I was now becoming anxious to make an escape as soon as possible: we were getting progressively weaker, due to the poor and insufficient food, and I knew that we should need all our strength for the journey through the lines. We were taken up to another pass, over this, and up a side track to a huge old Buddhist Monastery. It looked an excellent place to hide up in and I memorised its position with care. I think that our captors had hoped to billet themselves there, but the Chinese, who occupied positions in the hills above, did not seem anxious to have them. While the officers of our party were going through the rooms, several Chinese came down to investigate. A fierce argument arose and one of the

Chinese pushed a North Korean lieutenant away violently. I hoped to see a real fight begin, but another Chinese stepped forward as peacemaker. Through the interpreter we had with us, he explained some point at great length which seemed to satisfy both sides. We went back down the track to the road.

Our final resting place was a house in a village not more than a mile and a half down the road; we called it "Mother Reilly's" after the good-natured old Korean woman who lived in it. During the next day, she gave us what food she could spare—some old corn meal, which tasted of nothing but mould—but this is what she was living off herself, at the time. In this house, we were joined by a sergeant of the 1st ROK Division, a good fellow who had been captured only recently while on patrol. He was exceptionally angry when his captors took away his good American uniform, replacing it with rags; and when they took his boots off, I thought he was going to burst into tears. The guards tried to stop us from talking to him, but we managed to get news of the battle-line, and that we were to be marched north in ten days time to Pyongyang, the northern capital. The worst of our guards, a corporal we had nicknamed "Smiling Albert" because of his habitual expression, finally succeeded in having the sergeant removed from our room for the rest of the day, an act we revenged, during his absence at the latrine, by stealing the mirror in which he was forever examining his face.

Dusk saw us marching once more, the sign "3783" leading us along the route. The advance party had evidently been busy during the day. After continuing north-west for two miles, we turned due west again over a high pass that led us down into a large village, in which the North Korean regiment we marched with was billeted. Looking round, I decided that we had waited long enough to escape; had expected, perhaps, too good an opportunity. Discussing the matter with Fox and Graham during the next day, I said that we must make the next night but one a deadline for our "break", unless some exceptional circumstances prevented it. They were only too happy to accede. As we discussed final details, I called Morales over and asked him if he wished to join us. He said that he would. The four of us now made ready.

All is quiet; not even the sound of distant gunfire breaks the stillness to-night. On tiptoe, we leave the village, pausing every few yards to listen for sentries. Someone coughs nearby. We freeze in the shadows that hide us, waiting for a challenge or a step towards us. A voice calls out in Korean. We do not reply. Apparently, he is satisfied, for the challenge is not repeated. We reach the foot of the hill and begin the ascent. As we climb higher, the wind catches at our hair and torn garments. Now there are torches flashing below—is our escape discovered? We hurry on, careless of the thorn bushes that scratch us as we force our way through them. Fox is calling me.

"Sir, sir; we've lost Morales!"

I go back to look. There is no sign of Morales anywhere. I call his name quietly in the darkness; I go back through the bushes to the open slopes of the hill. The torches are still flashing below. We must go on. The inflexible rule of escapers, that an injured or lost man must be left, is invoked. Three of us continue the climb on to the wind-swept hill-top, hot, tired, breathless—but we are free again!

The next day was wet and cold. For the first few hours we lay stretched out on the soaking grass under cover of the bushes, our bodies camouflaged. At last, reasonably sure that our efforts to cover our tracks from the hill-top had been successful, we rose to our feet, exercised until we had restored some of the circulation in our chilled limbs, and sought shelter up a small re-entrant. Here the day was spent in warming one another between spells of vainly trying to strike a spark from a flint on to an old cigarette lighter wick; for we had sufficient grains of tobacco to roll one infinitesmal cigarette. At about four o'clock, we went over our plans for the night. We would retrace our steps towards "Mother Reilly's" house, where we would try to obtain more cornmeal, if her billets were unoccupied. Should the enemy be in residence, we would continue along the road to the old monastery, which would certainly provide a resting-place before we began the final journey back through the lines—and might provide food. There was another good reason for going to this area. I had an idea in the back of my mind that we were just north of the positions occupied by the Fifth Fusiliers during the New Year 1950/51. If I could identify any of the features, I should be able to plan my route through country with which I was familiar—a tremendous advantage.

Along the road leading to "Mother Reilly's", the Chinese were digging in more guns. We lost a great deal of time circumnavigating the individual guns and the command post, but eventually reached the old lady's village. The sky was completely obscured by clouds; the drizzle was constant. The rice paddy was a sea of mud which squelched loudly at every step. I was thankful to get on to the road, where we cleaned most of the mud clods from our boots. Leaving Fox and Graham by some mulberry trees, I went forward to the house. I could neither see nor hear sentries but this was not very surprising: the visibility was reduced to a few feet and the weather had probably driven any watcher into shelter. What actually warned me of cuckoos in the nest, was a man's voice talking in his sleep. I could not take the risk of investigating whether it was the enemy, or merely a boy friend who had looked in for a night's lodging. I went back to the mulberry trees to pass the news to the others.

Keeping to the roadside, which permitted us to walk in silence, we moved on towards the monastery. At the bridge, where we turned left, there was a sentry—an idle fellow, who was smoking. We cut off to the left of the road, to come out on the track beyond him. It was a slow approach now to the steps of the monastery, half a mile away; for we knew the Chinese were somewhere near, and we did not want to be challenged where it would be difficult to withdraw, with a deep stream on one side and a sheer cliff rising above us on the other. We felt, rather than saw, the monastery steps at last, and climbed them to the huge building above. For a short time, we rested in one of the many little rooms that ran off the main temple, then, growing bolder, began to explore the area. We were soaking wet and very cold. In the kitchen of the big hut belonging to the caretaker—an old woman who had made an appearance during our previous visit—we found the embers of a fire. Sitting round this, I decided to take a chance, while it was still dark enough to cover our flight if the alarm should be given: I began to knock gently on the door of the old caretaker's living-room.

For some time, there was no reply. Then the door was flung open suddenly and she appeared with a shovel of hot coals in her hand—a shovel she held very plainly for use as a weapon. She began to speak very quickly in Korean and her words were not words of welcome. I felt it was time we revealed our nationality.

"Yun-gook," I said, several times. "English."

She paused when she heard this, came forward cautiously, and peered into my face. My hopes rose as she put her shovel down and stepped down into the kitchen.

"Yun-gook?" she asked.

We all nodded, and she took a look at Fox and Graham. I am bound to admit that Graham's beard might have frightened anyone. In this case, it seemed to reassure her. She went back into her room, and reappeared with a small oil lamp, in the light of which she examined us all again. Now that she was satisfied that we were friends, she became, in the same instant, fearful for our safety. She signed to us to sit down by the fire, put a finger to her lips, and went outside into the cold. Very naturally, Fox wondered if we were about to be betrayed to the Chinese, but I felt sure that she could be trusted. On the previous visit, I had noticed how she kept herself as far as possible from both Chinese, and North Koreans. In a few minutes, she returned with a girl of about fifteen and a boy a good deal younger. They had brought a considerable quantity of food with them. Hiding us in a toolshed on the other side of her living-room, she commenced to cook this with all speed. We ate a hearty breakfast, sitting behind some old boxes, and were ready to settle ourselves in this spot for the hours of daylight when the boy beckoned us through the door. While the girl kept watch, he took us out across the main courtyard and into a temple, where, after darting to each door to ensure that we were not overlooked, he took out one of the huge wooden blocks that constituted the floor and disappeared below. We all went over to the opening and looked down. Beneath us lay a wood store, filled with huge logs, doubtless cut during the previous winter. The whole room had been cut out of the hillside, two adjoining walls being built against solid earth, the other two opening on to a lawn below the caretaker's house. Right in the centre, the boy had made a hideout for us, into which we descended. With tobacco and matches, an old blanket, and a bowl of fresh water from the stream, we were shut in for the rest of the day; three thoroughly contented men. The sound of the rain outside only enhanced the extreme comfort of our surroundings.

We rested and fed for two days. Each night I made a reconnaissance of the area. The more I saw, the more I became convinced that we were only a short distance north of the original positions held by the Brigade earlier in the year. I planned a route which would bring us on to the slopes of the massif, that would not only provide us with cover during the hours of daylight, but should also show us the way into Seoul. For the rest, I could only hope that the ROK sergeant's information was accurate when he told us that the capital was still in our hands. During the third day, alarmed by a North Korean police officer who had been snooping about the area, we withdrew onto a rock shelf at the back of the woodstore, seeking better cover amongst the tumbled mass of old beams, perpetually in deep shadow. Lying here, I briefed the other two on the journey that we should make that night.

Our normal evening meal of rice and beans appeared after dusk. By this time, I had written a certificate stating that the caretaker and her family had aided us during an escape, had thus placed herself in considerable personal danger for the sake of the United Nations' cause, and deserved a substantial reward. I felt that, should anything happen to us, the certificate would serve doubly to reward her and to give some indication as to our movements. For some reason unknown to me, the boy did not come back that night to collect our bowls and spoons. It had been my intention to give him the certificate then. As he had not appeared by the time we were ready to move, I decided to kill two birds with one stone: I would make a quick reconnaissance of the courtyards and path, and hand over the paper to the old lady at the same time. I left my boots by the trapdoor in the floor of the temple and walked out in stockinged feet; for the courtyards were flagged with stone and, without boots,

I could move swiftly over them when out of my hiding place. It was now getting on towards midnight. The Chinese had already been down from the hill to collect their water from the wells, and pick up their supplies from the road down by the bridge. The last mule and driver had returned to the hill, over an hour before. I ran through the courtyards past the great stone images of Buddha, checked the path to see that no sentry had been left to watch it, listened by the wells and the gate that led back to the hill above. There was no sound. Quickly I ran over to the caretaker's hut and knocked at the door. When she saw who it was, she dowsed the lamp and admitted me quickly. I said:

"Comupsom-nida", and handed her the certificate, tapping it as I repeated the word of thanks.

I think she understood me, for she smiled and took it, tucking it away behind an old box in the corner. I was about to leave, when we heard footsteps outside the door and a voice hailed her. The door shook as a hand knocked heavily upon it.

We looked at one another for a brief moment—a look of horror and surprise. She opened the door of the tool-shed and thrust me in, closing the door again at once. I watched the room I had left through a hole in the paper-covered wall, aware that my heart was beating wildly. The old caretaker had now opened her door and was temporising with the callers: it was plain that they were insisting on coming in. After a couple of minutes, they grew tired of the argument and forced their way into the room, throwing her to the floor as they entered. There were four men: three soldiers and what appeared to be an officer, the latter carrying a drawn pistol in one hand, a torch in the other. I sprang to the box in the corner, taking cover behind it. I had just concealed myself when the door of the tool-shed was flung open and I saw the beam of the torch circling the room. The sound of boxes and other articles being kicked aside came to my ears. I knew that my turn was coming. The box in front of me crashed to the ground, was removed and splintered by another mighty kick, and I lay exposed in the full light of the torch.

That was the end of that escape!

CHAPTER THREE

THE Chinese were furious! Two of the soldiers leapt on me and dragged me outside—there was no question of making my own way out. The officer and the remaining soldier ransacked the hut, throwing everything into the courtyards, until the living-room, the kitchen, and the tool-shed were completely stripped of their contents. The paving stones outside were littered with articles of ragged clothing, broken cooking pots, tools, shoes, mats. The old caretaker had been ejected at the outset, when she was savagely kicked by the third soldier. Moaning, she now lay on the stones, half-covered by the pitiful contents of her house. Satisfied that there was nothing more to find inside, the officer returned to the courtyard to deal with me. Seizing a piece of rope from amongst the articles about him, he made a noose which he placed round my neck, and bound my hands up in the small of my back with the running end. This device permitted me to ease my hands down a trifle at the expense of my neck, or loosen the rope from my neck at the expense of my wrists. It was a very effective device. He now began to shout at me, waving his pistol—the Mauser type—in my face. I observed that it was cocked, that the safety catch was off, and that he was exceptionally careless where his trigger finger lay. As I made no response, he led me into the lower courtyard, right under the wood-shed in which Fox and Graham were now doubtless listening with close attention. It was quite useless for them to try to assist me and I decided to give them what little warning I could. When I was next addressed, I said in as clear a voice as possible:

"There is no one here but me. I am the only one here."

The answer to this—principally, I believe, because he was exasperated beyond measure at being unable to understand me, any more than I could understand him—was a welt on the jaw that knocked me down on the paving stones. I was assisted to my feet by a kick from one of the guards. We climbed back up the path that led away from the monastery, and there, by a lean-to shed, I was made to kneel down and addressed again. A short silence ensued, only broken when one of the guards fired a burp-gun right behind my head. I was afraid that Fox and Graham, hearing that, would presume that I had been disposed of. I decided to keep talking if we passed that way again, in the hope that they would still be there.

My hopes were realized rather quickly. Tired of making no progress, my captors marched me back through the courtyards to the path leading to the road and bridge. I managed to say a few words as we passed the wood-shed and felt much easier in my mind once I had accomplished this. The officer gave an order to the guards and they made me double down the stony track.

There was one real snag in this: I had left my boots in the temple.

To my surprise, I was taken back to "Mother Reilly's" village—in fact, to a bunker dug into the hill right behind her house. The village was packed with Chinese troops, and seemed to be a Company Headquarters. The Company Commander was very stern when he saw me outside, and struck me several times across the face with the flat of his hand. However, when we got inside the bunker, he, himself, undid my bonds, patted me on the shoulder and bade me sit down. Throughout the night and next morning, I noticed that whenever we were alone together, or merely with his orderly, he was considerate. Only when others of his officers and men were present did he behave badly, shouting or threatening me with his pistol.

I was not sorry to leave them at mid-morning the next day. I had rested a little during the night, after realizing that my immediate escape opportunities were exceptionally poor; and I was now anxious to be away from this area, where there was a considerable number of soldiers. I hoped, too, to get food elsewhere. After two days of good meals, I did not want to lose my strength again.

A long and tiring march took up the remainder of the day. We journeyed from the Company to the Battalion Headquarters, from there to the Regimental Command Post, and so on. The terse grunts of my guards, the staring crowd of Oriental bumpkins, the heat of the day, and the fact that we lost our way at least once in every mile, all served to intensify the discomfort caused me by my blistered and cut feet. By the time we arrived at the Divisional Headquarters, I was in no mood to be civil to the first English-speaking Chinese that I had met. We parted on bad terms as I set off an hour later for Army Headquarters. I recall that he shouted after me that the victorious Chinese armies would invade Japan within a month. I was too tired to think of a suitably rude reply.

The Chinese Communist Forces do not possess that military formation we call a Corps. Thus I was evacuated direct from Division to Army control. The latter headquarters was about six miles further back. We managed to find it without losing our way more than twice; the guards who escorted me came from the Divisional Headquarters. After seeking the exact village uncertainly during the last half-hour of the trip, we were finally successful. I was searched, given some water, and led away to a small house round which there seemed to be eight sentries. Opening the door, I began to stumble my way across a floor covered with sleeping bodies.

"Who's that?" said a voice.

I identified myself.

"This is Kinne, sir, of the Northumberland Fusiliers. Can you find your way over?"

Thus began my association with a very remarkable young soldier.

The following morning, Kinne and I were able to take a look at one another, and continue the conversation we had had on the previous night.

From him, I learnt some of the details of the heavy fighting that had taken place on our right. The Rifles and the Fusiliers had fought a most difficult rearguard action on the road parallel to ours and had lost a considerable number of men. Kinne's Commanding Officer, Colonel Foster, had been one of those killed.

To my surprise, I found that Morales, the Puerto Rican, was with Kinne—he had been picked up by Chinese two days after our escape, having sprained his ankle on the hill. These two had been in the village for about eight days, prior to my arrival. I began to question them on the nature of the treatment since their arrival.

It seemed that the local Headquarters possessed a prisoner-of-war political unit, whose task was military interrogation and political indoctrination. The twelve ROKs who were held here with us were subjected daily to political lectures by a Korean-speaking Chinese. Kinne and Morales had had a mild political talk from the principal English-speaker—a man named Chen—but his real business with them had been a form of military interrogation. Strangely, they had not been asked the sort of questions that would provide the enemy with immediately useful information: the interrogator sought opinions rather than facts. For example, Chen had asked Kinne:

"Who was your company commander? What was your opinion of him? Did the troops under his command like him—if so, why? What did you think about before capture? Had you ever heard of the Chinese Peoples' Volunteers? What did you and your comrades think of the Chinese?"

Very properly, Kinne had refused to answer these questions, and had now been given two days to re-consider his decision. What would happen at the end of this time, if he continued to refuse, remained to be seen. The day passed without my seeing anyone who spoke English, and my requests for medical attention—even dressings—for my feet were ignored. At sundown, we all trooped into the courtyard of a Korean house to be fed on kaoliang—a kind of coarse barley—and beef stew. Kinne informed me that this rich addition to our fare was due to the fact that an F80 had strafed the village on the previous day, killing an ox in the process. It was this beast that we now enjoyed.

"I hope that F80 comes back, to-morrow," said Kinne. "We'll be eating beef for a month if they can hit the barn with the cows in."

I was going to my first proper interrogation. Walking ahead of the guard, I was taken up the side of the hill to a deep bunker. It seemed very dark inside after the sunlight and it was several minutes before I could adjust my eyes. At the far end, a man was sitting cross-legged on a mat. His brown eyes were not almond-shaped, but large and round. He had a pleasant face with a dark jowl, surprisingly heavy for a Chinese. His jet black hair was neatly cut in our own style, and parted on the left hand side.

"Sit down," he said, "I wish to talk to you: my name is Chen."

In reply to his questions, I gave him my number, rank and name. After pressing me for more for some little time, he said:

"Very well: I will not ask you for military information. We know you are one of the Adjutants. I have all the information I want." He paused and looked at some papers in front of him. "All I want you to tell me," he continued, "is your opinion of the Brigadier-General in command of your Brigade. What is his character? Is he best at attacking or defending? What do his superiors think of him in your Army?"

I protested that these were not questions that I could answer; that they were absolutely military questions. He attempted to refute this statement. Finally, thinking, perhaps, that I was fearful of discovery, he said:

"Do not worry. If you think these are secret things, we shall not give you away. Only the two of us will know that you have told me."

The argument continued for a short time, but ended when I refused to speak to him. After a long silence he said:

"The whole of your attitude to my questions is quite wrong. Let me explain to you how it is wrong—and why. When you understand this, you will be ready to co-operate with us, I am sure."

He began to explain how the capitalist states, fearful of imminent destruction by the oppressed working-people in the world, had engineered a war in Korea to whip up feeling against the "democratic" states of the Cominform block. It seemed that I was merely a pawn in the game; a pawn that might have lost its life, but for the fact that, by good fortune, I had been "liberated" from capitalist control, and was now in the hands of a truly democratic and humanitarian government.

He spoke excellent English with a slight American accent. It was plain, too, that he was speaking with the utmost sincerity—he really believed every word of the many fallacious premises he advanced. He continued this talk until it was dark, and then sent me back for my meal.

"We will go on again to-morrow," he said. "There is a great deal for you to learn."

I was recalled to the bunker on the following morning, when the lecture was resumed. We paused at noon for an hour. I took the opportunity of showing him my feet which were beginning to fester, and he was most considerate.

"We will send for the doctor," he said. "He will cure your trouble."

The doctor turned out to be a poker-faced man who wore a gauze mask throughout his ministrations to avoid breathing germs on to my feet, but seemed to overlook the fact that his hands were filthy. However, I was grateful to have dressings in place of the rags I had bound my wounds with. I was beginning to be thankful for small mercies. My physical needs cared for, I returned to the bunker to receive spiritual food.

We sat there for nine hours; I thought Chen would never tire. Late in the afternoon, six young Chinese were brought in—apprentice-commisars, as I later discovered—sitting themselves along either side wall of the bunker to listen to the words which would convert the dupe of the capitalists. I sat with my back to the entrance; the others, at ninety degrees to me on either side, gazed at Chen seated with his back to the rear wall. I began to feel as if we were all listening to some interminable after-dinner speaker; one of those men who can neither retain the interest of his audience, nor bring himself to sit down. I was able to stand it until he came to the subject of the British Commonwealth and, particularly, the United Kingdom. After he had spoken of the oppression of our people and the conditions of slave-labour that abounded throughout British industry, I could take no more. A great flood of words burst from me, which no protest of his could dam. I assured him that we did not believe every word published in the newspapers that we read—not even those who read the London *Daily Worker*, which was sold freely on the streets and in the factories for the comparatively few who would buy it. I reminded him that we had no political prisoners; and that offences for which we had given light terms of imprisonment to Mr. Willie Gallacher and his comrades, carried the death sentence in the U.S.S.R. I said a great deal more and I fear I spoke with a good deal of passion, so that before I realized it we were in the midst of a heated argument. By the time they allowed me to go back to the hut that I shared with Kinne and the other prisoners, the argument had arrived by a very devious route—as arguments will—at the Theory of Surplus Value!

I walked back through the darkness with my guards, calling myself all sorts of a fool. By design or accident, I had been drawn into an argument with my interrogators from which I should have remained aloof. Little did I know what the consequences of that midnight argument were to be.

Two days later, Chen sent Kinne and Morales away. He told me that I was unable to concentrate whilst they were there to give me companionship—that I would not begin to understand what he was trying to teach me while I could discuss superficial subjects with them. I must confess that I missed their company sadly. As a prisoner-of-war, in these circumstances, one did not know when one would see one's own kind again. I settled down to the routine of rising at dawn, spending the day in a bunker by myself, and listening each evening to Chen expounding his theories, against a background of the revolution in China or the Stock Market in New York: I preferred the hours of solitude. Three more days passed. I had resigned myself to going on in this way indefinitely when, a little before the normal hour for our second meal of the day—our second and last, usually taken in the twilight—Chen came hurrying down to my bunker to warn me that I was moving.

"It is with great regret that I see you go," he said. "I have every confidence that I should have convinced you of the truth before I had finished; you are politically conscious, without a doubt."

He sat with me while I ate my bowl of kaoliang—the beef had long since run out—making a final attempt to convert me by recounting his poverty-stricken youth as a student in Shanghai. As he touched with skill and sincerity upon each incident of his wretched early life, I watched his face. I have said that it was a pleasant face; it was more than that: it was a face filled with a sensitivity that must have rendered his many sufferings more acute. I realized to the full why he was such an ardent proselytiser, as more and more of his background appeared: he was an idealist, determined that he would convert the unenlightened, whether they liked it or not; for he knew what was good for them, better than they did themselves.

I was marched off in my stockinged feet once again. Chen's village disappeared below me, the remainder of a long climb up the stony path lay ahead. Accompanied by a non-commissioned officer and two guards, I was leaving for a prison camp in the north. Just before I left him, Chen seemed to reach a decision that he would tell me why I was being expelled so suddenly from school: the last of the prisoner columns was setting-out and I must join it. To miss this opportunity, Chen said, would be fatal. Ever mindful of my welfare, the Chinese authorities did not want to see me kept in the forward areas until the next column was formed; waiting there I might be recaptured by the Americans—my mortal enemies! When I protested that I was very willing to take this risk, he shook his head and remarked that I seemed incapable of understanding. Aside from the intellectual benefits awaiting me in the north, the material comforts must not be overlooked: good beds; eggs, butter, milk—to supplement our meat ration; all the tobacco we needed.

He really believed it all.

Our progress was slow; my left foot was now very swollen and causing me great pain. I felt better when, reaching a village in the next valley, we were joined by two more guards leading Kinne and Morales. They had not had a particularly happy time, for the guards had refused them water during the hot days: they had been lodged in a tiny, airless room, which had caused them to sweat heavily. I felt rather ashamed that my burden had been merely one of exasperation.

The guard commander was an elderly, bearded man who obviously wished to get us to the hand-over point as speedily as possible. I was in such pain, however, that I was unable to keep up with the other two, neither of whom were permitted to assist me at the outset. Little by little, the guard commander began to understand that I really was in difficulty. First, he allowed Kinne to drop back and give me the support of his arm and shoulder. Next, he got one of the guards to produce some rags from his pack to bind my feet. Finally, some hours after we left Kinne's village, he departed into the night to return with a pair of Chinese canvas and rubber half-boots into which I eased my bruised and swollen feet. It was, at least, a change for the better: I did not have to avoid every stone on the path.

We travelled throughout the night, resting at dawn in the nearest village we could find. This was to be our schedule for the next four days and nights, though the guards were changed after forty-eight hours. Marching back across the Imjin River, it became clear that this was the way in which the Chinese lines-of-communication existed: sleep by day; work by night. Our supremacy in the air permitted no other course.

About two hours after we had set out on the fourth night, we halted in a village street to drop off a group of nine ROK prisoners that we had picked up en route three days before. Once they had gone, we were marched back along the road for half a mile, and then led along a fresh track to a smaller village lying at the foot of a steep hill slope. There were the usual long conversations between our guards and those in the village, as they identified themselves; and the usual ceremony of handing over the scraps of paper that accompanied us from guard to guard, with a great deal of discussion and explanation. I always longed to tell the consignors to let the consignees read what the paper said for themselves: I began to wonder if Chinese could be the most ambiguous tongue in the world.

A Chinese with huge horn-rimmed spectacles had now joined our party, all of us standing before the veranda of a Korean house. He mumbled a few words of English rather shame-facedly—words that made no sense at all when joined together. An attempt to repeat these was interrupted by another voice, asking us our names in better English: a voice belonging to a podgy, pig-faced young Chinese, who had come up from the track. He began a long speech about obeying the rules and regulations of the guards under whom we were now placed, when I reminded him that it was late, we were tired, and that I had a poisoned foot.

I have a carrying voice, and for once it carried to good effect. In a room of the nearby veranda, some one had heard me speaking and called my name, adding:

"Is that you?"

I knew at once that it was the Colonel.

It was another of those strange reunions where one was happy to find friends alive and reasonably well, but troubled to see them prisoners-of-war: a bitter-sweet meeting.

I was separated from Kinne and Morales, who were taken off to another room as I joined the Colonel. On entering the tiny room in which he was lodged, I found Denis, and a ROK interpreter, all obviously awakened from sleep by my arrival. We spent about half an hour telling our stories of recapture, and exchanged what little news we had of the fighting. It appeared that Sam's column had marched north some days before, having dropped off Bob at the Imjin River with those wounded who were absolutely unable to get to their feet. They had had no news of D Company's success; and they had seen nothing of Privates Fox and Graham, whom I had left in the monastery. Bob was now with a group of other officers in the same house as ourselves; while round the corner of the mountain, concentrated in an adjacent group of houses, were about three hundred other ranks, about half of whom were Glosters —the remainder being made up of men from the Rifles, Fifth Fusiliers, Gunners, Eighth Hussars, and Sappers. We were all tired and decided to continue our talk the next day. There was one final exchange for the night, however. The Colonel's voice came quietly out of the darkness as we were dozing off on the board floor.

"Are you lousy?" he asked me.

"No, sir."

"Well, I'm sorry to say that you will be; Denis and I have been for several days!"

On the following morning the sun and blue sky were continually overcast with long, grey clouds. Breakfast consisted of kaoliang, and a minute portion of semi-cooked bean shoots. We had no proper mess kit; so we were fortunate in having old food tins, scoured out with sand; others had to make do with plates made from pieces of rag. After we had eaten, I was helped down the track leading to an open dug-out in a nearby hillside. Here all the officer-prisoners spent the hours of daylight, except for the Colonel, Denis, and the ROK, who were kept by themselves under close guard. Once separated from them that morning, I was not permitted to approach them or attempt to communicate with them in any way, except on two occasions when shortage of billets forced the guards to put us together. It had not taken the Chinese very long to realize that the Colonel and Denis wielded a great deal of influence with the remainder of the prisoners—an influence very naturally unacceptable to our captors.

There were many familiar faces in the dug-out: of the Gunners, Ronnie, Carl (who was wounded), and—surprisingly—Frank, whom I had mistakenly believed dead, and his Sergeant-Major, Askew; of the Glosters, Bob, Spike, Jumbo, Geoff, Mr. Hobbs and Sergeant-Majors Gallagher, Strong, and Ridlington. It seemed that I had only just missed Henry and Guido, who had escaped from the column two days before. And there were many others, made captive in the severe fighting that had gone on to the east of us: John and Sid, of the Fifth Fusiliers; from the Rifles, Paul, Max, Bert, and Peter—the latter wounded in the legs—and Doug, the Doctor of the Eight Hussars, whose half-track had been knocked into a ditch, at an inopportune moment, while he was driving it through an area already occupied by the enemy. With this band of British, were two other officers: Thomas, a young Filipino lieutenant, a veteran of the World War II campaign amongst his own islands; and Byron, an American Marine Air Force Captain. This officer was suffering terribly from burns; his entire face covered by suppurating scab, his hands, one arm, and part of his right leg raw from

116

the burning fuel which had been thrown back into his cockpit after his Corsair was hit by anti-aircraft fire. Bob's few dressings were almost exhausted and the Chinese had provided him with nothing since the march began. Yet, never once did Byron cry out, either at rest or on the march, as he was led—blind—along the rough hill tracks and rutted roads. I never heard him make a single complaint.

That morning was a happy one for me, although it rained frequently and we were all very hungry. It was happy because I was amongst comrades and, too, because I was able to get medical attention from two doctors in whom I had the greatest confidence. Bob and Doug examined my foot, released a little of the pus that had gathered, and dressed it with clean rags contributed by the members of our group. What worried me most was the fact that they said I must not walk on it. I knew that if I did not resume the march with my friends, my foot would either not get well at all, or keep me out of action for a very long time. In either case, I should not be in a position to escape again. As Bob, Spike, and I were anxious to go together on the next attempt, they decided to help me along as best they could.

We spent two more days in the village—principally, I think, because the Chinese, who had become tired of the slow pace imposed upon the march by the many sick and wounded, expected that a few days rest would refresh the latter sufficiently to continue at greater speed. What we needed, of course, as much, if not more than rest, was proper food and medical attention.

The march became increasingly difficult for me: after forty-eight hours, Bob and Doug decided that they must operate. As usual, we were marching by night and resting by day. At noon on this particular day, Bob gave me what little morphia he had been able to conceal from our captors and made ready the patient by getting Denis to hold me down at the top, Spike in the middle, while he held on to my ankles. The Colonel got up, remarking:

"I'm going outside, so you can swear as much as you like!"

Doug got to work with a Schick razor blade; and I regret to say I swore a great deal.

From then on, Bob and Spike half-carried me throughout the

night marches, until we reached the staging area known as the Mining Camp—a little North Korean gold-mining town, whose industry had been utterly destroyed by our aircraft. We arrived about an hour before dawn, to find that the room selected for our stay was so small that only the sick and wounded could lie down, while the remainder had to sit in an upright posture. Jammed into this dark chamber, we spent an unpleasant four hours until breakfast time, when the guards opened the doors to permit us to reach the can of kaoliang outside.

At the Mining Camp, Bob had his first and only real success in persuading the guard Company Commander to see reason in respect of the sick and wounded, who had managed to keep up so far, but were now becoming too sick to maintain the pace. His endeavours secured a promise to send us along by transport to the next major halting point; a promise that was kept. With a tall, effeminate Chinese named Su, I set off with one of the two parties of invalids. We lost our way at almost every conceivable point. Kinne, now suffering from dysentery, was almost put in a local prison, when he was caught looking for wireless parts in the rail centre at Sunchon; and Yates, the scout-car driver, ended the march by carrying me over two miles on his shoulders. It was an eventful journey.

The day came, finally, when we limped over a hill into a white-walled village, on the banks of the upper Taedong River, to find the remainder of the column resting again; a rest they really needed, now that the insufficient and poor quality of their diet was beginning to make itself felt. The Chinese told us that we had accomplished half of our journey; we called the village "Half-way House".

They took a group photograph of our dirty, bearded faces in this village and, later, removed the valuables—rings, watches, pens, and so on—from those who had not lost them at the front. I had been stripped by the North Koreans, except for some money I had hidden in my clothing, so the Chinese removed nothing of mine. They promised they would return the articles on our arrival at the northern prison-camps—a promise they kept with few exceptions—but so many of us had had our property stolen from us at one time or another after capture that we doubted this. Sergeant Sykes of the

Machine Guns stamped his watch into the ground, only to find that he was not permitted to do this with his own property. He was bound and placed in solitary confinement, until he agreed to read a self-criticism in front of the entire column concerning his action. It was full of cockney wit, which the Chinese were quite unable to appreciate—they listened very gravely, the interpreters asking various prisoners why they were smiling. I left this peculiar performance with a feeling of distaste; hearing Sergeant Sykes read a criticism of himself aroused in me a feeling of revulsion for the mentality of the authorities who had ordered it—a strange mentality that seemed alien and, in a sense, abnormal. An outlook which, sooner or later, we should clash with inevitably.

CHAPTER FOUR

ON the day that the main column marched north again, forty of us were taken out and sent to a village called Munha-ri, two miles to the south. Our party was a mixture of fairly fit men and invalids, so that with dysentery an ever-present danger to every one of us, to say nothing of all the other diseases with which Korea abounds, we were delighted to find Bob among us when we formed up to leave the the Half-way House. To my great disappointment, I was separated from Spike.

Munha-ri was quite a small village of no more than forty houses, lying below and up the side of a hill standing a quarter of a mile back from the Taedong River. To our great surprise, we found the remnant of Sam's column was in the village—mostly sick men, but including the Padre, our Gunner Battery Commander, Guy, and an American Air Force pilot, Duncan. Another reunion took place.

A new schoolhouse had been partly built near the river, the walls still unplastered, the windows unglazed, and the doors unhung. We were all crammed on to the dirt floor in a concentration which just left us room to lie down at night. A new routine commenced. Before dawn, our guards would begin to scream orders through the window in an effort to get us out of bed. Eventually, the fit would rise and form up outside for a check, preparatory to marching off. The hours of daylight would be spent on a hill about a mile away where, in the shelter of a pinewood, we received our breakfast of kaoliang—on three wonderful days, we had rice, as a treat—and half-cooked bean shoots. The two Chinese doctors in the village occasionally came to the schoolhouse to examine the sick and, now and again, gave Bob a few drugs to dispense. As the number of sick increased, we were told that it was due to our neglect of "personal sanitation"—for which they held no responsibility. They were quite unabashed when Bob pointed out that we were rarely allowed even to wash our hands and faces. Eventually he was permitted to remain behind each day to care for the sick, though the issue of drugs remained irregular, infrequent and inadequate.

On our first evening in the village we had been addressed by the guard company commander, a small, dapper, young Chinese, who called himself Tien Han. Through a pudding-faced female interpreter, he pointed out to us that though we had been spared death at the hands of the Chinese, we must not mistake this leniency for weakness. We were war-criminals who would now be given an opportunity to make recompense for our past misdeeds; absolute obedience to his authority would be the first way in which we must show that they had been justified in sparing us from death. Those who disobeyed the regulations must expect, at least, severe punishment in the form of rigorous imprisonment.

This little address was followed a few days later by a military interrogation. The only officer who was questioned seriously was Carl, whose identity as a technical expert they suspected, though, by good fortune, they never discovered that he had commanded a radar unit. Carl was brought up before the principal interrogators three times, and, remaining obdurate in the face of their threats, was bound and marched away to a small underground bunker where he remained night and day for a considerable period. He was not the first to be placed in this foul, deep hole. One of Frank's young Gunners, Ross, had already served a sentence in it, becoming so ill from the damp that he had contracted severe bronchitis. Sergeant

Sharp, the Intelligence Sergeant of the Fifth Fusiliers, soon joined Carl and we began to wonder which of us would be next.

I became convinced that the fact that I had argued politics with Chen had been reported to the headquarters controlling Munha-ri. On the first occasion that I was taken out, I was asked:

"Where did you receive your political training? Are you a political officer with your Army? Did you give political instruction to your unit?"

And when I made no reply to this, they said:

"What is it that you misunderstand about Marxism that makes you reject it?"

These questions were asked me by a very ugly, lisping Chinese called T'ang, who spoke English with a heavy accent. He was an unpleasant and dangerous character, ambitious to a degree; a man who boasted that, as the son of a landowner before the revolution, he had subsequently delivered both his parents into the hands of the authorities for execution as "enemies of the people". I was taken out twice, about this time, for an interview with T'ang, and spent most of the time listening to his opinions on international affairs and the change that might be expected in these now that China was becoming the most powerful nation in the world. They soon became tired of military interrogation and began to select small groups of prisoners to attend lectures on the Chinese Revolution and its significance. As an alternative, we had further addresses reminding us of our good fortune in having our lives spared; of the debt we owed to our Chinese captors for their "lenient treatment." They cannot have realized how bored we were at hearing the same nonsense repeated over and over again.

My foot was now healing fast, thanks to Bob. We made up a new escape party consisting of Bob, Thomas, the Filipino, Sid of the Fifth Fusiliers, and myself. Byron, the Marine, was also a member, as soon as Bob pronounced his burns sufficiently healed. Unquestionably, his former health had pulled him round, in spite of the absence of drugs and surgical treatment It was only later, after our strength had been sapped by long imprisonment, that we were to find it impossible to recover fully after sickness.

We went over our plans as we sat on the hillside each day, making what preparations we could from our limited resources. Just as we reached the point of being ready to go, Bob had to withdraw. It was at this time that he was allowed to look after the sick and wounded in what he called the "mediaeval pest-house" and he felt that he could not leave them to the mercy of the Chinese. It was a bitter disappointment to him—indeed, to us all. We prepared to go without him. Then the final blow fell.

One evening, after the second meal of the day, T'ang came into the schoolhouse and read out a long list of names, telling each man to move outside with his few possessions for a night march. When he had finished, we discovered that five of us were to remain in the village with a group of very sick men and the occupants of the bunker: Sergeant Sharp and Carl. This was a new Chinese puzzle which we were to spend many weeks in trying to solve.

Our little group returned to a house at the river end of the village, in which we were allotted a small room. Now, instead of leaving the village entirely for the hours of daylight, we were merely taken to the hill at the back of our hut where we lay under the trees. Each one of us had lost friends in the departure of the other column and I had lost all my escape associates. Our group consisted of Guy, the Padre, Duncan, Sergeant Fitzgerald of the Gunners, and me; and what we were all doing there was a mystery.

A possible solution to our retention in the village occurred on the fifth day after the column had left. On the afternoon of this day, we were bidden to the quarters of the guard company's officers and sat down to afternoon tea. This consisted of bowls of hot water being passed round, each of which contained about three green tea leaves which left the water lightly coloured but tasteless. Still, we were not even used to hot water at this time of day, and we were most curious to know what had occasioned this move. A packet of cigarettes was produced and passed round. We all smoked. Smiling, showing his perfect teeth in an affected way that he had, Tien Han, the company commander, addressed us through T'ang.

"All the others have gone except for the five of you and some very sick men. Undoubtedly, you are asking yourselves, why has this happened?"

122

We waited expectantly, wondering what was coming.

"We Chinese do not wish to be your enemies; we are your friends. It is your own leaders who are your enemies but you do not understand that yet. In time, you will come to have a full understanding of this problem. You require a great deal of education. In the meantime, if you have any doubts or worries, come to us to solve them. You may approach us at any time."

That was all, except to ask us to sing a national song of ours to them; an invitation we declined, though Guy was pressed so much towards the end that I felt sure he was going to oblige with "Screw Guns". We never attempted to follow up the proposal that we should approach them to discuss our "problems", whatever they might be; and, equally, for some time, they made no effort to contact us, except for the normal daily routine.

Then T'ang began lecturing us—the five fit as well as the sick men—on the subject of what he called "The New China". Each morning, he would appear, lisping and smiling, a changed personality from the scowling Chinese he had been less than a fortnight before. His scowl returned only once, in fact. One warm afternoon, we were sitting in the June sunshine on the hill, drowsing, as I recall it, when he suddenly appeared from nowhere like the Genie that materialized from Aladdin's wonderful lamp. In a shaking voice, his face twisted with rage, he pointed to the bound figures of Bob, Byron, and Thomas, who had been brought up the hillside.

"These men," he screamed, "tried to escape from the group marching north. But escape is impossible! We Chinese are all-powerful; you cannot evade us! Now these men will receive the severe punishment they deserve."

He led our three friends away, and we returned to our places, desolate that they had been recaptured.

Carl, Bob and Thomas were released three weeks later from their respective bunkers, and we had every hope that they would release Byron and Sergeant Sharp before very much longer. By this time, we had had a council-of-war about our position. We had very little to go on—Tien Han's little speech, certain hints dropped by T'ang, a few allusions to "study" made by Kan, T'ang's deputy. There was not really enough evidence to form an opinion as to the meaning of it all; but we decided that we must have a firm policy in case they started political indoctrination in earnest.

We knew from our own intelligence sources, prior to capture, that the Chinese and North Koreans had returned small batches of prisoners after lecturing to them for a time. I recalled that three of our men had been returned in February after capture in the New Year battle of the Rifles. Furthermore, they had received their "course" at a political school north-east of Pyongyang—the direction in which Munha-ri lay. Was this the school, we asked ourselves? If it was, what was our position? The real question came to this: if we felt that there was any prospect of our being sent back to our own lines, having the information we possessed about the battle, about the conditions along the line-of-communication, and about the treatment of prisoners, should we be prepared to listen to the seditious matter which would be put to us in the form of political lectures? My view was that we should listen to as much as they cared to give us, provided that we were not required to sign anything, write anything, record, or broadcast, or give lectures ourselves. We were all of the same mind, agreeing to suspend our escape projects for the time being. When Carl, Bob, and Thomas joined us, we put the same question to them, and they agreed with the policy. This was our outlook, then, when T'ang began to lecture us on the origins of the Korean war and the guilt which lay upon the shoulders of the Government of the United States. We sat down to listen, obediently, assuming expressions which we hoped would convey interest, surprise, even—when the worst accusations were made against our own Governments—horror. There were to be times when we required every ounce of self-control—sometimes to prevent us from assaulting the lecturer; sometimes to prevent us from bursting into screams of laughter! June ended, and July still found us sitting on our portion of the hillside, waiting to see what the next move of the Chinese would be.

As the summer advanced, three major incidents disturbed the dull routine of our lives. The first was that T'ang left us—"on promotion to a higher command", he said, smirking—and Kan became our lecturer-in-chief. Next, as Byron was released from the bunker, Bob, Sergeant Sharp, and all the sick party were sent north by truck, leaving Duncan, Guy, Carl, Thomas, Byron, the Padre, Sergeant Fitzgerald and myself. Last, Tien Han's company was relieved from duty in the village by the same company that had taken the Colonel's column north—the company of Commander Soong, whom we called "Mephy" because of his Mephistophelian eyebrows. Amongst the company officers who now supervised our life, the principal English-speaker was the pig-faced youth who had met me on the night that Kinne and I joined the Colonel's group in the south.

Kan, who belonged to the Regimental Headquarters, continued to visit us each morning to give his lectures, to bring political material for us to read, and to labour at the thankless task of getting us to work up a really good group-discussion on such themes as "The course of imperial aggression in the Far East since 1945." Somehow—though we tried so hard—we could not manage the right note of sincerity. In retrospect, I see that Kan came to realize little by little that our hearts were not in our work; that we took part in his classes only as a means to an end. By the time that August had arrived, his smile on parting rebuked us for not really wanting to be converted to Marxism: he could not understand us at all.

I became more and more impatient to see the end of the game that both sides were playing, so that I should not lose an opportunity to escape before the summer months were over. Carl felt the same, but was certainly not fit to try at that moment: he had contracted dysentery, which the few tablets the local doctor was prevailed upon to give him from time to time did nothing to cure. I, too, had been weakened by a bout of relapsing fever; a deceptive disease causing a high temperature, which apparently leaves the body only to return again with renewed strength four or five days later. The Padre's presence was a great comfort to me at this time—both spiritually and materially. He, Carl, and Byron washed my sweat-soaked clothes in the river during one hot day; and, strangely, when a third bout of fever was beginning, it left me as he said the prayer for the sick and laid his hands on my head.

I began to do simple physical-training exercises with Carl as soon as I felt better. Our diet had certainly improved, in that we now had potatoes, cabbage, or pumpkin to eat with our kaoliang. Twice, we had a wonderful flour and water pancake fried in bean oil. On the second occasion, Guy was caught by a guard hiding some extra ration of these under an old sack. He hastily explained that he was merely trying to keep the flies off them, but couldn't find any flies about when he was asked where they were!

We had been in Munha-ri nearly three months, when we were given notice to pack up one evening in late August.

In the middle of the guard company, accompanied by Pig-Face, the interpreter, and Chang, the company officer who had immediate charge of us, we set off from Munha-ri about an hour before the sun set. We were all tremendously excited; for we felt that, at last, with August almost over, we were going to discover why we had been kept back from the prison camps in the north. Besides, we were all sick of Munha-ri: sick of being harassed by the boy guards of sixteen and seventeen, whose hatred of us was stirred up daily by the company political officer; sick of the patch of hill we had been confined to for so many weary weeks; sick of waiting about to see what the Chinese were going to do next. As the leaders in the column took the path that led south from the village, eight hearts rose in eight breasts: south was the course, not north! Perhaps, after all, we really were going back to the front. With every step my hopes for an end to captivity increased; for if the long shot— release by the enemy—failed, every yard along our present course improved my chances of escape.

We fell into the familiar march-routine: breakfast at dusk and supper at dawn. Another series of villages provided billets for the column during the daylight hours. And all the time, our general direction continued southward.

We marched through the broken streets of Pyongyang, causing a mild stir, as our bearded unkempt figures were noticed by one and another of the groups in the crowded street. The population seemed to consist mostly of North Korean soldiers and workers—though we saw two cars carrying Russian military and naval personnel, who, we assumed, were part of the local Embassy staff. There were several European civilians, too, who quickly turned their heads away when they saw us. In the central area through which we marched, no more than thirty Chinese troops passed us, except for the many convoys of supply vehicles that awaited passage across the one bridge in operation.

Beyond Pyongyang, we took the road south-east that leads, eventually, to Suan. To our delight, Pig-Face, who was forever boasting of his courage and belittling ours, began to show his apprehension, as we marched along roads subject to air attack by our night bomber forces. The effect of his fears upon us was that he became more than usually unpleasant, removing our food before we had finished, on the excuse that we must get ready for the night march without further delay; preventing us from washing in a nearby stream, with the accusation that we were trying to signal to aircraft—when there was none to be seen or heard; and instructing the guard to prevent us from leaving the room in which we were confined, so that we could not go to the latrine. Of the many ways in which he could vent his spite on us, surely the worst was his habit of preventing us from resting in the mornings on those days when he had overeaten himself and was thus suffering from a bilious attack.

On the eighth night of the march, the column scattered from the road as the sounds of aircraft were heard close by. Everywhere the air-raid warning "Fiji—fiji-lella" went up, as we took cover on a boulder-strewn hillside. Some way down the road, one of our planes was firing its machine-guns beneath the light of parachute flares. As the last burst died away, another sound caught my ears. With the greatest pleasure I saw a pale, terrified Chinese lying near me in the ditch. It was Pig-Face being violently sick!

Ten days after we left Munha-ri, we reached our destination.

We had lost our way that night, as usual—not once, but many times. When, finally, we reached the rendezvous at a turning off the main road, the guide had forgotten the route by which he had come to meet us. In the pouring rain we stumbled through streams and rivers, up and down hillsides, in and out of valleys, inquiring at every village and hamlet through which we passed. It was almost dawn when we halted by a group of houses. The guards began to remove their packs with many mutterings of "Ta malega"—which is a very rude word in Chinese.

"This must be it," said Duncan, who, being an airman, hated the marching even more than we did.

"I won't believe it," said Carl, who was now walking in boots without soles.

But it was. We had arrived at the village which was to be our new home.

Having divested themselves of their packs and other equipment, our guards led us into the courtyard of a medium-sized Korean house, where the Company Headquarters' staff, already settled in the rooms, seemed to have filled the entire building. At that moment, Chang appeared with Pig-Face, indicating that we should enter two small storerooms, each about the size of a water-closet in an average British semi-detached house. The only way in which four of us could lie down simultaneously in one of these rooms, was to overlap legs and hips, taking it in turns as to whose legs should be on top! Carl, Byron, Duncan, and I settled in one of the boxes and were soon asleep after an exhausting night.

The weather had improved by the following morning, and we were able to dry out our damp clothes—already partly dried by the heat of our bodies. Apart from Carl's boots, we were not too badly equipped at that time: I had a pair of Chinese shoes; we each had one of the small handtowels the Chinese issued to their soldiers, a piece of soap, and a toothbrush. These articles had been given to us, with the explanation that we were not prisoners-of-war but merely uneducated fellows—backward boys, really—to whom they were trying to teach the truth. We had accepted the items without comment.

Another hillside gave us accommodation during the day from now on; a duller hillside than that at Munha-ri: it had no view beyond a few hundred yards of maize fields. The days passed as we sat waiting for some explanation or statement from our captors concerning the move and their intentions for our future. Nothing happened. Four days went by without a sign of Kan, Chang, or even

Pig-Face. We urgently needed the quack who served the Regiment as a doctor, and occasionally favoured us with his presence. We saw him in the distance once and called to him, but he hurried away as soon as he saw who we were. On the fifth day, Pig-Face appeared. We showed him Fitzgerald's feet, which were cut, and swollen with pus. Byron and Carl needed the doctor, too; their dysentery was considerably worse. Pig-Face reminded us that we were captives—perhaps he had forgotten we were "backward boys"—who were unentitled to medical treatment. For good measure, he told us that the peace talks, of which Kan had given us a very little news just before we left Munha-ri, had been broken off, and that the Chinese were now moving steadily south in a great offensive. He had so many unpleasant things to say that, after he had swaggered off along the path, we made a pact that we would ignore him in the future—a policy that was to achieve some success in irritating him. Meanwhile, we had to consider how things stood, in the light of his news about the peace talks.

We had never been very sanguine about these—Kan's information had made it plain that his side were out to wring every ounce of propaganda from them. It had occurred to us that the talks might enhance our prospects of return: the Chinese might want to give an appearance of good faith, by releasing a number of prisoners during the early stages of negotiations. Unless Pig-Face was lying —which was very possible—any hope of this had now disappeared. That day I decided I would begin preparations to escape, so as to be ready to meet any eventuality. My immediate problem was a partner.

Because of sickness or debility amongst the others, I decided that I would ask Duncan. He was a man of very strong character who, having put his hand to the plough, would not readily turn back. He was an unselfish companion, had a strong constitution, and, not least, was a good swimmer. That evening, I spoke quietly to Duncan, as we lay side by side in the box we shared, the only time when we were not under permanent observation by the guards. Duncan still believed that we had a prospect of release. Once he knew that there was no hope, he was ready to come with me, he said. I told him that I was already at work on my means of escape and would wait another three days. After that, I should have gone. He had three days to decide on what he wanted to do.

Two evenings later Kan appeared with "Hawk-Face", the Regimental Commander, and "Pudding-Face", the girl interpreter. Hawk-Face said how well we all looked. We must be careful not to get too fat! We were fatter, he declared, than when he had last seen us—what excellent care the company was taking of us! He looked into our accommodation and remarked that we were indeed lucky. He might have been Mr. Rackford Squeers, inspecting the school. I almost asked him why our kaoliang ration had been cut, why we had no doctor or medical kit for Fitzgerald and the others, and why we were treated like felons, instead of honourable prisoners-of-war. But I forbore; there were other things I wanted to ask Hawk-Face.

"We are very sorry to hear that the peace talks have been broken off," I began. It had to be put like that. To have asked a question would have been fruitless; he would merely have replied with the blandest of smiles that he did not know, he had not heard.

Hawk-Face glanced at Kan for a moment, then nodded. Kan muttered something to Pudding-Face.

"Yes," said Pudding-Face, "it is a setback for the true lovers of world peace everywhere. Now the world can see that it is the American Imperialists and their lackeys"—she added this for the benefit of her British audience—"who are the enemies of the people. You will see it, too, if you study."

Hawk-Face intervened here; he spoke quickly to her in Chinese and at some length, using his left hand to emphasise a point as he developed his subject. At last, Pudding-Face turned back to us.

"Go to your sleep, now," she said. "You need this for your health; you must take great care of your health, the Regimental Commander says. You have not worked hard at your study of the truth. You must now begin to study with sincerity. You should write a letter to your friends at home, telling them to act for peace in Korea. Soon, perhaps, you can pass on the truth to your friends in their camps in the north."

They bade us good night and we climbed into our sleeping boxes. I had heard enough to convince me that I had waited too long. When all was quiet, I paused in my work, and turned over to Duncan.

"What about it?" I whispered. "Are you coming?"

"You're damn right, I'm coming. When do we start?"

On the following night, my preparations bore fruit: Duncan and I slipped away from the village, heading west under a quarter-moon. We hoped never to see Pig-Face again, except at the end of a rope.

As the sun rose, we settled ourselves on a hill-top under the cover of the dwarf oaks and prepared to rest, having breakfasted off raw maize. We took it in turn to watch, the first turn falling to me. Lying there, listening to the noises that rose from a village far below, I realized that my whole body was filled with that splendid feeling which I had lost months before at the monastery: freedom! We had a long, long way to go and there were many difficulties to be overcome—not least, our physical weakness—but we were free again, and our anxiety to retain our freedom would strengthen us in every adversity.

Each night we moved as directly along our course as we could: the route was never easy. The hills were covered with bushes and dwarf oaks, which gave us splendid cover by day but impeded our movement by night. Many of the valleys contained rice fields which were flooded at this time of the year. We had to avoid main tracks, choosing, when possible, fields of maize or soya beans for our path, yet leaving these deliberately at intervals because of the clear trail that our passage unavoidably left in them.

On the fourth night we came to a river that lay directly across our route. We could not see the other shore. Searching for a ford, we set off along the bank and, a mile downstream, found a sand-bar stretching into the river, thrown up by a small stream which emptied here into the main waters. There was just a chance that the river had silted up sufficiently at this point to permit us to walk across. We walked along the spit to the water, wading in. The ground dropped away beneath us, the water reached our waists, our chests, our shoulders. The current caught us; there was no going back. Remembering my previous experience in the Imjin

131

River, I turned on to my back as I was swept away, keeping my arms under water, and kicking strongly with my feet. I was getting tired when my anxious foot touched bottom on the far side and I found that I had reached the base of an almost sheer cliff. I was about to leave the water when I heard Duncan's voice.

"Help!" he called. "Help! I'm drowning!"

Wading towards him, I saw that he was only a few yards from the shore.

"It's all right," I called back. "You're in shallow water. Stand up."

Doubtfully, he put his feet down to find that the water came up to his armpits. We met by the bank. It appeared that he had found the weight of water-filled boots too much for him—he still had his original leather pair—and, making the mistake of trying to take them off while swimming, sank, swallowing a great deal of water, as he began to sink a second time. He had come up for the third time when he called out. The shock and the cold river had set him shivering uncontrollably. I was feeling the cold also, but the scramble up a nearby re-entrant, that was very steep and filled with thick bushes, helped to restore our circulation. It was beginning to get light as we found ourselves near a wide track, bearing the imprint of tyres. Obviously this was no place for us; it was time to find a hiding-place for the day. We hurried away from the road and through a cultivated valley, made a detour of a village, and began the ascent of a hill. Half-way up we came across a series of platforms such as the Chinese dug out for themselves to sit on during the summer days. Above these, the hill was fortified with trenches and dug-outs, but they looked old and unused; the trench walls were falling in, many dugouts were flooded. The whole system had probably been dug during the withdrawal of the enemy to the Yalu the year before. It seemed unlikely that we should encounter troops here at this time, so we climbed on to the crest of the hill. In any case, it was well after dawn; it would have been difficult to get to another hill, unobserved by those in the many villages that we saw in the valleys on either side.

Our clothes were still saturated with water from the river crossing; there had been no time to wring them out. Unfortunately, it was an exceptionally overcast day and the strong wind was from the east. I squeezed the water from my outer garments and dressed again. Duncan, however, laid his things out to dry, clothing himself in his thin flying suit as a temporary measure. We were both feeling the effects of our long and tiring marches, the coarse food we had been given over so many months, and the uncooked maize which had done little more than ease our hunger pangs during the past three days. I decided that we must try to obtain food which would sustain us against the ten or twelve days of arduous marching that separated us from our destination, the coast. While Duncan was laying out the remainder of his clothes so that they would not be seen from the village below, I went off along the hill to select a house from which we might obtain sustenance

At the head of the valley that lay to the east of our hill I saw a small isolated house from whose one chimney smoke was rising. A path ran past the house, joining a wider track as it approached the village that stood on the valley floor—a village that was filled with Chinese soldiers. The advantage of the isolated house was that Duncan and I could descend the hillside under good cover to see who lived in it, and Duncan could watch the path for half a mile in either direction while I entered to seek food, if a civilian family were in occupation. We followed this plan exactly.

The moment came when I approached the open kitchen door, through which we had seen a young woman cooking at one of the pots. The kitchen darkened as I stood in the doorway, causing her to look up. I smiled and showed her that I held no weapon in my hands. Still watching me, she half-turned her head and called to her husband who was lying on a mat in the other room. She must have said something that alarmed them all, for the cries of the two children with whom he was playing ceased. For a moment all was quiet. Then he got up and came into the kitchen. From the doorway I looked down into their frightened brown eyes.

I made signs that I was hungry and pointed to the cooking pot. The man said something in Korean to me which I did not understand, adding,

"Migook?"—American?

133

I shook my head. "Yungook."

They continued to stare for some moments; then the man pointed to my eyes, turned to his wife, and laughed. She smiled. They had probably never seen a man with blue eyes before. On this basis of humour, the man seemed to become friendly. He spoke to his wife, who began to scoop up their breakfast from the cooking pot. At the same time, he joined me by the door and pointed down to the village.

"Chungook," he said. "Na pa." I was encouraged to find that he had a poor opinion of the Chinese; I felt bound to agree with him.

By this time, his wife had removed everything from the cooking-pot. With a feeling of shame I saw that we were taking all their poor breakfast—nine cobs of boiled maize. They thrust them into my hand and urged me back up the hillside with many expressions of alarm as they pointed to the valley.

"God bless you," I said in English, and left them. Duncan met me as I reached the cover on the hill.

At this point in our journey, I made a major error for which I can never forgive myself. As the soldier in the party, I should have known better than to have agreed to stay near one of the disused earth platforms on the hillside so that Duncan, who was chilled by the wind, could obtain shelter. Crouching against the hillside we ate our boiled corn—still warm—and enjoyed it thoroughly. At least this would not pass straight through our systems. I was about to say to Duncan, "We really must go after you've eaten that corn cob," when the sound of voices reached us. Within a few seconds five Chinese came through the trees from the direction of the village, searching for wood. They were unarmed, but two of them had long, thick sticks.

We had not time to hide properly—we were actually moving towards some bushes below a rock-face when they appeared.

"Lie still and they won't see us," I whispered to Duncan. The soldiers had certainly not seen us; they were fooling about, throwing stones at one another as they came towards us. Each minute seemed an hour as they picked up sticks or tore at branches hanging from the trees. I dared not turn my head to look at the three to my right from whom I expected at every moment to hear the shout which would herald discovery. The other two were now about twenty feet away, their backs to me as they lit cigarettes. I heard a whisper from Duncan, who lay six or eight feet to my left.

"What is it?"

"They'll spot us for sure. I'm going to make a break for it."

"Don't be an idiot," I said. "Keep still and they'll never see you. They aren't looking for us."

"I'm not going to take a chance," he said. "You stay if you want to. As I'm going, I'll try to lead them away from you."

He rose instantly to his feet and dashed away towards the corner of the platform we had just left; the sound of his feet on the leaves and dead branches seemed to crash upon my ears. The two men to my front whirled round, gave a mighty shout, and set up an excited chatter on seeing him; the other three came running across to join them. All five stood there, shouting and pointing. Duncan might have made good his escape, so long were they in recovering from their surprise, but he tripped over a root and fell. At that they gave chase and were closing on him as he disappeared round the shoulder of the hill.

If Duncan had done nothing else, he had kept his promise to lead them away from me. I did not intend to waste this opportunity now. Looking quickly about me, I made for the thick cover higher up the hillside, from whence I could observe the course of events.

They brought Duncan back about ten minutes later. It was his fair beard I saw first as he came through the trees with four of the soldiers. The fifth had preceded them by several minutes to report the news of his capture to the village. As the main party arrived in the village street, I saw the entire garrison crowding the road to look at him, before he was taken into a large house which I guessed to be the local headquarters. A few moments after he had disappeared into the courtyard I remembered that all Duncan's clothes were still on the hill-top.

135

WHEN I returned to the top of the hill, Duncan's clothes were dry; the morning wind had done its work. I gathered them in before returning to my observation post, where I sat down to think out the problem of getting the clothes back to him.

It was all-important that he had these. It was now September; the weather would soon be turning cold. The prospect of anyone spending a winter in North Korea in nothing but a thin summer flying suit was appalling; he would die. I decided that the best plan was to enlist the aid of the Koreans, by handing over the clothing bundle to them and trusting to their fear of the Chinese to have it delivered to the local headquarters. This also placed reliance in the Chinese to turn the clothes over to Duncan, but I faced that problem whatever I did—short of assaulting three armed guards in the centre of the village in daylight to return the clothes to him personally. I made my way to the edge of the village under cover of the trees and maize fields.

I spent many hours round the village trying to get some villager to come near enough to effect a hand-over, but without result. Gradually, very painfully, I accustomed myself to the idea that I should have to give myself up, hand over the clothes, and go through all the business of escaping again. In the late afternoon I was forced to a final decision, when I saw them marching Duncan out of the far end of the village. I stood up amongst the tall maize stalks, parted them, and stepped out on to the village path. Ten minutes later I was in the local headquarters, handing over Duncan's clothes.

The Chinese were very surprised to see me, for we had travelled a long way from our original village and their communications were very poor. Their immediate reaction must have been that we were the survivors of an aircraft, shot down close by; but my Chinese shoes and our two towels, identical to their own, made them realize that we were not. Whatever they thought, they understood that I had Duncan's clothes and that the two of us were associated. They made signs that I would join him shortly; and this was confirmed when a very dark-skinned, rat-faced Chinese appeared who spoke understandable, if limited, English. As dusk fell, he accompanied me from the village with three soldiers, chatting happily as we walked along, pausing after each sentence to see if the soldiers were watching. They were very impressed by his ability to speak to the queer foreigner in his own tongue, and he played up to them admirably.

An hour later we reached the village to which Duncan had been taken. I was only allowed a few moments with him and had been warned not to speak. I just said:

"Hallo, Duncan. I've brought your clothes," before they took me out again very quickly.

An interrogation followed, by a man whose English was so bad that I decided to give fatuous replies to his questions—the success of which so cheered me that I had quite recovered my spirits by the time I was taken to my lodging for the night. This was a straw stack in the barn adjoining a Korean house. I was told to lie down and remain lying down throughout the night. Two guards were posted within six feet and flashed a light on me every minute or so. I realized that an escape attempt at this time would be fool-hardy, and so made the best of my comfortable circumstances to enjoy a good night's rest.

The following afternoon Duncan and I were marched west to Namchon-jom, a town on the western railway. The few houses that were left standing had been requisitioned by the Chinese who seemed to provide the entire garrison; not a North Korean soldier was to be seen, apart from the local gendarmerie. The little rat-faced English-speaker was in charge of our escort. As we passed through bomb-shattered streets, he turned to Duncan to say:

"How many Korean women you have killed with your aero-planes!" Or, a little further on: "How many little Korean children are dead from your bombs!" His accusations increased so that, eventually, he uttered one every few paces. We became so tired of this nonsense that we began to reply:

"How many guns you have sheltered in these houses!" "How

many tons of explosives you have stored in this town!" "How many soldiers you have put into these buildings!"

This was always a sore spot with the Chinese: we received the standard answer they were taught to give by their newspapers, and by their political officers.

"That is different! We have a right to be here."

"If you do not want the Korean civilians to be bombed, why do you continue to occupy every village in the countryside?"

There was, of course, no answer to this; but he continued to repeat "That is different!" like a parrot. With soldiers and warlike stores all round us, in the houses and in caves dug into the hillsides around the town, he could not very well deny that his own forces had turned each village, each town, each city into a military target.

We left Namchon-jom in darkness, passengers in a truck half-filled with empty tins of various sizes lashed down beneath an old tarpaulin. The main western highway, that runs from the Chinese border to Pusan in the far south, was packed with motor vehicles of Chinese and Russian origin, those going south piled high with stores. Only sidelights were permitted, though drivers flashed their headlamps on, to negotiate the many traffic jams caused by accidents or lack of traffic control. I fumed inwardly at the thought of the targets which our aircraft were missing that night, although I knew their difficulties. And the Chinese were very alert for air-craft warnings. A rifle would crack from a hilltop where their spotters listened for the sound of aircraft engines. Even the side-lights on the vehicles would be dowsed; many vehicles would draw off the road into cover. The cry of "Fiji", or "Piangi", or "Fiji-lella" would be shouted from driving-cab to driving-cab. Where there were passengers, the cries would be chorussed. How I wished through that night drive that our air strength was even half of what our enemies attributed to us!

A mile beyond Sinmak, we turned down a track which led to the east. Our speed was now greatly reduced, as the surface of the road was exceptionally poor, and we were often ascending or descending considerable gradients among the mountains. Two of our guards were getting so sleepy that I was weighing up my chances of warning Duncan for a leap over the side into the pinewoods that ran right down to the road, when the truck halted with a jerk, the sentries woke up, and we were ordered to dismount.

In the beam of a flashlight I began to climb a winding path that led up the side of a hill, Duncan following. Half-way up, we came to two bunkers, in the doorways of which we saw iron bars set in stout pine-logs. We seemed to have arrived at a very secure prison.

A non-commissioned officer and two sentries were on duty at the bunkers, the doors of which faced one another at a distance of about four feet. One sentry opened the doors while the others covered him with their weapons. A moment later I was inside one bunker; Duncan was in the other. The doors were closed behind us and fastened with stout padlocks. Our escorts' footsteps died away along the path.

From the light of the sentries' torch outside, I saw that I was in a cell whose walls, ceiling, and floor were covered by thick pine logs which would take a great deal of cutting through. Two Chinese were returning to their rest after being disturbed by my entry. From their clothing and fear of the guards, I presumed them to be prisoners serving sentences. I, too, lay down to sleep.

Normally, I am a restless sleeper, turning constantly from side to side. I quickly learned that such habits were not tolerated here. At the slightest sound from the straw mats on which we lay, one of the guards would shine his torch through the bars of the door, while the other poked at the offending body or bodies with a sharp steel rod. My shoes having been removed, I received the point of this rod in the sole of my foot about ten minutes after I had entered the cell. For the remainder of the night I lay as still as I could, but turned involuntarily several times, to be awakened by the chastisement of the guards. It was an unpleasant night.

In the morning, we were allowed out to visit the latrine once, at the time when breakfast appeared—a breakfast of millet, accompanied by some hot, dirty water containing a cabbage leaf. Duncan had only one Chinese in his cell but, like mine, his fellow-prisoner was terrified of the guards, almost jumping out of his skin when they addressed him. We were not permitted to lie down, or even to

139

doze in a sitting position during the hours of daylight. I contrived to sit with my back against the wall in the deepest shadows of the bunker to catch upon my night's sleep. Fortunately, after a time, the guards got tired of trying to see whether I was awake or not, and I had a good nap, until one of my cell-mates reported me to the guard commander, when he came in to make the regulations clear with the toe of his boot. The informer got a dry biscuit from the guards for his trouble.

The evening meal of millet appeared; we made our second latrine run of the day. Another uneasy night was passed in the timbered cell. On the following morning, I began to feel that my escape might take rather longer than I had intended. At breakfast time, I managed to pass a few words to Duncan and we agreed that, if the opportunity arose, each must escape without waiting for the other. The morning and afternoon passed as before. The evening millet arrived, accompanied by a thin fish soup that was excellent: though it was tasteless, there was a distinct aroma of whiting as one bent down to the dish.

As I prepared to go back to my cell—Duncan had already been returned to his—a Chinese came down the pathway from the hill-top, carrying a paper which he handed to the guard commander. At the same time he indicated that I should remain where I was. Duncan was released from his cell and, with two other soldiers who appeared, we were marched away. Two more soldiers joined us, at the point where we had dismounted from the truck two nights before, and we set off in a party along the track. Soon we left this for a narrow path which we followed for about two miles, travelling north-west. Another Korean village received us; another company of Chinese soldiers took us over. Duncan and I were placed in separate bunkers, oil drums were rolled into the doorways, and we were left for the night. I was so tired that I fell asleep almost immediately.

The sun was up before I awoke. This was partly due to the fact that it was exceptionally dark inside my bunker, the only light coming in through a narrow space at the top and down one side of the oil drum in the doorway. I examined my surroundings. The bunker had been dug into the hillside at an angle of about forty-five degrees. The sides were unrivetted, but the roof had branches across it to prevent a fall of earth; on the floor a small amount of straw had been scattered. Its chief drawback was that I could not sit up in it; the ceiling was too low. I could either lie down, or half-sit, resting on my elbows. It was just wide enough for me to draw my knees up, which was a blessing; and long enough for me to stretch out full length, if I followed the slight curve of the wall towards the entrance. The absence of light was not entirely a drawback; it meant that the guard could only look in to see me by drawing the drum right back from the doorway—an act which gave me ample warning of his intentions. I peered through the crack at the side of the oil drum to watch the sentry's behaviour, and then made a closer inspection of my cell, with a view to finding a way out of it.

After breakfast that morning—millet again!—I was allowed to visit the latrine, and made the best use of my few minutes in the open to see how my bunker lay in relation to the outside world. I think that I first realized that I was sick when I went outside; I felt very faint when I stood up, and after a few paces vomited. Immediately I thought it was merely an attack of tonsilitis; my throat was becoming swollen and painful in a way I had experienced before. In addition to this, the cut in my foot, caused by the steel rod of the guards in my former cell, was turning septic. I decided to ask if there was a doctor or medical orderly in the village, showing the sentry my foot. He was a good-natured fellow, I am sure. He clicked his tongue, when he saw how swollen and inflamed the cut appeared, nodded when I drew a cross in the sand. My visit to the latrine had been extremely successful.

For two days I worked on a tunnel, carefully disposing the earth by scattering it over the bunker floor under the straw. On the second day, a medical orderly appeared as I returned from the morning visit to the latrine; a pleasant, smiling little man, who dressed my foot very competently but regretted that he had nothing to give me for my throat. I noticed that he looked at my eyes very closely after he had examined my throat, turning me round to face the sunlight so that he could see more clearly. I tried to ask him what he was so interested in but our sign language was insufficiently comprehensive for him to tell me. As I crawled back into my bunker, I reflected that he was probably merely curious at seeing a man with blue eyes.

Next day I could eat nothing, but knowing how badly I should need food, I stored it away against future needs, hoping that the millet would not turn sour.

On returning from the latrine in the morning, I was horrified to see two of the local officers inspecting the inside of the bunker with flashlights and poking at the walls. One of them came out and addressed me angrily in Chinese, shaking his finger at me. It was very difficult to pretend that I was at ease; my heart was beating violently. Why were they going over the bunker? Why was the outside now being examined? What had the Chinese said to me so threateningly? I sat down by the bunker to wait, knowing that they only had to pull away some stones to find the entrance to my tunnel. Even now, the second officer was emerging with a stone in his hand. He joined the man examining the outside of the bunker, engaged him in a short conversation and then—they both made off! The sentry returned me to the bunker where I lay for many hours like the most model prisoner, fearful that they were waiting for me to make a move that would reveal the tunnel. But no one returned and, after several hours of darkness, I returned to work.

Each evening, the bulk of the village garrison went up to the hillside opposite my bunker. There they followed a routine common amongst Chinese troops in Korea: they learned a song in praise of their leaders, or in denunciation of their enemies—in the latter case, the Americans were the favourite subject. Their evening exercise accomplished, they would round off the meeting with a few rousing choruses of those songs they had learnt previously. As my fourth night in the village drew on, I heard the troops pass along the path below my bunker with their rather slow marching step. Soon after, a pleasant tenor voice began to sing on the hill across the valley, the troops repeating the words after him, line by line. I approached the oil drum and put my eyes to the crack. By good fortune, the sentry was within my limited line of vision, standing by the tree, looking up at the heavens. There would never be a better opportunity than this. On my side, I crawled back to the far end of the bunker and removed the stones which had hidden the tunnel I had dug with my hands and a piece of sharp wood, torn from the roof-timbers. It was a small tunnel and I am a wide chap. I had measured off the width as best I could and physically tested the entrance by wriggling into it, but could not risk going further. I realized now that it was going to be a tight squeeze. I had to clear away about another foot of earth before I broke out on to the hillside and I knew that I must make at least one trip back into the bunker to see what the sentry was doing. I would have laboured in vain if I appeared on the far side of the tunnel to find him peering down to see what sort of a mole would emerge; for my point of exit lay on his beat. Yet I could not make the journey up and down the tunnel too many times—the sides or roof might well fall inwards from the hillside. As soon as I estimated that I had only a few more inches to clear, I wriggled back into the bunker to look for the sentry. It was now twilight: I could only just see the tree. The sentry was not there. I waited for some time, wondering where on earth he could be on the beat. A moment later, the crack at the side of the oil drum became dark and I heard the sound of his footsteps. He was standing right outside my bunker. If he came in now, my plans would be discovered! I sat in the darkness, waiting for him to move, expecting that the oil drum would be pulled back at any moment and the light of his torch shine in.

He was so close that I could hear him breathing. Time dragged in the darkness. I seemed to have been sitting there for hours. Then, hawking and spitting, he strolled on in the direction of Duncan's bunker. A few minutes later I could see his outline standing by the tree.

Now was the time to move quickly. I slid into the tunnel, and worked my body up it to the point where the earth sealed me off from the outside. I dug my wood spike into the earth, tore away with my hands, packing the earth into the sides of the tunnel. After about a minute the earth broke under my hand and I felt the chill night air on my flesh. I had reached the end of the tunnel! I got my shoulders through the opening and was able to look over the top of my bunker.

The sentry was talking to a friend nearby. He had his back to me—but it was a back less than twenty feet away. Slowly I emerged from the tunnel; the ground seemed to resound with every grain of earth that fell back behind me. I stole across the open to the maize which lay on the far side, entered it and crawled up the hill towards the bushes on the upper slopes. The cold, wet maize leaves ended, the bushes closed around me. Five minutes more and I reached a burial clearing just below the crest. I leapt up from the bushes, doubled across the open ground and ran as fast as I could along the path that led between the fields beyond, heading for the hill to the north. For the moment, my sickness was forgotten; I felt no fatigue. The night air smelt of freedom and filled my veins with fire!

CHAPTER SIX

I WAS still climbing when I heard a rifle shot from the valley I had just left—another followed, a few seconds later. It could only have been a short time before the wretched sentry, circling his beat, had become aware of a pile of loose earth on the hillside and had rolled the oil drum away from the bunker entrance to find the bird had flown! I reached the dense underbrush just below the hill-top, and sat down to see what line and form the enemy pursuit would take—if any: following a man in darkness on that hard ground was impossible, I believed.

Apparently, they thought that it was not. Ten minutes later I heard voices shouting from either side of the track that led due west. Torches began to flash. Once I heard the sound of dogs barking, and feared that they might have put some on my trail. A moment later I realized that this was nonsense: I had merely heard the village dogs demanding to know what all the excitement was about. The shouts died away as I went through the brush over the top of the hill, making for the pinewoods through which we had come on the truck from Sinmak. There I should find cover amongst the trees, deserted tracks, and water to quench the thirst that escaping had given me.

My journey to the west had begun!

There were many difficulties in making the journey to the coast. The flooded rice-paddy that I met again and again caused me to make detours in the early stages. There were rivers without fords or stepping stones, which had to be swum; and the effort involved taxed my few reserves of physical strength considerably. After three days I realized why the Chinese medical orderly had peered so curiously into my eyes: it was not the blue pupil which had interested him, but the yellow that had spread over the iris. From the colour of my urine I felt almost certain that I had jaundice; and when I looked at my reflection in a pool of clear water, I saw that I was right. My tonsilitis, too, was troubling me a good deal. I swallowed with difficulty the maize that I took from the fields each day. Throughout each night journey, the hills and valleys seemed determined to hinder me, forever lying across my course, never with it.

It took me two days to return to Sinmak; two days later, I was still only a dozen miles from it. Resting on some pine branches after my night march, I realized that I would have to devise a different system of travel, if I was to hope for success. Originally, I had based my calculations on a fifteen-day journey from the point of escape to the nearest suitable point on the coast. On arrival there, I had to be prepared to take anything up to three days to find a boat, bringing the total estimated time to eighteen days. The journey from there was a comparatively short one—perhaps only a few hours, if wind, tide, and current favoured me; but I could not bank on this. I estimated that I might well be at sea, needing sufficient strength to handle a boat single-handed, for anything up to two or three days. The grand total for all phases thus came up to twenty-one. Taking into account my sickness, and my diet of raw maize, I felt that three weeks was about the maximum period I might expect to remain active. It was now clear that I was not going to cover the distance in fifteen days, since I was not covering ten miles a day—the estimate on which I had based my calculations. For ten miles a day meant reducing the distance between me and the coast by ten miles, not the actual distance marched up hill and down dale to accomplish this—a much higher figure. In four days I had travelled, perhaps, twenty-four miles. Already I was sixteen miles behind schedule. As the sun rose and I ate my morning meal of maize, I decided on a new plan.

I slept until the sun was overhead. As usual, I had climbed at dawn to a high, thickly-wooded hill and would have remained there, under my previous plan, until late afternoon or early evening. On this day I rose on waking and climbed to the highest point I could find. From there I selected a route through the pine trees which I would travel in daylight; for I had decided that it was necessary to take this risk, in order to make up and keep to my time-plan. Although there was a chance of running into wooding parties, signallers laying telephone cable, or air-raid sentries, it soon became clear that this disadvantage was heavily outweighed. Selecting the route now took less time; I stopped only infrequently to check my direction. Moreover, now I could select my entire route each day; hitherto, I had been able to do this for the first part of the night march only, continuing by the stars across hill and valley, rarely finding a clear path, often making detours round rice paddy or thick bush.

Although I was anxious to make up for lost time, I realized, as I marched along during the afternoon, that I could hardly have risked moving in daylight before. East of the main highway that runs through Sinmak, every village was packed with troops or depots or both. In the area of the town there were many administrative units, including numbers of railway repair gangs, who lived in caves in the hills to the west as well as to the east: there were few buildings unbombed in Sinmak. Now, moving into the huge western peninsula, I saw very few soldiers; which accounted for Byron's information that we had established a bomb-line approximately ten miles west of the main highway, and that our aircraft were forbidden to operate west of this line apart from reconnaissance and special missions. I was fortunate, too, in that the general line of the hills began to favour me, at last, running towards the coast and not parallel to it, except for odd ranges which I often managed to avoid. In spite of the frequent river-crossings, I felt satisfied that my strength was going to last, for I was doing more than ten miles a day. After twelve days, I began to look over each hill for a sign of the sea.

About this time, my shoes began to cause me concern. I had marched part of the way to Munha-ri in them and all the way south to the village of Namchon-jom from which I had escaped. Escaping, I had travelled frequently over rough and precipitous ground. Now, to my dismay, the heel of my right foot split, and I lost two precious hours sewing it back on with wire from some old signal cable I had picked up on a track—a very clumsy piece of cobbling: my needle was a rusty nail! Whether due to slipping on the hillside when my heel went, or from some other cause, I discovered when I finally got up to walk on that the cut made in my foot by the rod of the Chinese jailers had opened. I bound it with a piece of rag and continued the journey, determined not to be set back at this stage.

The fifteenth day came and went; but there was still no sign of the sea. At dusk I made my bed as usual on and under pine branches, very tired, conscious that my legs were weakening, that my heart was now finding every climb a great effort. I had so hoped that I should see the sea that day. I dropped off to sleep, reminding myself that I must redouble my resolve at this stage. I was sure that I must reach the sea within another three days.

On the following morning I slept late. My long rest had refreshed me; my spirits were high. The sun warmed me, as I came through a small clearing in the silent woods. The scent of the pines seemed invigorating. I stopped at a small stream to wash and drink, eating my breakfast by it and hiding the cobs under some stones by a waterfall. The narrow path led straight up a slope to the top of the hill, where it passed out of sight between two huge boulders. I moved slowly towards these, wishing to avoid an unexpected encounter with anyone on the far side. Near the top I had to pause for rest; my heart was beating like a hammer after the short ascent, and I felt very faint. Recovering after some minutes, I reached the boulders, listened, and moved on between them to the edge of a small cliff. The path turned sharply left, descending the western slope through more pinewoods—but I did not take it. For there, through the few trees on the cliff edge, my eye was caught by the reflection of sun on water. Beyond the pinewoods, far below me, lay the sea!

I rested in a group of thick bushes a little way down the path. I could not bring myself to leave that view while I was resting. Proud Cortes did not look upon the Pacific Ocean with an eye more appreciative than mine, as I gazed on the Yellow Sea that morning. It was foolish of me, of course; but I had walked such a long, long way to see it.

Eventually I forced myself to get up to continue the rest of the march. I still had a considerable distance to go, and there was much to be done before nightfall—by which time I must reach a covered observation point. Now that I had arrived at the coast, my second problem arose: to find a boat, with a sail which I could manage myself. The tremendous tide along this coast—a rise and fall of thirty odd feet—and the problem of mud flats, thrown up by the estuary of the Taedong River, had to be reckoned with, too. I was thankful that the path now led downhill through the woods, for I realized that my reserves of strength were fast running out.

What happened next, I am unable to say. Some time later in the morning—it may even have been the afternoon by then—I found myself walking through an open field, sown, I think, with beans. Nearer, much nearer, was the sea; on it, two fishing boats with grey sails. I said aloud to myself: "What on earth are you doing here in the open? You'll be seen."

I walked across the fields into the trees, but cannot remember which way I went.

I next recall a track with fields of standing maize on either side. Again, I realized that I must seek shelter, and turned towards the stalks on one side of the road. Whether I reached them or not, I cannot say.

The smell of smoke was in my nostrils; beneath me, I felt a soft bed. When I opened my eyes I thought at first that it was night, for it seemed quite dark. Then I discerned some tiny cracks of light high upon my left side and, putting out my hand, I touched a light wall, which gave a little under the weight of my hand. My other hand found a wall to my right. I seemed to be in some sort of passage.

I did not care very much where I was: I just lay there, glad to be still and quiet. Presently, I heard voices beyond the left-hand wall: Korean voices. They continued talking for such a long time that I identified three adult voices and a child's. Two of the adults were women. I was still listening when the talk stopped. For a few minutes there was silence, except for a whisper. Then, half of the left hand wall slid back and the daylight came streaming in, blinding me momentarily.

There were three adults, as I had thought. The man was old in appearance; yet probably not more than forty. The Koreans age so swiftly from their incessant toil and poor food. The nearest woman looked old, too, though she was probably under fifty. Only the girl and the child—her child it seemed—were young; the mother under twenty, the little girl about four years old. Standing in the room of the mud house, they all stared at me as the light fell on my bearded face. There was no hostility in their eyes; only kindness, shyness, and curiosity. As much as five minutes passed before, finally, the old man spoke. He said something in Korean I did not understand at all, waited for a moment while I shook my head, and then pointed, first to his mouth and then to his stomach, which he rubbed. Thinking he meant food, I shook my head, meaning to say that I had had none for some time. They all moved then, the old man coming over to the sliding door he had opened—which formed part of my left wall—closing it to within a few inches of the end of the frame. He patted my arm through the crack that remained and stood there, smoking a long, thin metal pipe with a tiny bowl, such as all the old Korean men smoke. After another short interval, his wife returned with a heaped-up bowl of rice and some soup. The thought of eating rice made me feel like vomiting, but I managed to eat about half the soup before I lay back, doing my best

149

to keep it inside me—and succeeding. This was the first of many acts of kindness bestowed on me by these good people.

I stayed in that house for another six days, during which they fed and cared for me as if I was one of their own. The old man would come in to see me in the mornings and evenings, often taking my hand to lay it beside his own seamed and calloused one, running his finger tips over the comparative smoothness of my skin. After three days my appetite returned; on the fourth I got up after dark and walked round the courtyard behind locked doors. The old man was very conscious of my security. The cupboard in which I lived was always kept closed, unless one of the family was in the room; never once was the house empty, though I am sure that they needed all hands in the fields just then. After the evening meal, once I had got up, I would play with the child—games of penny-conjuring with an old Japanese coin, or peep-bo. But it was all done in whispers; all speech was in whispers. I had absolute faith in their friendship—the more so when I got from the old man the story of how he had found me beside the track, and brought me into his own house, when, without enmity, he could have left me there rather than take the risk of hiding and succouring me under pain of death. I, too, explained my position with many signs. As we grew to understand one another better, I pin-pointed my position fairly accurately and began to make preparations to move on.

The sea was about two li away—roughly, half a mile. He said that he would find me a boat to take me to Cho-Do, the big island nearby, which I had hoped to reach since the day of my escape with Duncan, almost a month ago. I cut open my clothing and gave him all the money I had so carefully put away months before; water-soaked, sweat-soaked, earth-stained money. I put it all into his hands and promised him the same amount again if we were successful. Reluctant to take it at first, he finally agreed and, with many "Comupsom-nidas", stowed it away in some hiding place.

I was still extremely weak, yet knew that every day spent there was not only a danger to me but to the old man and his family. The girl's husband had been killed at the front, I gathered—on which side he fought, I was not quite sure. There would be no one to say a word for them, if it became known that they had sheltered me. Each one of them, possibly even the child, if precedent in Korean punitive measures was applied, would be put to the sword. After two days' gentle exercise, to show the old man that I could walk to the shore, he agreed to send me off on the evening of the sixth day.

Early in the afternoon I was watching the track that ran past the house, as I had done since breakfast time, my eye peering through a crack in the back of the cupboard. Outside the house, sitting on the path that led down to the track, the child was playing with some little round mudballs which she had made the day before. All was quiet, except when some neighbour passed to exchange a greeting with her. The afternoon shadows were lengthening, when I saw a North Korean soldier coming from the direction of the sea, a burp-gun slung across one shoulder, his jacket open, a pack on his back. He stopped by the well to take a drink of water and called to the little girl to come over, producing from his pocket an apple which he held up to her. She went over with reluctance, the apple helping her to forget how shy she was. Munching a piece of apple each, she and the soldier began to talk. The Korean words were incomprehensible to me, but I could not take my eyes off the soldier. I longed for him to go. Suddenly, I heard the word "Yungook" spoken by the child amongst others. The soldier leant forward and took her by the shoulders questioning her. Then he got up, slung his burp-gun forward, and walked towards the house. Just short of the entrance to the courtyard he seemed to change his mind, for he ran back to the well, pulled on his pack, and went off down the track at a sharp pace. I had an idea that it was time for me to go.

The old man was in the courtyard as I came to the door. When he saw me standing there in daylight, he probably thought I had gone mad. He came hastily into the room, shutting the door. I tried to explain by signs what had happened, but realized that I was going much too fast to convey anything. After one more attempt I knew that it was hopeless trying to convey my many thoughts to him quickly by signs. I must leave, and trust to luck that I could find a boat on my own, if I did not manage to contact him again. Patting him on the shoulder reassuringly, I ran out through the door, through the courtyard, down the path. The area behind the house was open. Only the far side of the track contained good cover, where the maize stalks remained tall, leafy, and green, with some form of bean growing up round their roots. As I crossed the track, four armed Chinese came running round the bend further down, giving a hoarse shout as they saw me. I jumped into the maize, hurried along the narrow passage between the stalks, and had just decided that I would head east—away from the coast—for a short distance, when I saw some Chinese soldiers enter the far end of the maize field from the direction in which I was going. Footsteps approached me from both ends of the field, closing in on me. The last moments of my freedom were, even then, dying, within a quarter of a mile of the coast.

I was taken up to the village of Sosa-ri; a miserable journey on which I collapsed twice. Finally the escort, tired of accompanying me at a snail's pace, got me a lift on a passing military pony cart whose driver was a good fellow—unlike my scowling guards—and gave me a half of his tin of beef and six biscuits, despite their attempts to dissuade him. At Sosa-ri, the guards changed. A surly-faced non-commissioned officer and two privates took me on to the town of Songhwa, where an attempt was made to interrogate me by the North Korean police, through an interpreter who knew less English than I did Korean—a man who had evidently lived on a reputation as a linguist for a long time, without expecting to be called on to show his skill. The Chinese soon got tired of his efforts to make me understand him, and sent him packing. They put me on a Korean civil truck, with my three guards and a great number of Korean civilians and their luggage, which reached the main western railway two days later and dropped me off. It began to rain as the guards did their best to hurry me along the railway track, away from the main road. We took shelter for an hour in a small village inhabited by railway sappers. They were mostly older men, easily distinguishable by their blue uniforms, which many of the transport personnel wore. One group we joined had been having a party on saki—a rice wine—which they had got from one of the houses in the village. As we arrived a great argument was going on between the Chinese and an irate villager who was refusing them more wine. I stood there for some time, watching them, until, all at once, he noticed me. He was a nasty little man, wanting to jump on me with a knife to demonstrate to the Chinese how tough he was. Two of the soldiers, thinking it all a huge joke, threw him out of the house bodily, returning to give me a packet of cigarettes, some pipe tobacco, and a half box of matches. I refused saki, but had some of their beef. My pockets full of luxuries like tobacco and matches, eating my second meat meal in three days, I felt that things were looking up after my recapture. When, eventually, we continued our journey in light rain, I was in excellent spirits once more. Here I was, back at the railway line and highway. Well, no matter. With a bit of rest and some food, I could do it all over again. I began to watch the country carefully.

We left the railway, entering a long valley, stopping frequently to rest my wretchedly weak body. A path led us up to a pass, beyond which a large headquarters was dug into the hillsides. During the day, after giving my military particulars, and admitting to escaping from a column of prisoners marching northwards, I was asked, with great friendliness, if I wished to write a letter home. I had had this chance only once before—at Munha-ri one wet day in Bob's "mediaeval pest-house"—and had little hope that this letter had got past T'ang's inquisitive eyes. I said that I should be delighted to write, and spent half an hour with an unfamiliar pencil in my hand, writing on cheap white paper. That evening, when I came up for further interrogation, my inquisitor drew my letter from his pocket, when I refused to answer his questions, and asked me whether I wished to send my letter or not. I told him that I did want to send my letter home, but was not prepared to pay for the postage with military information. Thereupon he tore the letter up in front of me.

About ten minutes later I was packed off down the path leading east. I was very tired and hoped that we had not far to go. As it transpired, we had less than two miles to walk, but the guards lost their way three times during the journey, so that we actually covered four. Exhausted, I was led away from my escorts to a courtyard.

One side of a double wooden door was unlocked, the door opened, and I was put through it. Straw rustled under my feet; the stench of unwashed bodies filled the air. My foot touched someone's flank.

"Hell! is there any room in here?" I asked.

To my complete surprise, a very young, English voice replied: "Is that another Englishman?"

A minute later I was shaking hands warmly with Mike.

CHAPTER SEVEN

WE were both seized by that enthusiasm one experiences on meeting one's own kind, after being separated from them for a long period—an emotion intensified in this instance by being in the hands of a captor who insisted, much of the time, on treating one as a felon. It seemed to me that I was incredibly lucky, in finding a comrade so far away from the routes along which our enemies normally evacuated their prisoners; although it was less surprising when I discovered that Mike was a fighter pilot, shot down in a P51 while flying with the South African Squadron. After a short period of captivity, he had escaped and remained at large for about four days, only to be recaptured by a couple of stray Chinese who had come upon him by accident. When I learned that he had been shot down only six weeks before, I considered myself doubly fortunate; for here was not only a companion for the irksome life one led in captivity, a potential colleague in escape, but also a man who had all the news of the battle and the outside world—news that I had missed so much during the long days of enforced idleness at Munha-ri.

Lying there alongside Mike on the dirt floor, I questioned and he replied about all that had happened since that day in April when the battle began for us on the Imjin River. Mike had a good memory, and obviously took an interest in outside affairs; but I taxed him to the limit that night with my questions. Finally, we were both so tired that we agreed to go to sleep, covering our cold bodies with a ragged piece of straw matting. As we adjusted this to our mutual comfort, Mike said:

"By the way, have you got lice?"

I replied that I had rid myself of them some weeks before.

"I'm afraid I have them," he said. "I wish you'd tell me how to get rid of them."

"Mike," I said, "if you've got lice, you won't need me to tell you how to get rid of them. To-morrow morning, I'll be giving you a very necessary demonstration on myself!"

Next morning Mike turned out to be tall, ginger-haired, and a second-lieutenant. The two of us were taken up to a bunker in a nearby hill, immediately after our kaoliang breakfast, and thrust inside with a group of South Korean soldiers whose uniforms had long since been exchanged for rags. Whence these filthy, starved, dejected men had originated, neither Mike nor I discovered. We just managed to identify them as ROKs, after considerable sign-making, but this exhausted the conversational resources of both sides.

On the posting of a sentry and guard commander less hostile than their predecessors, the two of us contrived to get permission to leave the stinking, crowded bunker. Outside, we sat in the sunlight, discussing our exact location in relation to the most important thing that lay before us: escape. Undoubtedly, we were now about ten miles south of Sinmak, and a little to the east of the main western railway and highway, which run, broadly speaking, side by side. Escaping from this point, we could make for the coast again; or, in the light of Mike's knowledge of the Kaesong neutral zone established for the Truce Negotiations, we could head south. There were many factors to be considered before making a final choice: our immediate task was to break with our captors.

After we had eaten our kaoliang on the following night, I was taken out of the room I shared with Mike to a house on the western edge of the village. Sitting in one of the rooms, I found three Chinese—presumably officers—whom I named Adolescence, Smart-Alec, and Darkie. After a long silence, during which the three stared at me with almost unblinking eyes, Darkie opened the conversation.

It was the same old nonsense: I was a war criminal. My "attitude," revealed at the headquarters two days before, by my refusal to answer military questions, showed that I was not sorry for what I had done. My guilt was intensifying each day under these circumstances and I could not expect my captors to continue much longer with their "humanitarian treatment!"

This summary of the case for the prosecution was presented in its entirety by Darkie, who, after the prolix fashion of the Chinese Communist Forces, took something over an hour to state it. Immediately I began to reply, Adolescence jumped up, pointed a finger of accusation at me, and began a lengthy explanation of the causes and history of the Korean war. It was all deliberately melodramatic. He would rise, speak for several minutes, beating the air passionately with the hand that was not outstretched in accusation, conclude with a toss of his head, and sit down in complete composure while Darkie caught up with the translation. This done, Adolescence would switch on the melodrama again, even to assuming a special facial expression as he got to his feet. As the hours passed, it occurred to me that he had probably been preparing his subject since the day of my arrival—and this was confirmed when I caught him peeping at some notes in his pocket during one of the periods of translation.

The points that Adolescence made bear repeating, if only because they were identical with those put out by the Chinese Communist Government for internal and, not infrequently, external consumption on the subject of Korea. Thus they are the points that were made again and again to the United Nations prisoners-of-war in Korea, in the innumerable addresses they received during their captivity, and formed a part of the programme of attempted political indoctrination.

In the first place, said Adolescence, the American war-mongers—the more powerful members of the New York Stock Exchange on Wall Street—began the war in Korea for two reasons: they thirsted for bigger and better profits, which armaments would give them; and they wanted to blacken the name of the Cominform countries to dupe their own restless, oppressed workers. These two reasons were complementary. On looking round for a suitable battleground, they chose Korea, saying, in their duplicity, that the very people whom they were attacking by an act of wanton aggression were the cause of it all. If I needed evidence of the United States' guilt, said Adolescence, what better proof could I ask than that the arch-enemy of liberty—John Foster Dulles, himself!—was in South Korea just before it began. The most doubting of hearts could doubt no longer when confronted by such a fact.

Though greatly outnumbered, the North Koreans crushed the puppet forces of Syngman Rhee, whose remnant withdrew in disorder. Determined to end the threat of aggression from the south once and for all, and not least, to liberate those unhappy Koreans living under the Syngman Rhee regime, the North Korean Army marched on victoriously, overcoming the resistance that the regular American Forces attempted en route. Only later, when the whole Capitalist world had been mobilized against them, were the soldiers of the gallant North Korean Resistance Movement thrown back from the box formed round the Naktong River. Well knowing that the predatory forces following them up to the Yalu River intended to cross into China to continue the aggression there, the Chinese people, spontaneously, and independently of their Government, formed a military body, for the specific task of protecting their Motherland and aiding the North Koreans in their fight against American aggression. Armed with their democratic Marxist spirit, led by commanders enlightened by the Marx-Engels-Lenin-Stalinist philosophy, this body—the Chinese Peoples' Volunteers—had marched across the Yalu River, fallen upon the aggressors and driven them back. Any responsibility placed on Mao's Government for their formation, control, or supply was a calumny of the vilest kind.

It seemed, too, that any reference to the Chinese Fourth Field Army—in our terms, an Army Group—which had apparently volunteered for Korea to a man, under its commander, General Peng Teh Huai, was considered a calumny also. I was not permitted to raise the point again; though I tried to ask what they would have said, if the British Government had said that the 29th Independent Infantry Brigade Group was a volunteer force, released as such from the United Kingdom Order of Battle—with all their armament, equipment, vehicles, clothing and necessaries. I gathered that there was no answer on the written "crib" to this or any similar points.

Adolescence spoke for another hour, and I gave up attempting to argue with him. He had his speech prepared, and he was not going to be put off saying it. Switching the scowl from his face, he suddenly sat down and began to eat an apple. I believe he was still serving his apprenticeship as a politico and, secretly, was rather glad it was all over.

It was now the turn of Smart-Alec. As I had suspected, he was the most powerful of the three. In honeyed tones, he now suggested that I should sign a written confession of my guilt as a war-criminal —a confession that they would be delighted to assist me to prepare! —which would relieve me of responsibility for my former crimes. In the plainest possible terms, I told them that I would not. They threatened to separate me from Mike. I pointed out that he was, mentally, a sick man—he had been trying to convince them of this before my arrival as part of an escape plan—and that he would almost certainly become completely insane without my care. I cannot think they cared whether he was looked after or not, but whatever they felt, after a further prolonged argument about my confession, I was returned to Mike just before dawn. A full night had passed without either of us being able to work on our escape.

On the following day, we did not go down the hill, as usual, to our evening meal in a group with the ROKs. In the afternoon— about three o'clock—a non-commissioned officer and two soldiers collected us from our seat outside the bunker and took us into the centre of the village. There we were given as much kaoliang as we could eat, and an ample quantity of egg-plant soup. By the look of the kit that the guards had got together, we were going on a journey. The meal over, our escort led us out of the village to the headquarters where I had stayed five nights before. The interpreter who had torn up my letter met us.

"Come with me, both of you," he said. "Remember you should call our commander, 'sir'."

Neither of us had the slightest intention of calling him anything, so we prepared ourselves for an argument. We were thus very surprised to meet a very mild little Chinese, dressed in a well-cut khaki suit, but wearing a cap several sizes too large for him, who neither insisted that we should address him in any special way, nor expected anything of us that we were not prepared to give. The interpreter treated him with great respect, as we talked in a large, comparatively well-furnished, bunker. It actually had a glass sky-light with a wooden shutter, and was furnished with a bed, two chairs, a table, and an old tattered carpet. It seemed he must be an important man to have items of property like this in such an area—even if they had been appropriated locally. I decided that he was at least the commander of a district on the line-of-communication—probably the equivalent of a brigadier or major-general.

The little man bade us sit down, asked our ranks, and said he knew we were English. We made no comment. He told the interpreter to give us a cigarette each—he did not smoke, he said but "this comrade" had plenty. "This comrade" turned out his pockets as fast as he could and lit a match for us. Emboldened by his geniality and obvious authority, I asked:

"Why was my letter to my family torn up, because I did not wish to answer your questions?"

The commander looked at me for a moment from his little bright brown eyes before he said:

"That is an administrative matter. I hope you enjoy the journey." He got up to signify that the interview was over. We were hurried outside.

"Remember," said the interpreter, as we made our way down the hill to pick up the reinforced guard, "if you escape again, you will be shot."

We journeyed through the night to Pyongyang in an empty Chinese two-and-a-half ton truck, arriving at dawn, with many bruises from our frequent contact with its sides and floor as we passed over innumerable pot-holes and makeshift bridges, and round the edges of many bomb craters. The cut in my foot had opened after its pounding on the steel floor, and I found difficulty in walking from our debussing point to some houses in the extreme north of the city. After an hour's sleep, we had a breakfast of rice, and were ordered to continue on our way. We had not been on the road very long before it became apparent that we were lost, with the result that we spent the remainder of the morning moving backwards and forwards, until we reached a very large village about a mile and a half from our original starting point. Our escort handed us over to the village garrison, where we were searched and stripped of every one of our few possessions, including our shoes and belts. After a short wait, we found ourselves locked in a very strong cell, lined with stout timbers, and offering, as cell-mates, a Chinese boy of fifteen years and one of the filthiest men I have ever seen.

Through constant protest we managed to secure the removal of our cell-mates—who were literally crawling with lice—the issue of a covering to keep out the growing chill of the October nights, and a small measure of freedom to sit for a little while in the sun each day. On two occasions, we were actually allowed to wash and we worked hard at delousing. Our luck seemed to be turning a little, and we hoped it would continue as we made fresh plans to escape. On the fourth day, however, Mike was removed from the cell, and we had but a few moments to wish each other good fortune before he disappeared with the guards who had brought up his possessions. Although we had been together only a short time, his companion-ship had meant a great deal to me. Moreover, escape would once again become an individual business. I passed a lonely evening, which was not improved when the guard commander strengthened the wire round my cell.

On the following night I was really pleased to find that I, too, was to be moved on. I was put into the hands of a very cheerful officer, who had evidently not long removed the Red Star of the Chinese regular forces from his cap—a gesture to international custom on crossing the Yalu River into Korea. He was extremely friendly, presenting me with apples and the Chinese hard-ration biscuit during our night truck journey, and borrowing a padded greatcoat for me from our driver to keep out the cold wind which had risen shortly after our departure. But his kindness did not relax his vigilance. I arrived at Sinanju as fast a prisoner as I had left Pyong-yang.

At dawn on the following day I reached Chinju. The guards handed me over to a headquarters in a village just east of the town and departed. Once again I found myself confined in a small, mud-walled room; and, this time, I was not permitted to sit out in the morning sun. I spent the day trying to scratch a crossword on the wall under the puzzled eyes of the sentry, who came in every few minutes to make sure that I was not scratching a hole through to the other side! An hour before dusk the guard commander brought me an excellent meal of rice and a soup of potatoes, which had a liberal quantity of cooking oil floating on the top. I ate my fill of this rich dish, before being taken back to the centre of Chinju town. Accompanying our party was a Chinese officer who evidently spoke good Korean, from the fluency with which he conversed with two North Korean tank officers on the journey. The reason for his presence became clear when I found myself outside the local police station: I was handed over to be kept in their cells. After several hours of darkness I was relieved to find that it was not the intention to keep me there for the night. I was already chilled through in my unheated cell, when a police officer and two sergeants came to escort me down to the main cross-roads, where they joined a group of Chinese attempting to stop a vehicle for a lift.

No one stopped; several of those giving signals were almost run over. Eventually, they decided to give it up for the night. As my policemen were about to return me to the local lock-up, the Korean-speaking Chinese came running-up, said a few words to them, and instructed the Chinese to bring me along the road behind him that led us back to the east. I caught the word "Mi-goor"—American—in their conversation as we left the cross-roads, and was just wondering whether they were referring to an impending air-raid, when we came up to a small handcart in the middle of the road. Sitting on it, his crutches lying alongside his one leg, was an American. This was the "Mi-goor" to whom they had referred. His name was Tom.

When Tom and I left Chinju the following afternoon, it was a

161   F

special occasion. Tom was leaving the area in which he had spent his entire six months' captivity to date. The commander of an American F80 jet-fighter squadron, his aircraft had been hit by anti-aircraft fire in a raid on the Chinju rail yards. Jumping clear of his cockpit, his legs had been caught by the tailplane and injured. Fainting from pain and loss of blood, he had drifted to earth to be picked up by North Korean soldiers. For five days he had been given *nothing*—not even water to quench his raging thirst. Then, by God's grace, the local Chinese headquarters had learned of his whereabouts. Deciding that an Air Force Major was worth interrogating, they sent out a party to bring him into Chinju, but found that he was too weak to understand, let alone answer, their questions. They took him to a hospital—or what passed for one—a few miles away: a group of mud huts in a village filled with flies and filth that bred more flies and disease as the summer progressed. Fortunately Tom had a strong constitution. The Chinese feldshers amputated one of his legs in rough fashion, and, an hour afterwards, he had visitors: an interrogation team who plied him ceaselessly with questions about the organization of his squadron, group, wing and the Headquarters of the Far Eastern Air Force for over nine hours. Evidently his captors were not pleased with his replies to their questions: his leg remained unattended for a month, by which time the wound had become terribly infected. He was leaving Chinju prematurely now: the amputation was still only partly healed, but he had refused to write a letter to the United States calling for the end of the Korean war and thus was not considered worthy of further treatment.

In the late afternoon we reached Sinui-Ju.

Our truck drew up outside the main gates of a large, brick-walled enclosure. Inside, we could see several stone buildings and a huge bunker from which radio-aerials protruded. Behind these ran the main railway line that came across the Yalu river from Antung, the Chinese city that sits on the north bank opposite Sinuiju. As we entered the gates a huge locomotive steamed past on the embankment drawing a long line of boxcars.

At first, I thought we had come to a North Korean Army Headquarters. As we stood in the courtyard, however, I realized that all

162

the officers and men about us wore police uniforms; and the windows and doors of several of the stone buildings were barred in such a way as to leave me in no doubt: we were at the police headquarters and jail!

The Korean-speaking Chinese who had brought us came out of the main office building, glanced at us, and returned to the truck with the Chinese guards. Our escorts were now North Korean police officers, who took us over to a wooden structure nearby and bade us sit down. Tom and I began quietly to discuss why we had been transferred to the Koreans when he had been told at the hospital that he was going to one of the main prisoner-of-war camps. We were probably very stupid not to realize that his failure to answer military questions in the hospital provided the answer.

As darkness fell, we were taken into one of the cell blocks. The heavy, barred door was opened, closed, and relocked behind us. We found ourselves in a wide passage containing a bench, a chair and a desk. In the thick outer wall there was one small window, now blacked-out for the night, and a door at either end of the passage. In the other wall were set small, barred doors, too low for a man to enter, without bending almost double. Above each door, and running into the wall on its right, was a long barred window. Behind the doors and windows were wooden-floored, cement-walled rooms, thirty feet long, ten feet wide. These were the cells.

As soon as we entered the passage from the cold, fresh air, the warm stench of unwashed bodies met us. Yet, though it was obvious that the block must contain a considerable number of human beings, there was no sound, except for an occasional muffled cough—the sort of cough one might hear in a public library, when the cougher is afraid of making too much noise. Three warders—a second lieutenant and two warrant officers of the police—met us and took us into their charge. They had unpleasant, cunning faces; I called them Weasel, Ferret, and Stoat, hoping that, as is so often the case, their expressions hid kind hearts.

Weasel and Ferret—the warrant officers—began to search us. They removed everything from us, including our footwear, the draw-strings in our underwear, and Tom's rough crutches. A cell door was opened and we were put in. A bright, barred light shone down from high up in the roof ceiling upon the backs of twenty-one men and boys who sat on the floor, cross-legged, in absolute silence, their backs to the door and window in the passage wall. Not one man looked up as we entered; they seemed to be terrified of attracting the attention of the warders. From behind the barred window, Stoat spoke to two men who were sitting by—but not leaning on—the wall beneath the window. They scurried forward into two vacant places at the bottom of the cell, as we moved into their places, Tom hopping forward on his one leg, leaning on my shoulder. The cell door clanged to behind us; the key turned noisily in the lock.

CHAPTER EIGHT

WE soon learned the rules of the prison. At five o'clock in the morning the dense mass of bodies, overlapping one another on the wooden floor, responded like automatons to a single word of command from one of the warders. As one man, almost, without a second's pause, they would rise into a sitting position, their legs crossed, their shoulders drooping in an attitude of contrition, their heads bowed. At dawn, one man was permitted to stand up, in order to remove the cardboard blackout from the tiny window in the top, left-hand corner, at the far end of the cell. He would climb on the little, knee-high, rickety wooden screen which afforded all the privacy allowed to prisoners when they were permitted to visit the cell latrine—a square hole in the floor at the far end under the window.

Two or three hours later, the heads of the prisoners would move —just slightly; a move that could not be seen by an observer in the passage behind. In some way unknown to me, they knew that food was coming. For perhaps another five or ten minutes my straining ears could catch no sound at all. Surely, I would think, they must be wrong this time! Not even the faintest echo of a clattering food tin, or rattling of our crude, metal bowls could I hear. Yet a few minutes later I would hear the sound of preparation; a few minutes after that the food would come along. As the warder reached our door, my cell-companions scattered to form a large circle, their backs to the cell walls. From inside their filthy, ragged clothing, they produced chop-sticks—two little pieces of unsmoothed wood per man—and their own preparations for the meal were complete. Bowls of millet, kaoliang or maize—mostly the latter—were passed into the cell: half a bowl per man. Occasionally, there would be a little thin bean soup, and in anticipation of this delicacy the saliva almost ran from their eager mouths. Tom and I were lucky. The only concession made to us as prisoners-of-war was that our bowls were half-filled with cold rice (left over from the police dining-hall) and, sometimes, a little fish. When we could do so secretly, we shared our fish with those that sat near us; for they looked at it with such longing eyes, poor wretches. When we had finished our meal, the bowls were passed back through the serving-window in the cell door, places were instantly resumed, and the pattern of motionless bodies was re-established.

Day and night, the electric light shone down on us from the ceiling. At dusk, the cardboard black-out was replaced. The evening meal was brought along at five, the prisoners long since aware of its proximity; and at ten o'clock the second command of the day was shouted. Before the echo had died in the passage, the cell floor was covered with recumbent bodies, so closely packed that, even when lying on one's side, one's legs overlapped another prisoner. In this press Tom and I, almost lice-free on entry, speedily found ourselves crawling again, our clothes and hair providing fresh nests for the quickly multiplying creatures.

One of the prisoners is to be punished. The Weasel, creeping up and down the passage in his usual way, hoping to find someone disobeying the rules and regulations, thinks that he has discovered a man whispering to another in our cell. It is useless for the man to protest his very real innocence. He moved, and his clothing, rubbing against that of another man, has caused a slight noise. The Weasel believes—or pretends that he believes—that the prisoner is guilty of talking. He stands behind the passage window, rapping out questions, and what sound like threats, to the cringing prisoner, who, standing at the Weasel's order, is facing him, terrified. After a few minutes, he is sent to the end of the cell. Tom and I do not understand what is happening. He is raising his arms above his head. The Weasel shouts at him and he raises them higher; he is stretching them to the utmost. Slowly, the nature of his punishment becomes apparent to us. His back is now turned to the passage. He cannot tell whether or not he is still watched by his tormentor, and so, as his arms become tired, he cannot rest them, fearing worse punishment if he moves without orders. An hour passes. Now and again, Tom and I can just hear the Weasel's footsteps as he comes back; or sometimes we hear him cough slightly above us, and we realize that he has returned silently. Four hours pass. When the Weasel calls out to the defaulter, we see that his cheeks are wet with tears of agony as he turns to answer. Only when darkness falls, only when the tormented man is about to faint, does the Weasel give him permission to lower his arms and return to his place.

No one moves in the cell. No eyes are lifted in sympathy. No hand is raised to give him a friendly, comforting pat, as he resumes his cross-legged posture. From further up the cell block, there comes a swishing sound, followed by a cry of pain. The Weasel has transferred his centre of operations. I think it is a woman whose cries we hear.

Now and again, as the days passed, we were allowed to wash. That is to say, every third or fourth day, the door was opened about an hour before our first meal, and six men or women were allowed out from each cell in pairs to wash their hands and faces. Twice I was permitted to carry Tom pick-a-back down the passage, to the little room at the end where our feeding bowls were kept, and where there was a single tap from which ice-cold water constantly flowed. On those days when we were not lucky enough to wash, we were able to exchange a few words with our cell companions; for Stoat, Weasel, and Ferret were always busy on such occasions and could not watch all the cells. Besides, the next pair had always to be ready at the door, waiting their turn to run up to the wash-room as soon as the previous pair came back. In this way, we had warning of the warder's approach.

There was a boy in our cell who spoke a little English learned at a Korean high school. He was seized by a high fever two or three times a day, but received no medicine for it. He told us that he came from a town called Pyoktong where there were many prisoners, closely guarded by the Chinese. Mi-gook, Yun-gook—every kind of prisoner. He had been arrested for speaking to them as they passed. We asked him what his sentence was; he had no sentence. Arrested five months before, he had had no trial. How long would he be here? He did not know. Maybe till he died. This was a political prison. There were men there because they had been Christian leaders; men who had been members of the Communist Party, but had fallen from favour; others who had been arrested for no reason known to themselves—perhaps on the old system of a *lettre de cachet*. Trial? They had not been tried. They would not be tried. They would stay here until some powerful friend could get them released, until they were moved to another prison, or until they died. Tom and I tried to comfort them from our horror-stricken hearts, but though they were grateful, they were comfort-less. They knew better than we did what the future held.

Coming back down the passage after our second wash, we were followed to our cell by the Stoat, who began to question Tom about his leg. He thought it a great joke that Tom had to hop about, and that he found it difficult to visit the latrine hole with such a dis-ability. In this genial mood, he informed us that there was another European prisoner in the next cell down. Such were the circum-stances of our imprisonment, that he had been there all the time without our even suspecting his presence. Leaving us standing by the window, the Stoat went down the passage and began to talk to someone inside. A cheerful voice with a broad Australian accent answered.

"More prisoners-of-war, eh?" said the voice, evidently speaking for our benefit rather than to the Stoat. "Good-oh! Hope to get a chance to see 'em before long, eh? This place is a dinkum chamber-of-horrors!"

Now I realized what it was that one of the Koreans had been trying to tell me on the previous wash-day, when we had not been allowed out. He had repeated "Hoju" again and again. This was a word I had never heard before; it means, of course, "Australian".

Two days later, we heard the "Hoju" come out of his cell. It was meal time and, peering through the door bars, I caught a glimpse of a mass of curly hair and a huge, light brown beard.

"Just off," he called, apparently to a warder at the far end of the passage.

"God Save King George," I called back; and I was lucky that the Stoat was on duty and in a good humour. He kicked the door with the side of his boot, setting it rattling, but left his rebuke at that.

Ferret and Weasel are both in a foul temper. Although it is four days since anyone had a wash, no one has been allowed out this morning to the wash-house. They are looking for trouble: if there is no trouble, they will make it.

For a time, they vent their spleen in one of the cells further up the passage; cries and a sobbing voice are heard by us all. After a period of silence, Ferret's voice screams out from the window above where I sit with Tom. He has obviously slipped down to our cell, hoping to find someone to punish. He has found two or three, apparently; he and Weasel are not going to be content with tormenting just one man this morning.

First they pick on a little man sitting to the left and forward of me, who had been brought in two days ago after we had a clear-out. (Five men had left our cell, wired together with telephone cable. We received word from the boy that they were being taken to work in one of the coal mines.) Now this man has been chosen to teach the five newcomers a lesson in discipline. Neither Tom nor I can understand what he is accused of: we shall have to inquire later. It is probably for talking or visiting the latrine without good cause—these are favourite reasons for punishment by Weasel and Ferret. Whatever it is, they have called the prisoner over to the cell door. Yesterday, they kept a prisoner at that door for over an hour, taking it in turn to twist his arm, which they pulled through the bars. Turning it almost to the point where it broke, bringing

168

the prisoner to the verge of fainting, they would stop, rest him for a moment, then start on his other arm. This morning, the punishment seems to be quite mild: they are pulling his hair, twisting his ears and nose; punching his face through the bars. He dare not step back out of reach, but stands there, apparently willing to suffer these sadistic acts; in reality chained there by his fear of worse punishment.

Throughout this, Ferret keeps questioning him, giving more point to each query by a sharp tug at the handful of hair he has, or a hard rap on the nose. The prisoner answers in a whisper. Now another prisoner is called over, and Weasel transfers all his attention to him. Ten or fifteen minutes pass in this way; the remainder of the prisoners sit mutely by, hearing all, but seeing nothing; terrified that their names may be called at any moment. Our hearts burn because we are unable to do anything at all to aid these men.

A third man is called up; but not for punishment—yet. The two others are made to kneel down, their heads towards the far end of the cell. The third man is ordered to kick them and he does so— their seats, their sides, their legs. But his kicks, though hard enough to cause the two wretches to cry out, are not hard enough to satisfy Weasel and Ferret. With the steel rods they carry in their hands, they reach through the bars and begin to beat the third man, urging him to kick harder. The cries, the sound of the blows, and the swishing of the steel rods mingle in this way for about five minutes. Only then are the groaning men permitted to sit down again, a shout from Weasel silencing the exclamations of agony that their bruises cause them.

Outside in the courtyard flies the flag that represents the Democratic Peoples' Republic of Korea.

At last we were to move again. Fifteen days after our arrival, we were taken out of our cell and told to prepare for a journey. Our belts were returned, but my Chinese shoes had been stolen. After a great deal of fuss, threats, and argument, they contrived to find me a very old pair of canvas shoes. The little box of matches, and the few cigarettes that the Chinese truck-driver gave to me on the journey up from Chinju, were not returned to me.

How glad we were to climb on to a truck, even though my wrists were bound with wire and Tom's crutches had been removed from his reach. We looked back, as the truck drove off down the street, remembering the unfortunate ones who must stay behind. From the gateway emerged a long column of prisoners, taken from the cells at the same time as ourselves, wired together for their march to another prison or a labour camp.

At first we headed east, taking the road that runs parallel to and just south of the Yalu River. Northwards, we could see the huge jagged peaks of North-East China; southwards, the country alternated with rice paddy and low hills. Four nights later, after a crazy journey that had led us gradually south and then south-west, we found ourselves back in Pyongyang.

We reached a wooden police building about two o'clock in the morning but, to our delight, were not put into a cell. We dozed until daylight and, sometime after nine, were given breakfast of stale, cold rice and bean curd. Neither of us was very anxious to eat this stodgy, unappetising food: the last police station on the way down had given us, on the previous evening, our best meal for more than a month, but we ate all the bean curd because of the nourishment it provided. A young Korean in a cheap, European-style lounge suit brought the bowls of food down, and confided that he, too, was really a prisoner but was permitted to do small jobs about the area. He had been at Pyongyang high school for some time and spoke understandable, if limited English, though he seemed unable to tell us why he was in the hands of the police. It was plain that he did not wish to be caught talking to us, but we did manage to discover from him that the Peace Talks had started up again at Kaesong. He would say nothing more than that, and then changed the subject by saying that another American Air Force Officer had passed through this very building, on his way to a prisoner-of-war camp run by the North Koreans. We were probably going to the same camp in four or five days, he added.

At dusk, a lieutenant-colonel of the police, with a small escort, took us in his jeep along the road to Chinam-po. A few miles from the city we turned off the main highway on to a dirt track, which led us through several villages to a large Korean farm standing on the edge of a community of about forty houses. It had probably belonged to a Japanese formerly, for it had a brick barn and its rooms were spacious compared with others in the village. The colonel knocked on a huge double gate of wood, calling something out as he did so. As soon as the gate was open, we were ordered to leave the jeep and enter the courtyard. There was a sentry, armed with a burp-gun on the gate—the first North Korean private soldier of the infantry I had seen for a very long time. Near him was a corporal, who was receiving some sort of orders about us. Two or three minutes later, the corporal opened one of the double-doors of the barn and switched on an electric light. I was told to enter, Tom following on his crutches. Inside, lying on some straw, covered with a piece of matting was the "Hoju" from Sinuiju jail, and, with him, a freckle-faced young man wearing an American flying-suit. We had a warm welcome.

We made the final decision to escape while working on the hill one morning. After telling the story of my captivity to my new companions, very naturally the subject of another escape had arisen. With the rapid onset of the Korean winter, I had originally decided, after my discharge from Sinuiju jail, that I would take up winter quarters in a prison camp and make a fresh escape in the following spring. In any case I had Tom with me; and I had felt that I could not leave him alone with the North Koreans, knowing that he would suffer at least in part for my misdemeanour if I managed to get away. Now, talking to the two working with me— Jack, the young American flier, and Ron, the Australian—it seemed to me that circumstances had changed considerably from those on which I had based my former appreciation.

The first change had been that we found ourselves in a North Korean interrogation centre, and not in a prisoner-of-war camp. Though we had not expected to find any luxuries in the latter, we had anticipated sufficient food to maintain life throughout the winter. Here we were getting a diminishing ration of boiled millet daily with a very thin soup, containing a bean or a radish leaf to convince our stomachs of its authentic nourishment value. Worse,

171

Tom, who was under intensive interrogation, was being punished for his lack of response by being starved. His rations had been cut off completely, and they were now threatening to cut off his water supply. Our efforts to feed him from our own meagre issue of millet had been circumvented; at mealtimes we were supervised to the point where the guard commander or a sentry actually watched us eat.

In the second place, the barn in which we were quartered was now bitterly cold at nights. The North Korean troops in the village had all been issued with warm winter garments, but the interrogators made it clear that they would not issue clothing to those who did not co-operate with them. We were not co-operating and had no intention of doing so. It seemed as if the bitterest phase of the North Korean winter would find us in what threadbare garments we still possessed. Jack was the worst off. He had been shot down in mid-summer, wearing only thin underclothing and a summer flying suit. Ron, who had parachuted from a Meteor shot down over Sinuiju, was only better equipped to the extent of a woollen shirt.

The staff of the interrogation centre were the most unpleasant and unscrupulous captors I had encountered up to that time, being either fanatical Communists, sadists, or a combination of both. The commander was a lieutenant-colonel of the infantry who spoke a little English. After our arrival, he had pointed out that, as war criminals of the worst sort, we could not expect a proper ration of food while awaiting our turn to be interrogated, unless we worked for it. This meant, in fact, hard labour, constructing air-raid shelters for his headquarters, digging and removing earth and rocks, carrying water for cementing over a long distance, and carrying timber and bricks up to the hill from the village. We were all weak from the privations of our captivity, and on our coarse, poor diet we were expending strength we could ill-afford. There were sometimes additional tasks in the evening. For instance, the officer who dealt principally with us was an infantry major—referred to by Kim, the civilian interpreter, as the Young Major. He hated us bitterly. Whenever possible, he would find us unpleasant tasks, such as cleaning out the filthy head-

172

quarters latrine—a huge stone jar sunk in the earth which had to be emptied with a small can by hand into a leaking bucket. What enhanced his pleasure in setting us this duty was that he could refuse us permission to wash afterwards, so that we must return to our quarters filthy with latrine matter. On other occasions, we had to work the crude machine that cut fodder for the cattle, or clean up the animal-stalls—jobs we minded less because we were sometimes able to steal a diacon (a cross between a turnip and a radish), which, though raw and unpalatable, filled our empty bellies for a short time. I protested to Kim on my first two initial interrogations about this treatment, without result. He excused himself by saying that it was no affair of his, but betrayed his feelings, by replying to my remarks about the Geneva Convention and its Prisoner-of-War clauses, with a comment that the Convention was an instrument of bourgeois reaction which, anyway, was inapplicable to war-criminals such as ourselves. Kim was a vain man, who posed as an ex-professor in political economy at Seoul University, but let slip to Jack one day that he had really been an announcer on the Seoul Radio. He had a marked inferiority complex and, like the Young Major, was really a savage under a thin veneer of education.

These were the circumstances surrounding our captivity—with a prospect of deterioration. Before we met that morning to make our decision, however, one other important aspect had been considered: Tom's future as a lone captive in the hands of a group of men who hated him, as an American major of the regular service, perhaps more bitterly than the remainder of us. He was, to them, the epitome of all the power and abundance in life which they coveted so much, feared so much, and thus hated so profoundly. What had led me to consider leaving Tom at all was that our escape might make our captors afraid that the news of his treatment would become known to the outside world. If successful, we should actually institute such enquiries through Kaesong to ensure that he received the care a human being might expect. But both Tom and I knew that their fury on discovering our absence might be so unbridled that he would not survive it.

The night before we took the final decision, I rolled over on to my side and began to whisper in Tom's ear, putting to him the

173

prospect as I saw it and the hope that escape held for us. Tom said:

"Of course you must go. As the senior officer here, I order you to disregard my safety, if you feel you have a chance of making it."

I reminded Tom that he would be absolutely at the mercy of the Young Major's temper—a temper we knew to be demoniac in character.

"You must go," said Tom, again.

Knowing him, I should not have expected any other answer. On the following morning we reviewed the position and made our decision: I would begin work that night.

Initially, my interrogations had been conducted by Kim alone. These had been of an entirely political nature, in order to sound me out as a possible convert to their cause—or, at least, a co-operator. They had a young soldier elsewhere in the village, who had ostensibly accepted their views and supplied them with a certain amount of information after a terrible sickness which had left him looking like a skeleton. We saw him twice and he begged us, in a voice that might have belonged to a very old man, to abandon resistance to our captors. To his knowledge, he said, one American who had resisted them, had already been starved to death in the very building we now occupied. He was led away from us by U, his principal instructor, who urged him not to waste his time speaking to us.

On the very night that I was determined to begin work on breaking-out, I was called out after darkness for an interrogation by the Young Major, a Captain Li, and a lieutenant I called Poker-Face. Kim interpreted; the others spoke no English except for Li, whose vocabulary was extremely limited. As I followed Kim along one of the village paths to a hut just below the air-raid shelter on the hill, I wondered whether this was to be another political interrogation or military interrogation in earnest. If the latter, what would they ask me? I knew that the greater number of their questions to Tom were concerned with information he could not possibly have given them, even if he had been prepared to do so; for they had demanded all the details of the top-secret codes used by the Far Eastern Air Force Headquarters—insisting

174

that he must know these as a major flying with an operational squadron in Korea! The questions they asked me that night were even more fantastic. When I was brought before the Young Major, he asked me through Kim:

"Give us the organisation, means of recruitment and training, method of dispatch, and system of communication of the British Intelligence Services throughout Europe and the Far East."

I was so amused to think that they believed me to be intimately in the confidence of the War Office that I smiled. Captain Li began to hit me about the head with a heavy wooden ruler. After an hour of threats, blows, and a warning to reconsider my attitude during the next day, I was taken back to the barn.

At that particular time, the sentry on duty outside the barn door was an unpleasant youth with pimples whom we called "Hoju" because he used this term to Ron. We loathed him because he delighted in making our lives difficult. It was he who had caused the straw that we lay on to be removed; who had spied on us during meals and seen us hiding food to give to Tom; who prevented us from visiting the latrine. Whenever he was on duty, we were forced to talk in whispers, or he would get the guard commander to separate us in different corners, and insist that we neither lay down nor stood up, but sat up. At first, we had tried humouring, then ignoring, him; finally, we resisted his every command for as long as we could. I was glad to see him standing there on sentry, for I knew that before long he would be relieved. Though the attention he paid us was not directly intended to prevent us from escaping—it was merely a means of demonstrating to himself his power over us—his attention on this night might lead to disaster. I waited in the darkness until the new sentry came on, and then began my work.

I planned to cut a hole in the outside wall of the barn. The lower half of the wall was of brick and too hard for my poor tools; but the top half was of wattles and mud, running up between stout timbers from brick to roof. While working outside, I had picked up an old screwdriver and a rusty table-knife. With these tools and a Shick razor blade that I had secreted since the days at Munhari, I had to cut away the hard mud, bound with chopped straw, and to cut out the wattles on which the mud was mounted. The sentry was fifteen feet away, at the far, gable-end of the barn, by the main entrance to the courtyard. To enter the barn, if his suspicions were aroused, he would have to come into the courtyard—a matter of five paces—unlock the door, and switch on the light. If I kept a careful watch, I might have time to assume a sleeping pose but, after a certain point in my work, I would not be able to explain why there was the outline of a hole in the wall above us! Knowing that I should probably fail to cut my way through completely in one night, I decided to reach a point on the first night which might be explained, if noticed during the next day, by a fall of mud from the wall. Of course, I could not begin to cut the wattles but hoped to be able to look at the few I had exposed in daylight, so that I should be able to make a work plan for the following night.

The next morning, when the guard commander opened our door to bring in our bowls of millet, we all came near to heart failure. Looking at the wall, we saw that a large number of the wattles had been laid bare, and that the main area of mud removed was just about the size for a man to crawl through! It seemed that the great dark patch shrieked at the guard commander and sentries to be noticed.

The day passed in the normal way. When we returned from work, we at once asked Tom if anyone had taken an interest in the wall. Apparently, it had remained unnoticed. We ate our evening meal, and settled down for the night, ostensibly to sleep. Hoju was on guard immediately after dusk that night, so we knew he would not be on duty again for six hours. Shortly after he dismounted, I began work.

Tom, Ron and Jack lay back under the mats, listening to the talk of some of the officers of the interrogation centre, whose room was in the western half of the barn. Once I began to cut the wattles, we became absolutely committed to escaping that night, and I increased my speed as much as I dared. Every noise, however slight, seemed to echo through the room. I felt that, at any moment, there would be a cry of alarm from the officers next door, chairs would be thrown back, the doors opened, and a crowd of infuriated North

Koreans unleashed upon us. Now and again, the anxious voices of one of the others would reach me, asking for a progress report, and I would reassure them as best I could. I removed a complete section of wattles, after about two hours' work, and began to cut the hard mud away that lay beyond them. After about ten minutes, I made a disappointing discovery: there was another section of wattles between us and the outside. Though the room was very cold, the sweat ran from my forehead, face, and neck, as I cut, prised, pulled, and scraped as quickly as I could. Another hour passed before the second section was free. I pulled away the mud that remained on the far side, touched a smooth, flexible surface, pushed against it, and felt my hand slide through into the cold night air outside.

I returned to the floor, where the three were lying beneath their mats. Jack and Tom were talking in whispers. Ron had fallen asleep! Waking him, I went back to the hole and crawled through as quickly as I dared, dropping on to my hands on the far side. The wide ledge which ran along the outside wall was covered with empty bottles, buckets, tin cans, a motor-car tyre, and an old cast-iron wood stove. Standing on the ledge, I removed the bottles and the stove to one side to make way for Ron, who was the next to come out. His head appeared in the hole, his shoulders, his hips. Suddenly, he lost his balance. He fell forward, swept the ledge with his arms, and knocked the stove on to the track below. A loud crash rang through the village.

Nearby was an ox, lying in its stable. As Ron disappeared back through the hole in the wall, I ran across to the ox and lay down behind him, waiting for the reaction to the alarm. Several minutes passed, but no sound came above the heavy breathing of the sleeping ox. After ten minutes, I returned to the hole and called to Ron in a whisper. This time he managed to get right out of the hole before knocking a bottle off the ledge but I caught it before it could fall. Jack followed. The three of us moved, as planned, to a stack of dried corn stalks about eighty yards from the barn. Here, Jack and Ron concealed themselves, while I returned to the courtyard. We had completed the break-out.

In a corner of the courtyard was a pile of old padded jackets and a pair of padded trousers. It was most desirable that we should have these, because of the lightness of Jack's and Ron's clothing—I was afraid that Jack, especially, might suffer from cold shock once we reached the coast. I crawled back into the courtyard through an opening in the wall, normally used to pass fodder through to the cattle-shed. Laden with clothing, I returned the same way to the corn-stalks.

Both Jack and Ron felt much better when they had donned their new clothing. I took the old black raincoat that Jack had discarded and we set off across the rice paddy on a course that led north-west to the mountains. Neither shots nor other sounds of alarm reached us, as we crossed the main Chinam-po highway, and left the interrogation centre behind a hill—free men once more.

CHAPTER NINE

BY morning, we had put twelve miles between us and our prison; Pyongyang, a broad stretch of the Taedong River, and the fertile Taedong valley lay below us in the morning sun. Our hill-top gave us ample cover in which to rest from the night march. We ate our raw diacons, taken from the fields far back, as we discussed the route to the coast.

North of Chinam-po, we knew the seashore was covered with soft mud that often ran out for more than five miles, even at high water. But there were deep-water inlets northwards, and the port of Chinam-po would be about twenty miles south of the point at which we expected to find the sea. Ron and Jack agreed with me that we should turn north on reaching the coast, and seek the deep-water inlets and the fishermen's craft that lay in them rather than risk the sentinels of Chinam-po. Once we got to the sea, we could only hope that wind and tide would not be against us. The problem of water for the journey was one that concerned me most; for I felt that, in our present condition, we should not be able to handle the boat effectively, if we remained at sea for more than a week without water.

After a second careful reconnaissance, we descended from our hill at dusk, with a stream and valley to cross before climbing a range on the far side which led to the sea. The brown and yellow leaves lay everywhere, as we passed through the woods on the lower slopes. There had been plenty of chestnuts here, but the village boys had taken them all, leaving the spiky cases strewn beneath the trees. Reaching the rice-paddy in the valley, we made a detour round the first village that lay on our course. Beyond, the stream flowed fast and deep between high banks of soft mud. I was hoping that we should find a crossing place higher up, for I was anxious that we should not get our clothes wet; the heavy night frost would certainly freeze them, and we could not count on a sunny day to dry them out before another night fell.

A young civilian came suddenly upon us from a tiny side-path, glancing curiously at us as we passed. We continued across the valley without looking back until he was out of sight, when we quickly ran back along the track we had crossed, changed our direction and took the small, disused footpath that led along the river bank. As soon as we reached good cover, I led the way into the bushes to see if we were being followed. Sitting there on the cold earth, we could hear nothing but the river noise below us. Only after ten or fifteen minutes did we hear light footsteps. Looking through the branches, I saw the civilian we had passed earlier coming along the footpath, looking carefully about him as he went. He passed without seeing us and I watched him take a path that led to the main track running to our right. Half an hour went by; he did not return. I decided to go on.

We made another detour to avoid the next village, and were about to descend to the stream again when we were challenged. I heard the action of a rifle bolt close by, and, as the moon emerged at that moment from the clouds, saw a sentry about twenty-five yards away, his rifle covering us. Jack and Ron were behind me. It was foolish of us all to get recaptured; their chance of with-drawal was better than mine. Signalling to them to crawl away along a rice paddy bank nearby, I walked slowly towards the sentry, speaking in a normal voice, hoping to distract his attention.

Attending to me, he did not spot the other two. He halted me firmly when I was about ten paces from him. Each of us stared at the other: he did not know what to make of me; I wondered how I could slip away from the weapon that covered me.

The guard turned out. I was led into the guard-room in a nearby village, which we had not observed in our daylight reconnaissance because it lay in a re-entrant. By this time I had decided to attempt a bluff and, in the friendliest voice I could raise, I said "Tovarich!" pointing delightedly at a coloured picture of Stalin on the wall.

The soldiers looked at me in puzzlement for a few moments. They regarded my black raincoat and the Chinese Communist cap that Tom had given me for the escape; they indicated my beard and blue eyes to one another as they discussed me amongst themselves. One of them came forward and said a few words to me in what I believed to be elementary Russian, and I replied heartily in gibberish, ending as many of my words as possible with "ski", "shi", "ish", and "off". As their brown eyes grew friendlier, I began to indicate that I must be on my way, pointing to their watches as if asking the time. I really believed that I was going to get away with it; for they were smiling now and two men shook my hand. With luck, they might take me out on to the path and escort me to the edge of the village. I was about to light a cigarette offered to me, when the door opened and a North Korean police captain entered. He stepped towards me, speaking rapidly and apparently fluently, in a language that was certainly neither Korean nor Chinese. After a couple more sentences I realized that the game was up: he was evidently a Russian interpreter. I took a good pull on the cigarette and said in English:

"I'm afraid there seems to have been some sort of mistake."

By the look on his face, I could see that he intended to rectify it. I left the guard room with my arms bound tightly behind me.

I spent a very unpleasant night, being wakened every half hour or so by the guard, just to make sure that I had not slipped out of my clothes and crawled through a crack in the floorboards. Two or three hours after sunrise, the door of my cell in the local police-station opened and I looked up to see the commander of the interrogation centre standing above me.

"Ah," he said, greeting me with a friendly kick. "So it is you they have caught. I wondered which one it was."

I was removed from the cell, still bound, and taken into another village, where Kim and a lieutenant-colonel of the police were waiting for me. As I approached, Kim looked up to say:

"You have been very foolish. You must be killed for this, I think." His face was twisted with rage.

The whole party of seven or eight who had come out to fetch me breakfasted in a house while I remained outside. Their meal over, I was brought in for a preliminary examination. In order to infuse the proper spirit into all concerned, the police lieutenant-colonel cocked his pistol, brandished it in my face, and then began to hit me over the head with it. He had made sure that my hands and arms were securely bound before he began.

We had agreed on the tale to be told if any one or all of us were caught. First, we should insist that Tom knew nothing of our plans to escape; that we had cut through the wall and slipped out whilst he slept. In this way, we hoped to save him any further retribution. Next, someone had to take the blame for devising and planning the escape, and, as the senior officer in the party, it was my duty to assume this responsibility. Finally, at all costs, we were determined to conceal from them that we had intended to seize a boat and escape by sea, as we were most anxious to avoid any special watch being kept on boats in the future.

This was the story I now told. I told it during the first examination in the village; and I told it again at the Central Police Headquarters in Pyongyang in the afternoon of the same day. By this time I was sitting in an office containing three colonels of police, who, to my surprise, seemed to have nothing better to do than question a wretched escaped prisoner-of-war. It may have been, of course, that the prospect of losing prisoners who would report the conditions of captivity to the outside world was sufficient to command their personal attention. Whatever the reason, my interview with them that afternoon imposed on them at least a measure of responsibility for what followed.

Before I was taken from the room, an incident occurred which was typical of their irrationality. The first Colonel, seated at a desk, said:

"You say you tried to escape because we treated you badly, gave you no winter clothing, and so on."—this was part of our story. "Well, we have no food, clothing, or medical supplies to spare. The inhuman bombing by the American aggressors in violation of all the laws of decency has withheld supplies from us. You must not blame us; blame your own side."

No sooner had Kim translated this than the second Colonel spoke. Without reference to the previous remarks, he completely contradicted them.

"We have plenty of supplies: the bombing of the American aggressors has had no effect on our war effort. But we only give these things to those who understand the truth and co-operate with us. If you co-operate, you will receive the same as any other person."

As if this contradiction was not enough, the third Colonel apparently decided that yet another was necessary.

"You can never have such things from us. You are a war criminal, and thus have no status except as a criminal. Only because of our goodness has your life been spared."

Having translated these three statements, Kim led me from the room. Perhaps the Colonels wanted to argue out who should have spoken and what he should have said. I was taken to a square stone building nearby where the Young Major settled down to question me himself. Poker-Face (the lieutenant) and Kim were with us. I had a feeling that the interview would not be a pleasant one.

Now, although we had agreed to tell a set story and I had told this, I had refused to say in what direction Jack and Ron continued when I was recaptured. At first, I considered giving them a false scent, but realized there was really no point in this. I was not going to give them the information and I might as well say so. At each examination I pointed out that I was a British Officer, and could hardly be expected to provide them with details that would assist them to recapture my comrades. The Young Major now informed me that it was his intention that I should do so. An argument that

182

lasted for about half an hour began. At the end, Kim was given instructions by the Young Major, which he translated to me.

"You think you can trick us with your lies; but you will never be able to do so. We are armed with the knowledge of scientific Marxist Socialism and, scientifically, analyze your words. Furthermore, your attitude reveals your insincerity. You refuse to co-operate with us and show yourself to be our bitter enemy. The Young Major now gives you your last opportunity to redeem your crime of making an escape and of forcing the others to do so by using the rank you held in the forces of the aggressors. If you do not take it, we shall have to adopt severe measures."

When he had finished, they all looked at me. I said: "I have told you how things stand. I have nothing more to say."

When Kim had translated this back to the Young Major, the latter rose to his feet and said what I believed to be the only English word he knew:

"O.K.," he said, making for the door. "O.K."

His drawn pistol covering me, Poker-Face intimated that I should follow and, with Kim, we left the room.

The Young Major had set off down a passage. Almost at the end of this, on the left hand side, was a steel door which had two handles on it of the lever type—levers six or more inches long, whose inner ends locked into recesses in the door lintels. As we passed through this door, I saw that it was very thick, and that the greater portion between the two steel faces appeared to be packed with fabric of some sort. Poker-Face closed the door, locking it with the two inside levers and moved round to join the Young Major.

"Strip to the waist," said Kim.

My mind could not conceive the truth that my senses offered. We were all standing in a small square room, with cement-faced walls and a concrete floor. High above us, from a wooden ceiling, ropes trailed from metal rings. There were two more such rings in the left hand wall. Under the right wall was a large barrel of water. One little chair, such as a child might use at a kindergarten, was beside it; across its back lay more ropes, in a tangle. In the light of a single bright electric lamp that burned in the ceiling, I saw that there were stains on the floor and walls that looked very much like blood.

As I stripped off my filthy, lousy, shirt and jersey, I knew that I was in a torture chamber.

Yet, my mind could not conceive it. I was living in the twentieth century—the year A.D. nineteen hundred and fifty-one. Surely, these three men could never bring themselves to torture me in cold blood. Looking round at their faces, I saw neither passion nor compassion in any one of them. I threw my clothes to the floor, and Kim kicked them into the corner as Poker-Face tied my wrists again. The Young Major spoke to Kim, who said.

"Kneel down."

Kneeling there, looking up at them, still unable to comprehend that this was really happening to me, I saw the Young Major's hand come round to strike me on the temple, as the first of a series of blows that he and Poker-Face released upon me. Kim joined them when they began to kick; and it was he who covered my face, when the Young Major saw that I was anticipating some of the blows and ducking. Just before the cloth came down over my eyes, I saw to my horror that the Young Major's face had assumed an expression of savage pleasure: he was really enjoying my suffering.

In my innocence, I had thought this maltreatment was to be either my punishment, or a means of inducing me to give information about Jack and Ron. I discovered that it was merely the overture. The covering was removed and I was assisted by Kim and Poker-Face into the tiny chair. I almost thanked them for what seemed to be an act of remorse or compassion. It was neither. They now bound my legs to the front of the chair, my arms to the two uprights at the back. My wrists, still secured, were tied down with a second piece of rope to the cross-piece between the two back legs. The Young Major kicked me in the chest and the chair fell over, with me, on to its back.

Poker-Face now produced a towel, as the Young Major threw two or three dippers of ice-cold water over my face and neck, drawn from the barrel in the corner. Still I did not understand, thinking, as I lay shivering with the cold, that I was to be chilled to the bone by repeated dousing. But Poker-Face placed the towel over my face and, a second later, more water was thrown over me. When I tried to rise—a pitiful attempt in which I just managed to lift my head forward a little—the Young Major put his boot on my mouth and shoved my head back again. More water struck the towel, some running off on to my bare chest—but some was absorbed. I tried to blow out some of the water which had seeped through in to my nostrils and mouth. If they are not careful, I thought, they're going to choke me. And then, instantly, comprehension followed. That was exactly what they intended to do. I think I had never been so frightened in my life.

It was such a simple but effective torture. The towel completely covered my face, its ends resting on my chest below and on my hair above. The first application of water provided just sufficient moisture to make the towel cling lightly to my flesh, and so hold it in place. Thus, every breath I drew was drawn through the towelling, the process of inhaling only serving to draw the material more tightly on to my face. While the towel was reasonably dry, I could breath adequately. But as its water content increased towards saturation point, each successive breath provided less and less oxygen for my labouring lungs. My mouth and nostrils began to fill with water. I realized that I was dying as I shook my head from side to side in a last despairing effort to throw off the clinging towel-mask. Poker-Face or Kim took my head between their hands and held it steady as the Young Major poured on more water. I suffered another short, terrible struggle to breathe before sinking into a delicious, shadow-filled tranquility.

Of course, I had thought they meant to kill me. The violence of their treatment had been such that I had not hoped to live when I understood their purpose. But they were more experienced than I.

The Young Major must have known exactly when to stop—perhaps the moment I became unconscious. I came to, still lashed to the little chair but now upright, the water pouring from my nose and mouth down my chest. I had come round rather quickly because the Young Major was applying the end of a lighted cigarette to my back at frequent intervals. I saw that he was smiling. It was not a pleasant smile. He was good enough to desist, when Kim began to ask me for the information they wanted. About ten minutes later, the process began all over again: I experienced the same terror; my expectation of death was the same as before, yet concerned me less than the agony of finding my breath dying in my lungs. When, eventually, I was dragged from the room, they had tortured me in this way three times.

Scarcely able to walk, I left the building between two police officers who had been called in. They took me through the cold, overcast night to a concrete cell block about two hundred yards away, and handed me over to the warrant-officer who was on duty. The cells were constructed on much the same lines as those at Sinui-ju; the prisoners were sitting inside in the same way. The only difference I perceived then or later was that this appeared to be more modern and more strongly constructed. Two warders took me down the long passage that led past the cells, opened a door at the end, and guided me along an extension by the light of an electric torch. Finally, almost at the end of the passage, we came to an unlighted cell. A push sent me to the floor, where my legs were bound and the knots on my wrists strengthened. Satisfied that I was securely roped, the warders departed. The metal rang, as the door closed behind them and the key turned in the padlock. Their footsteps echoed as they withdrew along the passage. The door to the main passage closed; the last vestige of light disappeared. For the time being, my tormentors were content to leave me, if not in peace, at least alone.

That was the first day. They came for me on the second day, but not on the third; again on the fourth day; again on the sixth. In between times, I lay on the concrete floor, taking refuge in a corner from the water that covered most of the cell. Each morning I was brought a bowl of boiled maize, but had no water to drink. So that I could eat, my wrists were released, but not my sore, throbbing ankles. Though I asked to go to a latrine, I was not allowed to do so. As I had contracted enteritis from either the diacons or the maize, my clothes were soon fouled; but the lice did not seem to mind. Day and night, as I lay there, they wriggled across my flesh, setting up considerable irritation wherever they feasted on my blood. Sometimes, it seemed to me that my whole body was alive with millions of them, eating my flesh away. It was impossible to remain in one position for more than a few minutes at a time: the discomfort became almost unbearable; my joints seemed to be on fire. There was no light during those six days, except when I was led out to the torture chamber, or when my food was brought in. I lay forever listening for the sound of footsteps that would take me back to the little room with the water-barrel in the corner.

When they brought me back on the evening of the sixth day, my spirits were lower than they had ever been before. I could not disguise from myself that my resistance was weakening. Now I was reduced to the state where I said that I would endure it for one more time; and when that time came, for one more time again. I experienced that night periods of light-headedness, due, I think, to the severe beatings. Periodically, I began to hear voices in my ears, and have vivid dreams of being with my family again. That day Kim had said to me:

"If we do not find them, I think you will be tortured to death. We have many ways of killing you slowly."

Some time on the seventh day, I realized that I had taken almost all that my mind and body could take. I prayed very hard; and I think my faith in God was never stronger. Within an hour, my circumstances improved.

The door to the main passage opened and I saw a flashlight coming towards the cell. Another was switched on as three men reached my doorway. For a moment I thought that I was to be taken out again: Captain Li from the Interrogation Centre came into the cell and stood over me, calling my name.

"You are very lucky," he said. "To-morrow you will be shot."

Such was my condition that I was glad—grateful that I was going to die a clean death that was in keeping with my profession, instead of dying vilely, in fear and agony in the torture chamber, with my own cries in my ears. I confess I am not of that breed of men who manage to remain silent under torture: I swore and shouted at the inquisitors each time, as long as I had breath.

Captain Li departed, but not the other two. I saw that a Korean

187

police officer stood outside with one of the warders, watching me turning over and over restlessly, seeking for ease that was never there. He spoke to the warder, who entered the cell and, bending over me, unfastened my wrists and ankles; then departed, relocking the cell door. Unsteadily, unused to this freedom of movement, I stood up. Two of my ribs were cracked from kicks; my head, shoulders, and thighs were sore and bruised; my back was covered with cigarette burns, which smarted at the slightest touch from my filthy clothes—but I was free to move again! If I wanted to move a leg, I could move it! I could raise my arms and lower them at will! For several minutes I experimented happily under the eye of the watching policeman, though I had forgotten him. He called me over to the barred window, where we stood face to face. He was a man of middle height, clad in the uniform of a captain of the police. In the torchlight, I saw that he wore spectacles.

"Tambay, eso?" he asked, after a moment. I shook my head; he knew I had no tobacco. He drew three cigarettes from his pocket and passed them through the bars and found some matches to give me. As I stood in front of him, smoking my first cigarette for many weeks, he shook his head, smiling at me with obvious sympathy.

After all that had happened, this simple act of compassion was too much for my self-control. The tears rolled down my bearded cheeks as we stood, in silence, regarding one another.

When Captain Li came into my cell on the following morning, my mind was at rest. The preceding hours had been passed comparatively comfortably, on a piece of matting that had been brought to the cell by another prisoner—apparently permitted some measure of freedom in return for doing chores for the warders. He was a Korean national of Chinese parentage who had spent some years at a high school in Harbin. His English was quite good, and we had a whispered chat. It seemed that I was in the political block of the jail—a bad block to be in, beause its inmates were made to work longer hours than the ordinary criminals. Would the Americans rescue me? I said that I feared they had other commitments of a higher priority. He brought me some old rags, and with these I

188

endeavoured to clean some of the filth from my body. I scrapped my underclothing, feeling that I should not be requiring it very much longer. My greatest regret was that I had neither cap nor comb, so that I should appear rather an unkempt soldier before the firing-squad. As a great luxury, I sat down on my little rice-straw mat in the corner, leaning my elbows on my knees.

I now had a little light, which, however faint, made a great improvement to the cell; for, shortly after being unbound on the previous day, some covering on the roof had been removed, revealing a small shaft about the diameter of a penny. Gradually, my eyes took full advantage of it. Sitting in the corner, I went over my life, realizing how lucky I had been to have had so much happiness. I felt sure that I had had far more in my years than any other occupant of the block. I hoped my family would be informed of my death without too much delay, so that there would not be prolonged anxiety.

When Captain Li appeared, I rose, picking up Jack's black raincoat which had been thrown into the cell on the previous day. I thought it would cover my ragged clothes.

"Where you are going," said Captain Li, "you will not need that."

He was probably right. I let it drop back on to the mat and preceded him through the door. We marched back down the passage, emerging into a fine November morning. The sun was shining from a blue sky; the wind was light; the air was keen but not too cold now that the sun was up. Beyond the doorway, standing at ease on a mud square, I saw a file of soldiers armed with rifles. I wondered how far I should march with this firing squad before we reached the place of execution.

Captain Li said: "Go on," motioning towards the soldiers with his pistol. Saying the 23rd Psalm over to myself, I walked over to them, and was marched to the road that ran towards the centre of Pyongyang. At that moment I was astonished to see Jack coming out of a nearby building.

"Do not talk," said Captain Li. Three soldiers with him separated us on either side of the road, before we could exchange more than a greeting. I was just wondering whether Jack was to be shot, too, and

189

if so, who would be shot first, when everyone with us except Captain Li and the three men walking with him wheeled to the right and disappeared. We continued to walk along the sunlit road without a word, heading for the wooded hill which stands in the centre of Pyongyang City, overlooking the airfield across the river.

It was when we were crossing an open space of rice paddy between one suburb and another, that an opportunity occurred to talk. Captain Li saw a friend whom he ran after, calling on him to stop. They began an animated conversation some distance away. The guards drew together in a group to light cigarettes and have a chat. Jack and I worked along the paddy bund towards one another and sat down.

"Where are we going?" asked Jack.

"I don't know," I replied. "Are you going to be shot?"

Obviously, he had not thought of this. "Can't say," he said, after thinking it over. As the guards continued to disregard us, we decided to settle a few more points. Jack told me that he had been caught with Ron two days before. After a short wait with their captors, they had been taken back to the Interrogation Centre where they had spent a miserable time. Both he and Ron had been badly beaten up, in spite of "confessing" to our story. In addition, Jack had been made to kneel for hours with a heavy board held up by his arms behind his back, receiving a rain of blows every time he moved. Tom was recovering from several heavy beatings. Apparently six of them had considered it safe to attack a one-legged man after removing his crutches, while two men had covered him with pistols, in case he leapt to his foot and overcame them. He was still very weak from this and through his former starvation— concluded two days ago—and from a fever, given him by being drenched with cold water and left in a bitter wind. Both he and Ron had been taken off that morning in a jeep with the Young Major to an unknown destination. Kim had remained at the farm, while Li had brought Jack on foot to the Central Police Station. He was just telling me that he and Ron had turned south at the coast instead of north, when Captain Li returned. To my surprise, he did not seem annoyed that Jack was near me and obviously con-

190

versing. Instead, he made a remark that sent my hopes soaring to the blue sky.

"You understand," he said, tapping his pistol and looking at me very directly, "if you try to escape again, I shall shoot you."

Things seemed to be looking up!

We had a long, hot march—the more fatiguing because we were both weak and had had no food that day. South-east of the city, we came to a small coal-mining town where we met a jeep at the main cross-roads. My spirits were not so high when I saw that the Young Major was sitting in it.

He was very affable, nodding and smiling at us; but we did not return his courtesy. After a few minutes conversation, he got out and entered a restaurant, leaving us to climb into the jeep with Captain Li. I was very pleased to leave the Young Major behind us and continue the journey on wheels.

After some miles of open country, where we passed at intervals Chinese-manned flak batteries, presumably defending Pyongyang, we drew up at the entrance to a disused coal mine. Captain Li handed us over to North Korean soldiers at an office, suddenly became very friendly, and handed us all the cigarettes in his packet as he departed for Pyongyang.

"What do you make of that?" said Jack, as he disappeared. "Two nights back that bastard was beating the hell out of me!"

We marched across the principal mine road to another office on the far side of the hill, where our names were taken by two North Korean Army officers. Then we were escorted towards a group of huts nearby. As we reached the doorway of the last hut, there was a great shout; welcoming words greeted us; on all sides friendly faces appeared; Henry, Spike, Mike, the South African, Ronnie our Gunner, Tom, Ron—and new friends, British, American, French. It was almost a second homecoming as we were borne inside.

CHAPTER TEN

I T was a miserable little prison camp, part of the unworked coal-mining settlement of Kang-dong, and known formerly by prisoners as "The Caves." In 1950 and until the summer of 1951, many United Nations prisoners had been crowded into old tunnels in the hillsides round about, often drenched by the water that ran in from underground streams. The numbers of men who had died in these black holes in the ground will never be known exactly. In cross-checking to find our friends, we accounted for over two hundred and fifty deaths; but this is not the total figure.

Of all the many stories of gallantry and selflessness on the part of prisoners in these caves, I will recount only one here: a story that was told us later by men who had formed part of it; a story which provided us with inspiration to continue resistance to our captors during the most difficult moments. Terry—the last remaining platoon commander of 'A' Company—was taken to "The Caves" in the summer of 1951. He had been a member of a column of seriously wounded captives which had marched slowly north from the Imjin River some little time after the two main columns had set off. Though he was in great pain from a wound in his leg and a terrible head injury, Terry set a splendid example on the march, caring, as best he could, for other serious casualties with him. By the time they reached "The Caves", the condition of many prisoners had deteriorated dangerously; for they had had no medical attention of any sort en route and many still wore the dressings, by now ragged and filthy, placed on their wounds by our own medical staffs before capture.

Terry, and Sergeant Hoper of the Machine-gun Platoon, were placed with a number of others from the column in a cave already crowded with Koreans—themselves dying of starvation and disease. Except when their two daily meals of boiled maize were handed through the opening, they sat in almost total darkness. A subterranean stream ran through the cave to add to their discomfort, and, in these conditions, it was often difficult to distinguish the dead from the dying.

192

One day, a North Korean colonel visited them to put forward a proposition.

"We realize," he said, "that your conditions here are uncomfortable. We sympathize. I, myself, am powerless to help you—unless you are prepared to help us. If you care to join the Peace Movement to fight American aggression in Korea, we can take you to a proper camp where, in addition to better rations and improved accommodation, your wounds will be cared for by a surgeon."

Our men refused this offer, individually. But Terry, seeing their condition, their numbers dwindling, came to a decision on which he acted the next morning. He drew Sergeant Hoper to one side and said:

"I have thought this business over and have decided that you must go over to the 'Peace-Fighters' Camp. Most of you will die if you stay here. Go over, do as little as you can; and remember always that you are British soldiers."

"What about you, sir?" asked Hoper.

"It is different for me," said Terry. "I am an officer; I cannot go. But I order you to go and to take our men with you."

Terry remained firm in his decision; and when the North Korean colonel returned, as they had guessed he would, Sergeant Hoper and his party left "The Caves" with a group of American soldiers. The colonel pressed Terry to accompany them, advising him that he would not accept a final refusal just then but would return later.

He returned four times. Armed with promises of an operation on Terry's wounds by a surgeon, and of a special diet of eggs, milk and meat in place of the boiled maize, he failed each time.

Terry was a young subaltern, not long out of the Royal Military Academy, Sandhurst. Yet, irrespective of his service and youth, he was, he saw clearly, an officer representing the British Commonwealth in enemy country: by his actions, the Commonwealth's reputation would be judged. Quite simply, he was given a choice: life, and agreement to reject, at least outwardly, the principles for which he was fighting in Korea; or a steadfast adherence to those principles—and death. Coolly, loyally, like the gallant officer he was, Terry chose death. And so he died.

Things were improved now: the caves were empty. We were in the quarters once occupied by the miners under the Japanese; quarters long since fallen into disrepair, and quite inadequate for the severe winter temperatures which were yet to come. Already, in November, the cold kept us awake at night, though the rooms were overcrowded. The food was poor: three meals a day of mixed corn and rice—very little rice—or a bowl of fresh, watery rice as an alternative, and a half bowl of thin cabbage or diacon soup. Occasionally—a recent innovation—there would be a small issue of the strong Korean tobacco, sufficient to make two or three cigarettes per man; but there was only one such issue during my stay. Yet, in spite of the poverty of our standard of living, Kang-dong Camp was a palace to me—a palace filled with the good things of life! After the Interrogation Centre and, more recently, the inside of Pyongyang jail, to have three meals a day, to be given a few grains of tobacco, above all, to be able to sit outside in the sun and talk with one's own kind, were luxuries indeed.

All these men—my comrades in the camp—had been collected from many different places: isolated headquarters and units, prisons and Interrogation Centres over a fifty-mile radius round Pyongyang, including the notorious "Pak's Palace" where the methods employed by the chief interrogator, Major Pak of the North Korean Army, had led to many deaths. All our own officers had been brought down from a Chinese camp on the Yalu River to Pak's Palace for interrogation by the North Korean Army. Mr. Day—a Quartermaster-Sergeant-Instructor of the Royal Marine Commando—Corporal Peskett, and four Marines had been captured on the east coast near Wonsan, and had drifted slowly towards Pyongyang and the hospitality offered by Pak. Colonel Mac, a red-bearded American pilot, had been held in solitary confinement for many months before being brought into an interrogation centre. Mike had joined him there on leaving me just north of Pyongyang. Fabian and Jaquette were two members of the renowned French Battalion, who had suffered many privations during the months spent under interrogation in Pyongyang. There was not one man fit for a long march when, a few days after my arrival, we were taken out and searched, before setting off on the road to the

Yalu River two hundred miles away. The few articles of padded clothing which had been distributed amongst us were removed, in spite of our protests, and many airmen left to endure the November winds in summer flying kit.

Our escorts were all officers! Second lieutenants carried burp-guns, the lieutenant in charge a pistol. We set off in the afternoon, carrying our special rations of rice and melki—little fish like white-bait that are caught off the east coast of Korea—which had probably been given to us to keep us fit for the march. In the rear of the column came a cart, on which sat Tom, a sick American called Harold, who was only semi-conscious most of the time, and Madden, an Australian soldier who was so thin that he looked like a skeleton covered with a little skin. I was very worried about Ronnie, who still had every sign of beri-beri. Henry, too, and many of the Americans caused us concern because of their dysentery. There was a little medicine available: aspirins. A fat girl-soldier accompanied the column, as medical orderly to issue the aspirins to those who were very sick; but there were always too many sick men for the ration of aspirins available. As the march continued I realized that my strength had been so sapped by my experiences in the jail at Pyongyang that I could not continue to walk. Placed on the cart, my condition continued to deteriorate: I found to my horror that the relapsing fever I had thrown off in Munha-ri during the summer months had returned.

The remainder of the march was a nightmare. Each night our cart would reach the billeting area long after the marching column, having been held back by the escorts, who stopped to eat in restaurants along the way. The result of this dawdling was that they frequently missed the way, and would leave us in the biting wind while they searched for the village concerned. Lying in the wind outside a restaurant, while they ate, in the daytime was bad enough; at night it was appalling. Our clothes were all ragged, and quite inadequate even for this stage of the winter. Spike and the others tried to give us portions of their own clothing and the few blankets available, but we could not accept all that was offered; to have done so would have caused them to fall sick themselves. Harold died on the second day of the march, after lying for two

195

hours in a ditch outside a house in which the escorts were disporting themselves. A few nights later, Ronnie and I each fell into a coma, from which only I emerged alive. In the light of a candle stub begged of our guards, Spike, Mr. Day and Corporal Peskett worked hard to revive our chilled bodies. But Ronnie had died during the last minutes of the journey through the night. We were to miss him sadly.

By the time we reached the village one march from Chiang-song —our immediate destination twenty-three miles distant—three more had joined our cart: Henry, Ace, an Air Force lieutenant, and Dick, an American rifle platoon commander captured almost a year previously; all were weakened to the point of absolute exhaustion by dysentery. With these additions, the sick cart carried only those completely incapable of walking and many men had to be literally carried between their comrades for long distances each day. Fortunately, the ration bags were now much lighter, though their contents had been changed miles back along the road. The Lieutenant of the escort had sold our rice at villages as we marched, receiving cash and a like weight of maize and a little barley in return. The substitute for the melki was cabbage at each halt—a very little cabbage: perhaps one leaf between thirty men.

The sick remained almost two nights in this village. It had snowed during the first night, and our guards decided to stop a truck to carry us to Chiang-song. Late on the second night, in a snow-storm, we were dragged down to the cross-roads and thrown aboard. Henry was now quite unconscious, and died during the journey through the night. I would not, could not, believe that he was dead, though his body lay in the ditch right by me, cold and lifeless. Yet my thoughts had to turn from him: I had no shoes and my feet were beginning to freeze.

It was Tom, of course, who remonstrated with our North Korean escorts. Knowing that we could not escape, two of them went into the warmth of a house, while the third departed into the centre of the town to find a billet for the night. Tom demanded shelter and got it, caring for us as he had done so splendidly throughout that terrible journey. Though he was not sick, he was weak from his past privations and, above all, he had only one leg. How he managed to look after as many as seven sick men at one time I do not know. Only his great strength of character and courage made this possible.

The guards accommodated themselves in what passes for an hotel in North Korea and ate their fill on arrival. We were dumped in a disused corner and left supperless. We fed on the following afternoon only because Tom had been given a little money derived from the sale of a concealed watch—the property of a Texan pilot, who had earlier given half the proceeds to Tom for emergencies amongst the sick party. The hotel proprietor sold us the scraps that were left from the mid-day meal, and some of our party were able to eat a little cold rice and luke-warm soup. I could hardly face even the soup, though Tom rightly insisted that I eat a few mouthfuls. We had just finished the meal when the senior second-lieutenant told us to come out to continue the journey.

I remember very little of what followed. I recall seeing a column of Europeans march past in blue uniforms, as we crawled out to a Chinese pony-cart a little way up the street. There were some friendly cries from the column—fellow captives—but I could not make sense of them. We drove on through the early dusk in a bitter wind, our cramped bodies packed tightly on the cart. When we stopped and Tom alighted, we were chilled to the bone, two of us quite unable to move. A voice in English said:

"What are your names?"

Ace, who was left with me, answered a little before me. I felt myself lifted up on to the back of a broad Chinese, who took me down a path between mud huts to a courtyard. There was an open door and a floor covered with blankets. Tom was there, and Madden, the Australian. Dick was sitting by the glowing charcoal in a tiny brazier. Ace joined me on the blankets. Five of us were left of the eight men who had been unable to march.

A Chinese face appeared in the doorway; spectacles gleamed in the light of a flashlamp.

"You are lucky to have come this day," said a voice. "Tomorrow is Thanksgiving Day."

The days that followed were filled with tragedy and setbacks along the road to recovery. We had arrived at a hospital; by which I mean a collection of mud huts in a Korean village, the floors covered with rice-straw mats and the walls papered with old copies of *The Shanghai News*. With two exceptions, the nurses and orderlies spat on the floor, rubbing the mucus in with their feet; they attended us with hands that were washed at the most twice in a day. The rooms filled with smoke whenever the fires were lit beneath the floors to drive out the bitter cold. Yet there were compensations. Two of the nurses—Chinese girls—had been trained at a European hospital in Shanghai. They were devoted to their profession, and gave us their best without caring whether we were friend or foe. Similarly, two of the doctors were sincerely concerned with making us well. We were provided with clean, lice-free clothing and the blue, cotton, padded uniforms and quilts that the Chinese had issued throughout the camps that winter. And, at last, we were fed food fit for human beings: rice, white bread, and a little meat each day; or bean curd, potatoes, occasionally onions, and—especially welcome to the British patients—a bowl of green leaf tea every other day. For the dangerously ill patients there were eggs and powdered milk. There were even medicines— penicillin, sulfa compositions, vitamin compounds, and so on in small quantities. But we were so sick, so weak, that it seemed as if these good things had come too late—except for Tom; and he was soon sent away along the road to the east.

One by one, the remainder of the group died. Ace became unconscious on Thanksgiving Day, and died the following after-noon: Madden died a few days later. Dick lingered on until Christ-mas time, but was too far gone with beri-beri to recover. In the house up near the doctors' quarters, someone died almost every day; men whose skeleton bodies had been starved or maltreated beyond the point of response to their improved circumstances. When I raised this question with Mr. Li, the hospital interpreter, he informed me with a ready smile that it was due to the American bombing; they had been unable to bring the supplies in. And when I asked him why the services of the International Red Cross to remedy this had been refused, he smiled even more blandly:

"That is another matter," he said, "I must go now; I have other duties."

Mr. Li was a naval architect by trade; in character, a hypocrite; a professed Marxist who did not love his fellow-men. It was his duty to conduct political lectures and discussion groups for those patients who were fit enough to get up each day. He forbade me to attend these, as he knew that I was priming the men attending them on the questions they should ask and the answers they should give to his questions. He announced publicly that I should not take part in any way. We were always polite to one another: he called me by my rank as well as by my surname; and in return for this courtesy, I called him *Mister* Li. We had many long political arguments, walking slowly along the shore of the frozen Yalu River inlet by the hospital, or in the hut I occupied. And always, when I asked a question which he was unable to answer without admitting one or another of the many fallacies inherent in Marxism, he would reply: "That is another matter. I must go now. I have other duties." And he would smile his bland smile.

My recovery had been a long and difficult struggle. Early on, I had made up my mind that to remain on my bed day after day might be literally fatal. I decided that I had to get up each day, if only for a little while, and walk a few paces. I could hardly stand the first day; it was cold outside and warm within my hut; dressing was a great effort. Yet each day I managed to push myself outside the hut and walk a set number of paces: twenty-five the first day, thirty the next, and so on, increasing my walk by five paces a day. By the spring, I must be fit again to escape. I forced myself to eat the food which, at first, I could not even smell without feeling sick. But by Christmas Day I was a walking patient and able to visit the wards to say a prayer and sing two carols with a small group of die-hards.

I was lucky in having good companions. There was a group of American infantry sergeants who were sterling characters: Hensen, Strong, and Barkovic. The last-named had suffered three operations on his leg without an anæsthetic; and, though often in great pain and constant discomfort, he retained a cheery spirit which helped many of his comrades through dark hours. There was Tremlett from C Company of my own Battalion—captured at the Imjin

199

River battle. And there was Fowler, a young north-country National Serviceman of the Rifles, who had a sharp Geordie country wit and remarkable strength of character. In my own hut I was lucky to have most pleasant companions in five American soldiers, one of whom was a Scottish emigrant, an ex-Glaswegian named John McCracken. He and I passed many a weary day of blizzards or high winds walking up and down Sauchiehall Street in imagination or discussing the respective merits of one or another brand of whisky.

The day came when I was asked to pay my hospital fees. There had been a first demand about two weeks before, when we had been asked to send a New Year's greeting to Mao Tse Tung and Kim Il Sung. I had informed all the patients that we should not do so. Then we were asked to fill in a so-called International Red Cross form in respect of the two doctors and nurses who had Red Cross membership cards. In the faint hope that our names might be delivered to the International Red Cross Committee, I wrote:

"Dr. X and Dr. Y, Nurse A and Nurse B, members of the Chinese Red Cross. have attended me at the Headquarters of Prisoner-of-War Camp No. 3 during the period in which I have been recovering from recurring fever and malnutrition."

I signed this. I then dictated the same thing to Sergeant Hensen and got him to include the number, rank, and name of every patient in the hospital. Mr. Li said that it was not sufficient but saw that he would get nothing more after we had argued for about an hour and let it go at that. But I knew then that the time was approaching for a reckoning.

One sunny morning, I was strolling down towards the frozen shore. I had just seen the better of the two good doctors, who had told me that I should stay in the hospital for about six more weeks. He was concerned about the weakness of my limbs, and the pain I still got from the ribs that the Young Major had cracked with his boots. Though I was restless to rejoin my friends in the Officers' Camp somewhere to the east, I felt that six more weeks would really improve my condition so that, in spite of the poor diet in the camps, I should be ready to escape when the time came. My thoughts were disturbed by a hail from a little, sharp-eyed Chinese who had evidently been looking for me. He carried a camera in his hand.

"I think you are getting very well," he said, without bothering to say who he was. I agreed that the condition of my health had improved.

"I think this is due to the skill of the comrades of the Chinese Peoples' Volunteers. I think you are very grateful to them."

With the memory of Henry and Ronnie, and the many, many others still fresh in my mind, I replied:

"I think that the Chinese Peoples' Volunteers are merely mending what they have broken."

But he was not to be put off in this way.

"I think you shall write for us a day-by-day account of your recovery, explaining how each member of the staff has helped you."

"I'm afraid I cannot do that."

He might not have heard me.

"Yes, and you shall have some pictures taken with the staff. I shall take some pictures with this camera now. We will find the doctors and the nurses."

I felt that he had to be told plainly how I felt: I told him. We had a hot argument, both became angry, and finally parted when he told me that he gave me twenty-four hours to think it over. On the following day he returned at about eleven o'clock and asked me how I felt.

I said: "You had my answer yesterday. It is the same answer to-day."

He looked at me angrily with his bright little brown eyes as we stood in the courtyard outside the door to my hut.

"You are not grateful for all we have done. You do not deserve to get well," he said.

It may have been the purest coincidence that, on the evening of the same day, I was told that the doctors had changed their mind about my condition: they were going to discharge me the following day. I felt that they might have added, Reason for Discharge: failure to pay hospital fees.

About a week before I left, Sergeant McCracken had a letter from his family. It was his first letter after eight months as a prisoner, and he hugged it to his great chest before opening it. It had taken less than a month to reach him and gave him the glad news that his name had been read out from the list of prisoners-of-war declared by the North Koreans and Chinese. That letter did McCracken more good than a year's hospital treatment.

The important thing, as far as I was concerned, was that the forms we had filled in on the 18th December, giving—for the umpteenth time—our numbers, ranks, and names, had really been of some use at last. Mr. Li had told us at Christmas time that there was to be an exchange of names, but I had not dared to believe him. For once, he had told us the truth.

This knowledge was a source of great comfort to me, as I said goodbye early one morning to McCracken and climbed on board a truck bound for Pyoktong. It was the 15th January, 1952: the fifteenth day of a New Year that I hoped and prayed would see me a free man again. Even if I was not completely fit, it was a great joy to think that I was going to rejoin so many of my comrades from the Battalion.

Pyoktong is a small town on a southern inlet of the Yalu River. Its houses run down one side of a rocky spur jutting out into the clear water; a picturesque little town, when seen from afar, dominated by the old temple above it. In addition to accommodating General Wang Yang Kung, the Commander of the Prisoner-of-War Camps, and his staff, it had been for many months a high-powered interrogation centre and a camp for non-Korean captives. McCracken had spent the greater part of the previous year there, and confirmed the stories I had heard at Kang-dong of the appalling death-rate. Every day during the late spring and early summer, McCracken told me, fifteen to twenty men died; men whose last strength had been used up in fighting for life during the terrible winter of 1950-51 when there had been neither accommodation nor food nor clothing for such temperatures, and the North Koreans and Chinese had refused to permit the International Red Cross to come in with any form of comforts for the prisoners. Those under interrogation who did not answer satisfactorily, or others who resisted or spoke against political indoctrination by the Chinese, suffered the punishment of the "ice-box"—a reinforced concrete hut where the wretched offender was placed in sub-arctic temperatures to "consider" his errors. Sometimes, he did not "reconsider" in time, and was removed to the hill to join in the growing mound of unburied corpses. When spring came, the "ice-box" gave way to the "sweat-box" where errors were "considered" in little hutches in which a man could neither sit nor draw his legs up but lay continuously, night and day, on the ground.

Having heard all this from the men who had been there, either through the winter, or during the later period when the effects of the winter were becoming daily more evident, I looked at Pyoktong with great interest as we approached by barge across the waters of the inlet, the wheels of our lorry held to its deck in token only by four pieces of rice-straw rope. At the headquarters I was received by an English-speaking Chinese and two girls, who gave me a seat and were very polite while they waited for my documents. One of the girls, little more than a child, began to converse in very good English which she said she had learned in Chunking. She asked me if it was true that conditions of life in Britain were really as bad as she had been told. Were people really starving to death? How could we stand such conditions, such oppression from our Government? Why didn't we back the Communist Party's Liberation Movement? I began to tell her that Mr. Harry Pollitt could not get popular support for his Movement—Liberation or otherwise— because people felt that he had nothing better to offer them than they had already; that many suspected he had a good deal less. She could not believe this. With her own eyes she had read details of the hunger of the workers—hunger that her Chinese comrades had known to the full before Liberation and the establishment of the New China under Chairman Mao. Of course, she added modestly, deprecatingly, she was not a true worker but came from the bourgeoisie; but she was trying hard to live it down. Her blushes were swept away by a flush of enthusiasm as she began to tell me of the success they had experienced in solving China's old, old problem of famine.

"What will your mother and wife do this year in England when the floods spread over your rice paddy?" she asked. "What will your family find to eat?"

Before I could reply to this interesting question, documents arrived; and the young Chinese, after reading them, seemed rather less cordial than before. I was taken away to a hut just outside the main camp and left alone with a small pamphlet that the girl insisted I should read. It was called "One step forward, two steps back," and was written by the late V.I. Lenin.

Glancing at the title, I had a feeling that V. I. Lenin must have had one or two experiences in common with me.

My hut was unheated but I had a blanket, a padded greatcoat, and my blue padded uniform. I awoke after a comfortable night to find a squat Chinese in the doorway holding an enamel wash-bowl of kaoliang and diacon soup. He ladled a portion into my two china bowls and shuffled off.

The day passed slowly. I could see but little of my surroundings because the sentry had put a baulk of timber against the door and all observation had to be made through holes in the paper that covered it. By three o'clock in the afternoon I had improved my position, however. The sentry on duty had acceded to my request to be allowed to sit in the sun—the interior of my room was dark and very cold. I sat on the narrow wooden verandah, enjoying the warmth and light, taking this opportunity to see how the land lay.

Sitting there, I was approached by a middle-aged Chinese who asked me my opinion of the progress of the Peace Talks at Kaesong. I replied that, having no news of them, I was unable to form an opinion. He did not rise to this bait but changed the subject to the political pamphlet lying by my side.

"Where did you get that?" he asked.

I nodded towards the reception office to which I had been taken on arrival.

"The young lady in there gave it to me," I said.

" 'Young lady!' " he repeated, horrified. " 'Lady' is a term like 'gentleman' which you use for your ruling classes—your aristocrats. There are no 'ladies' in China!"

As he left me to converse with a passing friend, I could not but reflect that, apart from impugning the character of Chinese women-folk, he had probably provided a new variation to a very old music-hall joke.

By now, the guard soldiers had settled down to their afternoon lessons. Further down the street, those who could find a place on a sunny veranda were squatting or sitting in groups of half-a-dozen, clutching elementary readers in their hands. One of their number—more advanced than his fellows—would conduct the class.

"You see," said the middle-aged Chinese, who had returned, "in the New China, everyone must learn to read and write. This is the new Happy Life."

"Very commendable," I observed.

"Not commendable," he rejoined. "This is a necessary thing, I think. If our people cannot read, how else shall they study the books and newspapers we give them. Talking alone is no good. This is not enough."

"Perhaps, when they have learnt to read they may also read the books and newspapers that *we* print," I said.

He smiled, pityingly.

"Ah, no. Once they have read our words they will know the Truth. Why, then, should they want to see the lies spread by your side?"

He strolled away down the street and turned a corner.

For some time I had been hoping to see some of our own fellows in order to find out what news, if any, they had from Kaesong. I knew it would be difficult, for I was an isolated prisoner, forbidden to communicate with others, as they were forbidden to do with me. At length, three young Europeans passed near to me and, the guards being idle at that moment, we exchanged a few words. It seemed that the third and fourth points on the agenda were still under discussion. The conversation was just developing when what I may only describe as a howl of rage came from the gable end of my hut. A tall Chinese with spectacles in blue-tinted frames, came running towards us in a fury. Pointing down the street, he hissed at three luckless listeners:

"Go back to your company!"

Then he turned to me. He was so angry that he could scarcely speak coherently. How dare I speak to other men without permission! The guard and the guard commander were called; I was flung into my cheerless little room, the door was slammed, two baulks of timber were placed against it, and the sentry glared in every five or ten seconds. I felt that I had probably been sent to bed without any supper.

Much to my surprise, therefore, at about four o'clock, the Chinese mess-orderly returned with another wash-pan of food. I was in the middle of eating this when the man who had received me the previous morning came down with a guard. I was told to pack up at once and when I objected that I had not finished my meal, this was removed from me. The hint was too plain to ignore: I packed up.

The guard took me through the narrow side-streets up to the main road, and then up the hill to the hospital in the old temple. But we had come to the wrong place and had to go back once again to the road below. I climbed on to the truck waiting there. Amongst the crowd of soldiers standing in the back were four Europeans in prison blue. They helped me aboard, and we examined one another in the dusk.

They were all Americans. Phil and I had met before at Kangdong. His knowledge of Japanese had helped us considerably on the march north, when he had acted as the liaison officer with the North Koreans. Charlie was a Marine pilot, William P. and the other man were infantry platoon commanders from the Reserve. All four were discharged hospital patients. William P. had had a terrible time with beri-beri, contracted after spending months in a small, dark, filthy stable near Sunchon where he had been fed on one bowl of old maize daily. He owed his life to the fact that he had contracted to render safe some unexploded bombs in the area for the Chinese in exchange for rations for himself and two men. The bombs were already perfectly safe, but William P. made a great show of working on these, one at a time—the contract said, "one bomb, one meal," and he was very hungry. Unfortunately, his scheme only succeeded in saving himself; the other two men were fed too late and died. It was said of William P. that he had remained alive only because he was what the Americans call "ornery", and I believe they were right.

We drove along the snow and ice-bound roads in the darkness. The moon was waning; only the pale starlight showed us the outlines of hills and valleys, of scattered villages and hamlets along the way. After about an hour we drew up in a village street. The guards indicated that we should alight and led the way over a ploughed field to a large Korean house. This was the receiving point for the camp to which we had been consigned. After filling in our registration forms, we had a meal of cold rice and potatoes—we all protested that we had not eaten, and none more vehemently than I, remembering the bowls that had been snatched away. Then we waited for over three hours, sitting round a stove which smoked abominably. At last, at about half past ten, we were led through a barbed wire fence, searched at a house called "the company headquarters" by two very irritable Chinese who had been awakened to do it, led on into a compound and thrust into a small house.

William P., the other infantry lieutenant and I were put into a room in which there were already three men. They sat up in their blankets, blinking in the dim electric light. I was delighted to see that one of the faces belonged to Anthony, the Intelligence Officer of the Fifth Fusiliers. I realized that my hopes had been fulfilled: I had reached the Camp containing my friends.

CHAPTER ELEVEN

WE had arrived on a Saturday evening; a good time to start life in the Camp, we discovered, since there was no early reveille on a Sunday, nor any compulsory political study. On that day, too, the meals were the best of the week. There was a minute portion of pork per man which was served as pork soup in the morning and pork stew—a thicker soup—with beans, in the evening, and two loaves of bread per man instead of rice. In my own case, these Sunday treats were overshadowed, however, by the joy of reunion with my friends. The Colonel and all the officers and warrant-officers taken in the 29th Brigade battle on the Imjin River in April 1951 were there, except for Ronnie, Henry, Beverley, and Terry, who had died. With them were the officers captured from the Brigade in the New Year, 1951, when we had fought a rearguard action north of Seoul. From the Rifles, I found Joe, James, Robin, and Sandy, their Doctor; and from the Gunners, Spud, whose comrade had died on the march north. These five had suffered terribly as prisoners in the bitter cold of January and February, 1951; and at one time or another had suffered, too, from the cruelty of their captors. Spud, for instance, had been strung up by his thumbs at Pak's Palace and, worse, experienced the agony of pins being thrust underneath his finger-nails. In spite of it all, they were relatively fit, thanks to an improvement in the diet since the preceding Thanksgiving Day and, not least, to their own splendid spirit. Only Denis was actually sick, lying at that moment in the Camp "Hospital" with pneumonia. I looked in on Tom, Ron, and Jack, whom I had not seen since November; and found Duncan, whom I had left in his bunker the previous September when I escaped to the coast. They had kept him there for a further seventy days, during which time he never once came outside even to make a visit to the latrine. He had swollen up with beri-beri as a result though, by now, he was on the road to recovery.

Sam, our Support Company Commander, decided to take me on a tour of the Camp. He explained that the compound was based on the main schoolhouse in Pyn-chong-ni, a village ten miles east of Pyoktong and four miles south of the Yalu River. The schoolhouse ran approximately east/west, a long building of timber and mud constructed during the Japanese regime. A corridor ran its entire length at the rear and, off this, sliding doors opened on what had once been classrooms. At the western end was a double classroom known as "The Library", which contained, in addition to portraits of all the Communist Party leaders throughout the world, all of twenty books and a few three-month-old copies of *The Shanghai News*, The London and New York *Daily Worker*, and the San Francisco *Peoples' World*. As the books were all either treatises on Marxism or translations of Russian novels, one may say fairly that "The Library" had a definite political bias. The other classrooms were used as sleeping-quarters, each room having a central alley, on either side of which the floor was covered with rice-straw mats. On these, at night, the prisoners lay, each covering himself with a padded quilt, a blanket, and a greatcoat as protection against the penetrating cold. Outside each door, a stove stood in the passage for which a small ration of wood was provided to heat water for washing clothes and bodies.

The main entrance to the building was in the centre, where a wide passage ran back to the classroom corridor and an exit to the rear. As we stood in the doorway—there were no doors—Sam pointed out to me a huge red star and two white peace doves which had been hung above it by the Chinese as Christmas decorations. The word "Peace" had been placed there, too. The prisoners had protested at this decoration, taking the view that the red star was no symbol of theirs, and that peace doves and the slogan "Peace" should really mean Peace and not be used as an instrument of propaganda. They had torn the word down secretly. Sam and I agreed that we would remove the star and pigeons at the earliest opportunity.

Below the main entrance was a large mud playground, covering about half the area of a full-size soccer pitch; now an exercise and parade ground for us. The schoolhouse stood on a higher level and, to reach the mud rectangle, one had to cross a promenade about fifteen feet wide and descend a flight of concrete steps. From the promenade, which ran the whole length of the exercise ground or "square", there were three flights of steps leading down: one below the main entrance, one at the western end by the exit gate to the Chinese headquarters, and one at the eastern end which led to the cook-house. We walked east along the promenade and descended to the kitchen.

This Camp had been established in the previous October, when all officer and warrant-officer prisoners not held back for further interrogation had been concentrated in it, with a few non-commissioned officers of the United Nations Command Air Forces. The cook-house had been built at this time, a long partitioned building containing a kitchen with nine huge cast-iron cooking pots heated by wood fires, a small room to accommodate the fourteen cooks, and a communal bath-house which had been built so inefficiently that it had never been serviceable. Sid and Tony, and Sergeant-Majors Gallagher and Morton were the British representatives working as cooks under Mac, the American Major in charge. The kitchen was more often than not filled with smoke as the chimneys drew off only half of it, the remainder finding its way out through air vents in the roof, as in mediaeval times. Our eyes watering, Sam and I returned to the schoolhouse by the main entrance and came to the back of the building, by way of the rear exit.

A few yards behind, there was another, higher platform, on which stood a short promenade and a number of Korean dwelling houses. Originally, these had been the quarters of the school staff. Now they housed the overflow of prisoners from the schoolhouse who had named the area of their residence "Snob Hill". I discovered that I and the other four new arrivals were quartered in this area which was now almost filled to capacity.

Perhaps the most important residence on "Snob Hill" was the Barbers' Shop. In this snug little room were a stove, a table, two home-made chairs, and three home-made barbers: one engineer, one marine, one airman. They had built a little empire there; an empire which provided a weekly shave with a cut-throat razor, a monthly haircut, and unlimited repartee. As in many a small town, the Barbers' Shop provided a sounding-board for all matters of controversy in the community. The time came when the barbers constituted a self-appointed board of assessment for all rumours relating to the peace talks, which many took more seriously than they cared to admit.

The daily routine in the Camp, though often irksome, was very simple. Within a week, a newcomer felt that he had been following it for months.

At dawn, the compound was roused by the Chinese and assembled on the square for physical training exercises or, occasionally, taken for a short, escorted walk along the road. What made this so tiresome was that after returning, washing, and tidying one's quarters, there was a wait of two and a half hours until breakfast. After the meal, the school bell was rung for morning political study. A lunch break followed—there was no lunch—and the afternoon study session commenced at two o'clock, ending at four. The second meal was at half past; and this was followed, again, by further study in small groups. At nine o'clock, the lights were extinguished at the main. This was the weekday routine.

On Mondays, Wednesdays, and Fridays, the fare was the same at both meals: rice—very bad rice in those winter days—and diacon soup. On Tuesdays we had rice and beans for the evening meal and two and a half buns of bread. On Saturdays, though we had no bread, there were beans to relieve the monotony of the diet in the evening. And on Sundays and Thursdays—what a feast we had! Rice and pork soup in the morning; pork stew and bread in the evening.

Every ten days, there was a small issue of sugar to each man, and a packet of tobacco. With this came two sheets of paper, each equal to four foolscap sheets: one for the latrine, one for smoking. As some men had the tobacco of non-smoking friends, but not their paper, any newspaper, lecture syllabus, or periodical left about for a moment would disappear instantly. Paper was at a premium.

Each evening, the six platoons in which we were organized would gather at the foot of the steps leading up to the main entrance to receive an address by the company commander—an elderly, grey-haired Chinese we called More-in-Sorrow-than-in-Anger on account of his reproachful look—or by one of the "vice-company commanders", of whom our favourite, for the fun he provided, was a man with a squint known as Tilt. Two interpreters, Zee and Gen, spoke abominable English—Zee particularly. Flanked by sallow-faced Chinese, the speaker would begin his address in his own tongue, continue for about five minutes and then pause for the translation.

"Say, you guys," Zee would say, "to-morrow is Thursday"—or whatever day it was. "The Company Commander, he say you gotta get outa your goddam beds. O.K."

There would be another torrent of Chinese, another brief translation into English, sometimes unintelligible. The meeting would break up and another day would be almost over.

On the surface, this was the dull and irksome life of a prisoner; bearable, if tedious. Really, it was not like that at all. Every hour of the day, we were at the mercy of evil, political extremists who could—and did—reach into the Camp to take out those whom they wished to exploit for their own uses, and those who led and organized the demand for proper treatment as human beings. The real danger to a prisoner's body—and mind—began when one of the Chinese staff came in to his room to say:

"You are wanted by the Headquarters. Pack your everything and come with me."

Or when a Chinese came into a room to say:

"Which is so-and-so's kit?" and begin packing it, heedless of the questions of the individual's friends as to his whereabouts, as to his future.

The name of the Camp Commander was Ding. He was of medium height, pale skinned with fine bones and long fingers. His eyes were narrow even for a Chinese and glittered like a snake's. He was a fanatical Communist; his staff were terrified of him; he hated us if only because we rejected the political indoctrination programme and remained loyal to our own Governments.

Ding's Headquarters staff was extraordinarily large for the care of about three hundred and fifty prisoners. There were seventeen different staff officers, in addition to a deputy camp commander and an assistant deputy commander. Of this group, there were five with whom we had real contact as prisoners normally inside the compound: Wong, Chen Chung Hwei, Sun, Big Chu, Little Chu, and Niu. Wong was a big man, almost six feet tall, and broad. He swaggered about the camp, tried to bully any prisoner he got on his own, and lost no opportunity—however small—to have us punished. In the early days of captivity under the Chinese, Wong had lectured in his American-English both to Camp 5 at Pyoktong and Camp 1 at Chiangsong on the prospects for those who refused to take part in political study.

"No one knows you are our prisoners," he reminded his sick and starved audience, "no one knows you are here. If you resist us, we shall put you in a deep hole where you will remain for forty years—and your bones will rot. The world will forget you."

On another occasion, he demanded at the end of a lecture given to the officers that they should hand over all erotic photographs they possessed.

"We know," he said confidently, "that you officers purchase many such pictures to keep with you. Everyone will hand them in at once."

As there was no move to comply, each prisoner was searched but without result. It was suspected that Wong had hoped to make up a collection of these items and he thus earned the name "Dirty Picture" or "DP Wong".

Chen Chung Hwei was a little man with a twisted body and a twisted mind. His spine was misshapen, hunching and bending forward his tiny shoulders. His face was scarred by a childhood burn. Walking along, his big eyes darting from side to side—pools of gravy in white saucers, the Padre called them—he resembled an evil gnome. A poor schoolmaster before the Communist Revolution, he had seized the opportunity to gain power and was prepared to go to any length to hold it. He was the staff officer concerned with maintaining order in the Camp; a task he loved, I think, because it involved spying on us.

Sun was also a little man, almost girlish in his mannerisms. Of all the staff he was, perhaps, the most sincere Communist; and he believed in the maxim that "the means are justified by the end." For many months he had been the organizer of the political study programme, and it had been obvious to him from the outset that his programme was an absolute failure. As lectures were read out, certain passages—"the people of America are starving", "Soviet Russia alone defeated Germany and Japan"—were greeted with boos, derision and genuine laughter. Sun's little yellow face would darken as he cried:

"Keep silent! You do not want to hear the truth!"

Little Chu was a jack-of-all trades: he dealt with the mail; he helped Chen Chung Hwei with discipline; he kept the prisoners' records. A short, slight, frog-eyed Chinese, he was a willing

213

assistant in any unpleasantness that was inflicted on the prisoners.

Big Chu came into a different category. He was the staff member who undertook affairs of special significance: interrogation, discipline, even propaganda were his fields, providing that some important aspect was involved. Slim, about five feet ten high, he walked with a peculiar bouncing gait. When Big Chu paid a visit to a prisoner to converse in excellent English with a heavy Chinese accent, it usually meant that the Camp Commandant was concerned in his call.

The only other member of Ding's staff who was of importance in our lives was Niu. Niu's likeness to an Oscar Wilde Clergyman was astounding. He could have played Dr. Chasuble without difficulty. He spoke slow but good English with an affected accent; he was intense about "culture"; he was never less than polite; and he was a thorough-going liar. Niu never became involved in any nastiness; he faded out of the picture before it began. His task, which began in the Spring of 1952, was to control our entertainment and recreation. In this he succeeded.

The Chinese made feasts of the American Thanksgiving Day and Christmas in 1951—a decision perhaps not entirely unaffected by the resumption of the peace talks and the international outcry following the publication of the Hanley Report on the treatment of prisoners-of-war by the Communist Command. Official photographers arrived to take pictures of all the jollity; every effort was made, without success, to get individual prisoners to write articles for the Communist Press in praise of the Chinese for all their good treatment and especially for the Christmas and Thanksgiving feasts. The photographers found it impossible to take a good picture, for the prisoners covered their faces whenever they appeared. The Press representatives found that none of the prisoners could write. At Christmas time, they attempted a new tactic: they insisted that the prisoners should send Christmas Greetings to General Peng Teh Huai—the commander of the Chinese Communist Forces in Korea—and to Ding. The prisoners Daily Life Committee refused to do so.

On arrival at the Camp, the prisoners had "elected" this committee, at the insistence of the Chinese, to deal with the day-to-day administration of the compound. As all the captives were members of their respective naval and military corps, there was no question of "electing" anyone. Naturally, a choice was made from amongst the senior officers, and their names were circulated amongst the remainder as candidates to be "elected". In this way, we secured our own nominations to the committee; Colonel B and Denis being the American and British senior representatives respectively. Because of the long spell of solitary confinement our own Colonel —as the Senior United Nations Officer—had undergone in 1951, he was kept off the committee. He was universally respected by all nationalities in the Camp, and it was desired to keep him available if some major issue arose.

As soon as the Christmas festivities were over and the last photographer and Press representative had departed, Colonel B was arrested for heading an "underground resistance movement" opposed to Chinese discipline, military interrogation, and political study. There was also the matter of withholding the prisoners' Christmas Greetings for the Commander-in-Chief and Ding!— apparently a secondary, but actually a principal charge. In forty degrees of frost, he was placed without either greatcoat or bedding in an open cell in the centre of the village under close guard. He began slowly to freeze to death. An American major, a member of the committee, made representations to the Chinese for his release and was himself arrested. The two remaining members of the main committee, a marine and an engineer major, were arrested together. Denis, discharged from hospital after seven days' treatment for his pneumonia, was arrested a few hours after his return to the compound. Finally, our own Colonel was arrested seven days after my arrival in the Camp. On 8th February, 1952, their "trial" began.

We were all ushered into the Library, where the walls were lined with armed guards and the Camp and Company Headquarters staffs. Squatting on the floor, we saw the Colonel, Colonel B, the three American Majors, and Denis come in. Denis was deathly pale and we saw that both his wrists had dropped. One at a time, beginning with Colonel B, the defendants came forward to read their "confessions" to the crimes of opposing the humanitarian policies of our captors. The words they read were in stilted English, quite obviously partly dictated by the Chinese; and what was even more pitiable was that we knew that the majority of the crimes to which they "confessed" were non-existent—illusions in the minds of the Chinese. With a word of warning to any potential offenders among us, the Chinese departed, having informed us that the punishments would be decided by higher authority and promulgated in due course. The "trial" was over. There had been no need for an arraignment, or for a defence: the defendants had "freely confessed" their guilt before us all. Leaving the library, we commented to one another that this was a pattern of judicial procedure which we had observed before at rather longer range. It seemed that what we had read about it in the "reactionary" Press had been true.

I do not know exactly how all the confessions were extracted before that trial; but I do know, in detail, what happened to Denis.

Initially, in spite of considerable pressure, he refused to say a word when charged with being a conspirator in a plot against the plans of the Chinese to improve our Daily Life—the Chinese term—and to teach us the Truth as our captors professed to see it.

Having no success with this stratagem, a new line was adopted. Denis was asked to sign a document in which he acknowledged the Colonel's responsibility for his actions. Very naturally, he refused. Then it was put to him that he could ameliorate the Colonel's position by "confessing" his own guilt—and the wording of this confession was "suggested" to him. Thus, in an attempt to release the Colonel from implication, he made a statement assuming full responsibility for all he had done to ensure that the British element in the compound voted properly in the committee elections and followed the instructions of the Daily Life Committee. In this way, a confession was secured which gave the Chinese enough evidence to dispose of Denis for some time, though, in the event, they ignored that part of it which vindicated the Colonel. Denis now being in their grasp, they decided to follow up their advantage before the

216

trial and obtain a certificate from him that he would give military information freely.

Ding dealt personally with this case, as he had dealt personally with the Colonel in securing a "confession". Denis was brought before him, a proposition was made, and turned down. As Ding never personally supervised physical pressure on prisoners, it was Sun who took Denis away to an out-house and had him strung up to a beam, arranging it so that Denis's hands were secured so far up behind his back that he had to stand on tip-toe. Every hour, for four hours, Sun returned to ask Denis if he had changed his mind: Denis had not. Sun left him until the morning, when he was cut down. The next night began with another refusal to sign the certificate, after which Sun left Denis, stripped to the waist, outside Ding's house until he was blue with cold and too chilled to speak. After being taken back to a warm room for a time, he was sufficiently revived to utter another refusal. Sun took him to a cell down in the centre of the village and tied him again to a beam in the same way as on the previous night. This time, however, he realized that Denis's resistance was stronger than they had anticipated. After returning twice to give him an opportunity to change his mind, Sun left him for good. In the morning the Guard Commander untied him and the matter of the certificate was not raised again. This was the reason why Denis's wrists had dropped when we saw him at the trial.

Some days later, the varying, long sentences were announced in the Library, amidst booing: the Colonel, Colonel B and Denis got six months imprisonment each. The three American Majors were each sentenced to three months. By this time, hope was high that the peace talks might succeed before the longer sentences expired.

In and around the village were other prisoners, quartered singly or in pairs: men who had been removed from the compound for renewed military interrogation; men who had never been into a compound with other prisoners and were deliberately kept in permanent solitary confinement in an attempt to prise information from them; men who had seen too much since their capture and were thus too dangerous to release to a compound; all sorts of men in little rooms, and holes in the ground, living under varying conditions of discomfort. These men were seen only occasionally when a party of men from the main compound passed on a ration detail or to collect wood. An unknown, bearded face might appear in a doorway, pass down an alley to a latrine, accompanied by one or two guards; unable even to smile in reply to the greetings of comrades as he passed.

This was the life to which the six sentenced officers were now committed.

CHAPTER TWELVE

BY the time I arrived in the Camp, almost all my friends had had mail. Every two or three weeks, mail would be issued—old letters that had taken but a few days to reach the exchange point at Panmunjon, and over two months to cover the few hundred miles north to the Yalu River. Some men were lucky, receiving one or two letters by every post: others were less fortunate. Try as we might, we could see no plan behind the issue of letters. Bill, Denis's second-in-command, and Carl, the Gunner, had both served terms of solitary confinement, yet never failed to receive something. Others who had been in far less trouble received letters infrequently.

The outgoing mail, too, was a mystery. About a quarter of those in our compound had received acknowledgment from their families of ten or twenty letters since the Chinese had commenced to hand these over in apparent earnest. But, as late as May 1952, men who wrote regularly three times a month—the regulation maximum—had not succeeded in communicating with their next-of-kin or other addresses.

The Chinese had a simple, consistent answer to men who complained about lack of mail, or the pointlessness of writing letters that never reached their destination.

"The American bombing is responsible. Your mail is destroyed so often that only a little gets through to the neutral zone."

One morning, a huge pile of mail we had written earlier was brought into the Library to prove their words concerning air attack on the mail trucks. Sure enough, all of it was spoiled, at least half of each letter having been burnt. The two Chinese with it, Little Chu and a sulky youth named Tien, would not let us have our letters back, saying that they were of no further use. However, by one means or another, four men managed to take a closer look. The top pile contained mail posted over seven weeks before; but another pile had letters posted on the *previous day*!

On another occasion, Bob, Spike, and I were working outside the fence near the Camp Headquarters by an old air-raid shelter. The remains of what had been a considerable bonfire was smoking nearby. On the edge of the fire, were a number of half-burned pieces of paper—the remains of letters from the United States. It is true that they were only the envelopes, but where were the contents? Letters delivered to prisoners were always issued in their envelopes—even though the wrong letters were sometimes put back by the censors.

Finally, there is the case of Chuck, an American 1st Lieutenant of the Chemical Corps. Called out for a brief interrogation, he was shown two letters of comparatively recent origin, addressed to himself. He was informed that he could have his letters when he answered the questions put to him. He came back without the letters and, in front of his platoon, demanded of the interpreter when he was going to get them. No attempt was made to deny that they were held by the Camp staff: the interpreter merely replied that it was not his business to interfere. Other officers had similar experiences. None of them received those particular letters.

I became so depressed at attending each issue of mail without getting anything that I gave it up. One day in May, I was washing down by the bath-house during mail call, when Ron, the Australian, came running down to find me.

"You've got a letter! You've got a letter," he called.

I ran up to the Library, hardly daring to hope that it was true. Someone thrust a letter from my wife into my hand; the first one

I had received in fourteen months of captivity. By that time, my wife had written me over three hundred letters.

In late February, an epidemic of influenza spread through the compound. Overcrowding in the rooms, and lowered powers of resistance served to increase the casualty rate. About half a dozen men got pneumonia; I was one.

Frank and Bob helped me up to Snob Hill—I had recently moved down to Bob's room in the schoolhouse—where the pneumonia cases were put together in a little room. Bob and two of the American doctors remonstrated with the Chinese medical officer so much that he began to take the matter seriously. Hitherto, the pneumonia patients had been left unattended. We called this Chinese M.O. the "Dirty Doctor"; a suitable appellation for a man who practised with filthy hands and had a habit of spitting freely on the floor. What his training had been we never discovered. From his actions in the Camp, he seemed capable of diagnosing little more than a cold—but this may have been due to a lack of interest. His surgery, like himself, was forever grimy, but there were clean white coats, surgeon's cap, rubber gloves, and aprons in the Camp. For one day Geoff was called over to have the hand dressed from which he had lost three fingers in a bombing raid the previous autumn—a hand that had long since healed. He found doctor, nurses, and orderlies all in white with dressings and a few instruments laid out on a covered table. The medical staff, smiling pleasantly, grouped themselves round his hand, which the doctor began to examine. A cameraman appeared, pictures were taken, and the performance ended. The medical staff put their white clothing carefully away. Geoff returned to the compound fuming, having been an unwilling accomplice in a propaganda stunt.

Fortunately for me, the "Dirty Doctor" was not alone this time. A younger Chinese doctor, who seemed more capable and was certainly more interested in us as patients, had recently joined the medical staff. He began to visit us regularly and I saw the old man only once before I was pronounced fit to go back to my room. There was no period of convalescence and, however conscientious the young doctor was, he would not—perhaps could not—give us permission to miss the political study periods. We joined the remainder in the draughty library to hear more passages from "The Twilight of World Capitalism" under the arrangements of Sun.

The history of the attempts at political subversion of the United Nations captives by the Chinese and North Koreans may yet form the subject of a separate work; it certainly demands more comprehensive treatment than may be given here. Let it merely be said, then, that in April 1951 there were nine and a half hours of compulsory study each day, a year later only four hours. It began with "comrades" like DP Wong threatening the student body with severe punishment—a threat that was executed—for those who did not perceive the "truth"; and ended with "comrades" like Sun calling on us to "keep silent" when we booed an unusually crass statement; for though Sun would have liked to have given all those who actually rejected his instruction the same treatment as he gave Denis, he was prevented from doing so by his masters who were aware that the world beyond the Iron Curtain was beginning to ask what was happening in the prison camps. By Easter 1952, the whole programme had failed so manifestly and met with such opposition, that the decision was reached to drop compulsory study. In order to save face, we were informed that there would be "spring-cleaning" of the quarters and general area before the summer heat began; that this "honourable labour" would take place in study hours for the time being. The question of resuming study was left open.

New latrines were needed; old ones had to be filled in. There were many potential breeding grounds for flies—filthy ditches and bunkers—which had remained frozen in the winter but could no longer be overlooked now that the sub-tropical summer was approaching. Fortunately, our own doctors directed our efforts. Once we had destroyed the danger-spots in and around our quarters—and as far outside the compounds as we were permitted to go—we began to slack off, spinning out the remaining, quite useless work, hoping to avoid a return to political study. Efforts were made by the Camp Headquarters to induce us to line the paths with whitewashed stones, to pick out Picasso peace-doves with

221

stones in flower beds, and to erect "Peace" slogans. There was another camp some miles to the east of ours, a show camp occupied by ROK prisoners to which some of our number were sent to see how it should be done. On their return, they reported that not only had all these measures been carried out there but that, in many rooms, little pots of flowers had been placed under the portraits of Mao Tse Tung and Kim Il Sung—standard items of furniture throughout the living quarters. They had been rewarded, the ROK prisoners said, by extra food and tobacco, and by seeing a special illustrated article about their camp in a Chinese magazine!

One or two members of our camp were rather angry with the ROKs for co-operating in this way; but I recalled a ROK sergeant whom I met in the south at the village where I first met Kinne. One day, after a long lecture from a Chinese on the advantages of Communism, he said to me quietly:

"The Chinese come and they say, 'Communism looks after the people. Learn the truth and you will have much food and good houses and plenty of land for yourself.'

"And we say. 'Yes. Yes. Communism is very good, very nice.' And they give us cigarettes and maybe some more food."

Then the sergeant had looked at me from the corner of his narrow, dark eyes to say a very rude word.

"That's what we think of Communism," he said.

I had a shrewd suspicion that his brother-ROKs were saying that up in the show camp even now.

A Mr. Jack Gaster came out from England to China and, whilst there, was invited by the North Korean Government to visit the prisoner-of-war camps on the Yalu River to see how his fellow-countrymen in captivity were faring. He was described by the *Shanghai News* as a lawyer, though this was not the description we gave him after reading a newspaper report about his visit. Expressing himself as entirely satisfied with the conditions he had seen in the camps—he had certainly not been to our camp—he was quoted as follows:

"The food I have seen our men eating would make a British housewife's mouth water."

It may be that he was unaware that he was seeing a specially prepared meal when he passed this comment; a meal that would not be repeated until another visitor—such as Mrs. Monica Felton —came to provide gratuitous propaganda for the Queen's enemies that would help to conceal the true nature of our imprisonment from the outside world. It may be that the sharpness of Mr. Gaster's skill as a lawyer in examining evidence had been temporarily blunted by his sojourn in China. I cannot say how he came to make this statement at Pyoktong, where the bodies of captives who had died of maltreatment and neglect were buried in thousands. I only know that on the morning when we read it—the 15th April 1952—Anthony and I had just finished the compound breakfast of spoiled rice and diacon soup. However bad things were in Imperialist Britain, we felt sure that no British housewife's mouth would water over our meal—one that was repeated daily for two-thirds of every week.

The Chinese had special plans for Easter. Every camp would have extra food; there would be a small issue of 'saki' (rice spirit) per man; and there would be cigarettes, pea-nuts, and a few boiled sweets. They might have added that there would be photographers, too, on a lavish scale; for our captors provided these luxuries more for their benefit than ours.

We had had some very good entertainment in the camp on a previous occasion since my arrival, but it had been run chiefly by the Americans. Several of us amongst the British thought that we should try out our native talent and so we got up a pantomime. As one of those concerned, I took the matter up with Sulky Tien. It was not simply a matter of saying that we wanted to give an entertainment at Easter and asking for a few simple items with which to make stage properties. Before anything could be done, the script had to be censored by a process of explaining, line by line, what was meant, in case any satire on the Chinese in Korea or outside Korea, her allies in other countries, Marx, Engels, Lenin, or Stalin, was intended. Sitting in Tien's office after he had read through the script, each page would be examined in this way.

Tien: (turning to the next page and pointing)

What is this?

Us: That is a joke.

Tien: What is this joke?

Us: Well, you see, two men meet. The fat man says (pointing) "Have you seen a fat man about here?"

Tien: Why does he say that?

Us: It's part of the joke. Then the second man says "No."

Tien: But he has seen the fat man.

Us: Yes, of course. That's why the fat man says, "Well, if you haven't seen a fat man about here, I must be lost."

Tien: But he is not lost.

Us: (exhausted after three hours of this) But it's a joke, don't you see? Not a very good joke—just a pantomime joke!

Tien: This is some plot against the Chinese People's Volunteers. You are trying to say that there are no fat men here because we do not feed you; you must remove it from the drama!

The Padre went through a similar experience when submitting his proposals for Church Services. He had to explain every line of every prayer, every psalm and hymn. When he asked for a little wine to celebrate Holy Communion on Easter Sunday, Chen Chung Hwei said:

"What is Easter? I have asked many men in the compound what is this Easter and they say they do not know. We think it is a trick you are playing to stir up other prisoners to make them discontented with their Daily Life." There was much more in this vein, including a story that he, Chen, had visited our Colonel to ask him what Easter meant.

"Even he did not know," said Chen. "This is an unreasonable request. You may have your usual Sunday Service."

Fortunately, they were anxious that nothing should go wrong during these celebrations. They relented at the last moment and gave the Padre permission to hold the service and, at the last moment, the materials.

The Easter festivities included an unannounced item: on Good Friday, two Australian pilots, Vance and Bruce, escaped in company with three Americans.

Not long after Easter, the North Korean Army sent an interrogation team to the village. Each day, several men would go out, swelling the numbers that the Chinese had already under interrogation in the secret community of isolated prisoners. Joe, now the senior British Officer, was sent for after a few days and handed over to a lieutenant-colonel. He did not return to the compound that week; in fact he did not return at all. After two months, we managed to obtain a message that he was having a rough time but managing to hold out. Later still, we discovered that the North Koreans had tired of his stubbornness and had returned him to the Chinese. But the Chinese knew how great was his authority amongst his fellow-captives, as much by virtue of his splendid character as of his seniority, and they led him away to a small new community of prisoners then forming in another valley! Even here, he was too much of a thorn in their side. They trumped up a charge against him of assaulting a sentry and threw him into solitary confinement—his third spell since his capture.

The Good Friday escape party were caught within a few days and brought back into the village where they were lodged in the old fire-station. They remained there for over a month before being brought to trial; a trial in which they were not the principal defendants.

After the farcical proceedings which had followed the arrest of the Colonel, Denis, Colonel B and the three American Majors, we had been asked by the Chinese what our impressions had been of their confessions. We informed them plainly that we considered the whole thing a dreadful hoax, and that they had not the remotest idea how judicial proceedings should be conducted. As a result of this, their next "trial" was an attempt at court martial procedure as we understand it.

One morning, representatives were taken from each squad to a large house in the village to witness the second public trial. They found Zee, armed to the teeth, performing the duties of usher in a court-room marked "Military Court—no talking!" Seated in the well of the court-room, they were joined shortly by Ding and two of his henchmen, who comprised the President and Members respectively; Chen Chung Hwei, was labelled "Public Prosecutor"! and sundry assistants, guards, and orderlies were in attendance. The trial began.

There was a long list of prisoners. An American Air Force Captain was charged with offences he had not only been punished for once before but—on one indictment—twice before. This treatment was excused on the grounds that he was "not penitent".

Two Americans were charged with tearing down the Red Star from the schoolhouse doorway, which, in fact, Sam and I had removed—they had confessed to it!—and with moving the school bell to the latrine.

Two others had irreverently disfigured or torn down the portraits of the Communist Party Leaders throughout the world which had graced the Library. Dave, an American pilot, was charged with inducing others to escape.

All of them were accused of having a "hostile attitude" to the Chinese Peoples' Volunteers: a useful charge which is easy to assert and difficult to deny.

The defendants were charged, asked if they identified their confessions in the hands of the Public Prosecutor and, having read these, were officially found guilty. The Court adjourned to consider sentence and returned two or three minutes later to pick up from the table a detailed, typewritten list of *awards which had been lying there throughout the trial!* There was no defence case, no plea in mitigation. There was no defence counsel or representative. Sentences ranged from four months to ten months' solitary confinement. The escapees, less Dave, brought in at the end together with a Puerto Rican officer who was also a minor offender, had their cases referred back to the Company Commander for punishment. He awarded them a month's imprisonment "in accordance with the Geneva Convention".

Less than three months previously, DP Wong, translating for Ding, had reminded us that the penalty for escape under "International Law" was death; a penalty they would not hesitate to invoke in serious cases, and that the Geneva Convention was but an instrument of bourgeois trickery. But at that time, they had not

226

begun their campaign of counter-accusation concerning the treatment of prisoners in the hands of the United Nations Command. At the time of the second "trial", the Geneva Convention had come into fashion. It was constantly quoted by leading Chinese newspapers as the minimum standard by which all prisoners-of-war might expect to be treated!

At the end of their three month sentences, two of the three majors sentenced with Denis were released and sent back to the compound. The third was given a further three months because he had exhibited an "incorrect attitude" during his punishment! It transpired subsequently that his behaviour had been no worse than either of the other two until the very last day when his sense of humour overcame his sense of propriety and, for a chance remark, he was sent back for a further three months to reflect on the inadvisability of making jokes about serious matters.

The additions to the compound were soon balanced. Spike and an American named Bud were arrested for inciting a strike down on the shore of the reservoir, where they had been working in a labour party hauling wood to the road. Spike was knocked down by the company commander for his part in the affair and, with Bud, given a trying time on his return to the village. They were locked up together in the cell behind the North Korean Police Station; we wondered if they would be in there long enough for Spike to tell Bud every one of his many anecdotes.

Mine apparently was one of many escape parties which had been held back by the bright prospect of success in the peace talks during the late spring and early summer. After reviewing the situation, Sam and Guy agreed that my party should escape in late July or early August. They passed the news to the Marine Colonel—the senior officer in the camp—and we made ready.

The party was a large one—Sid, Mr. Hobbs, Mr. Day of the Marines, Sergeants-Major Gallagher, Strong, Morton, and an American Gunner-Officer named Smoky—too large to escape at one point through the heavily patrolled fences. The choice therefore lay between an escape by night via several points or an escape in daylight—which meant that we should have to employ a "confidence trick." I chose the latter method.

The water used inside the compound for washing and bathing was brought by hand from the stream that ran on the south side of Pyn-chong-ni. To reach it, the water-carriers had to leave the compound by the main gate and walk three hundred yards down a path between fields of ripening maize to the nearest point suitable for dipping their buckets. The system employed to control them during this process was a simple one. First, the water-carriers had badges: red arm-bands bearing Chinese characters which the sentries recognised and accepted as a pass in and out of the gates. Secondly, one guard and one member of the compound staff took up a position overlooking the water dipping-point during the hours appointed for water-collection. To get out of the gate, Robin, one of the Rifles officers, counterfeited the arm bands issued daily to the carriers, using a red flag stolen from the Chinese. The next problem was to escape from the water-point without being observed by the two men on duty nearby. We watched them carefully for some time, and reached two conclusions. On a rainy day, the two men squatted miserably beneath a shelter, paying very little attention to the carriers. Given reasonable luck, a quick move would take the escaper into the tall maize stalks, when he would be instantly hidden from view. On a fine day, we could only hope to get away unobserved if one or more parties had been allowed out to the river to wash their blankets or bathe. These parties were checked carefully in and out, but if, having made our exit as water-carriers, we mingled with them on the river bank near the maize, we should certainly find a chance to dodge into it. Both courses possessed the advantage that, though we would be missed on evening roll-call, the Chinese would not know when we had gone, or where we had gone. The "confidence trick" in passing through the gate as water-carriers permitted us to walk out without any check at all.

The remaining task, after I had decided on the method and briefed the remainder, was to carry out the supplies and items of escape gear which we had collected together, including a compass, the product of Carl's genius. We each had a makeshift pack-load.

Over a period of several days, we took our stuff out and hid it in the beans growing at the foot of the maize, or, in the case of food-stuffs which might attract animals, beneath heavy rocks along the river bank. Only a few items remained—the most perishable—by the morning of the 26th of July. By then we had been without rain for five days at the height of what was normally the rainiest period of the summer.

The 27th was a hot, dry day; but towards evening, dark clouds gathered and our hopes rose. On the 28th it poured all day. At four o'clock, half the water-carriers on duty assembled by the kitchen awaiting the Chinese guard to take them through the gate on their first trip and to assume his position in the shelter near the water-point. The remaining half of the carriers was made up from my party. Time passed; there was no sign of the Chinese. Eventually, the chief water-carrier went up to the Chinese company headquarters to inquire where he had got to. It appeared that it was too wet to come out—nobody wanted to wash, he said. The gates remained closed, we dispersed our perishable kit amongst various hiding places, and returned to the Library. That was that.

It was the 4th of August before we had got our kit ready to move again. By that time, several developments had taken place.

The 1st of August is a Chinese festival and they decided to let us share in the festivities by issuing, on August 3rd, a half ration of pork, some peanuts, boiled sweets, and saki. We decided that we would have a party and drink a toast in saki to our new young Queen, whose accession we had heard of comparatively recently. The British element gathered in the Library to find that all the American Naval and Marine officers in the compound were having a party too. We each took half the room and the Americans began to sing "The Star-Spangled Banner". They had barely finished when Hector, the senior South African Officer began to sing "God Save the Queen" in a strong voice, speedily joined by the remainder, including the Americans. Near me, Johnny Rotor-head, an American naval helicopter pilot, was singing splendidly, the words rolling from his tongue as well as from any member of the Commonwealth present. When it was over, Hector led the assembly out on to the square in a conga. Five minutes later, Sam was summoned to the company headquarters.

The company commander was furious. He was a nasty little man with an unpronounceable name; a man who had told us in a speech shortly after his arrival, in place of More-in-Sorrow-Than-in-Anger, that "your God cannot help you now. Only the Chinese Volunteers can give you what you need." He spoke to Sam through Chang, a new interpreter who spoke better English than anyone else on the compound staff.

Although the company commander was so angry, he was also a frightened man. He had never previously seen the conga danced and believed that the entire camp was about to riot under the influence of saki. In these circumstances, knowing the great respect in which Sam was held by all, he told him to go back and prevent such an incident. As Sam well knew that there was nothing to prevent, he left without passing any further comment; and we were glad, if surprised, to see him back. Sam's activities against the Chinese were notorious: he lived permanently on a razor's edge.

The 4th of August was a fine, sunny day—a grand day for washing blankets down by the river—and one of tension for us, relieved by a number of very amusing incidents.

Sergeant-Major Gallagher was told to walk down the school-house corridor to collect the last items of food he was to carry out. He left the Library and commenced to pass the first of the sleeping quarters. As he continued on his way, he found that many class-room doors slid quickly open to reveal a pair of hands grasping some item of provisions which was dumped into his hands. After using up all his pockets to hide these things, he arrived at the far end of the corridor bulging in the most extraordinary places, and walking with an unaccustomed limp.

Sergeant-Major Morton's figure looked like the Gibson Girl's before putting on his blue jacket. Mr. Hobbs had coiled round him a long piece of rope stolen from a Chinese tent, corseting his figure in the most elegant fashion. But it was done so effectively the first time that Sergeant-Major Morton was not only unable to breathe but almost cut in two.

Down by the kitchen door I met Sid. I checked with him that Sergeant-Major Strong had just taken out the remainder of his kit before passing on.

"I'm going over to the latrine, Sid," I said. "You coming that way?"

"No, thanks," he replied. "I've been fifteen times to-day already!"

At last the moment came. With Sergeants-Major Morton and Gallagher, I passed through the main gates on the south side of the square, wearing my red armband, swinging two buckets in my hands. These buckets were brought back under blankets by a party returning from the stream. Sergeant-Major Bates, Sergeant Wilkins of the American Air Force and a group of other sergeants with him had preceded us by half an hour especially for this task.

Down by the river, Robin and Spud were drawing water. The compound staff and guards were chatting up on the little cliff; below them, downstream, parties from two of the platoons were washing their blankets and clothes. While Sergeant-Major Morton awaited his opportunity to come downstream to join us, Sergeant-Major Gallagher and I moved towards the maize. We both entered and he began to stack a last item of the baggage beneath some stones. At that moment, I saw the maize moving; a movement that was not caused by the wind. Looking up, I saw that a sentry was standing there watching us. Behind him was one of the compound staff.

Sergeant-Major Gallagher called out to me: "Sir, they've spotted us! Someone is coming down from the cliff."

We both pretended that we were making an urgent call to the latrine and, after a moment or so, sauntered back out on to the river bank as if nothing had happened. But the sentry had shown the others the package Gallagher had hidden and, subsequently, kit on the river shore beneath an old jersey. Gallagher was arrested and taken back to the compound, just after Robin had managed to convey the warning to the others inside, who were awaiting the signal to leave. Shortly after, Morton was arrested, following the discovery of a letter amongst the kit in the middle of the field of maize. I carried water back to the compound, still a relatively free man.

231

Sid was awaiting me in the kitchen with Tony. I told them what had happened and said that we must put everything we still had back into a hiding place and lie low for a day or two. Tony took the map and compass I had; the other kit was quickly dispersed. The stuff in the maize field was, of course, a write-off.

Nothing further was said that evening, and roll-call passed off in the usual way. It was later, at about eight o'clock, that the final consequences of the day became known.

Sam, Guy, Anthony and I were walking up and down outside a small schoolhouse we then occupied on the hillside some distance above Snob Hill. The playground there was very small and we paced only twelve steps back and forth. Our platoon interpreter—Old Yang—came towards us from the Chinese staff hut nearby, calling Sam's name. The two of them went back into the hut and we continued our walk. Ten minutes later, one of the Chinese orderlies came to collect Sam's kit and we knew that he was under arrest.

Geoff, Anthony, and I packed up the kit and sent it away. But it was still too hot to go to sleep in the hut and I was in no mood to rest after the failure of my plan and the arrest of my friends We had resumed our walk when the old Chinese came back again. This time, it was my name he called. I accompanied him back to his hut and was thrust through the door. Inside were the company commander and Chang. The door closed behind me.

The Company Commander smoked through a whole cigarette before addressing me through Chang. Then he said:

"You have conspired to make men escape. You have used your former rank to order men to disobey the regulations."

I said nothing; we had already made plans for such a contingency as this and it was necessary to await further developments. The company commander poured out a torrent of angry Chinese which contained a repetition of his former accusations, more accusations, and a few threats. Finally, seeing that I did not respond, the little company commander threw his cap dramatically on to his desk and said:

"I withdraw your privileges of tobacco, liberty, and sugar."

232

He obviously placed their value in that order. The final word of my arrest had been spoken. Accompanied by a guard and the orderly, I was taken out into the warm moonlit night.

Escorted to Camp Headquarters, I stood outside the main building. Chen Chung Hwei came out and asked me my name.

"Confess," he said dramatically. "We know everything! What happened?"

This childish behaviour and his own misshapen little figure gave the whole scene in the moonlight an unreal quality. I felt for a moment that I was watching a puppet performing on a stage. The illusion vanished a moment later as one of the couriers in the Headquarters appeared.

"Follow this comrade," said Chen, disappearing back into his room.

"This comrade" took me down to a cell, searched me, and locked me in for the night under the eye of one of the jail sentries. I had had a good run for my money, between cells.

CHAPTER THIRTEEN

WHEN the morning came, I discovered that my cell was in the North Korean police station, the very cell which Spike and Bud had occupied immediately following their arrest. All that remained of their occupation was an inscription on the wall. With a nail, they had scratched "Spike" and "Bud" and put the date underneath: "27th July 1952". I found a loose nail and added my own name and the date below theirs, the last entries in a long list of names and dates.

The cell was about eight feet long and four across; its walls were timbered on three sides with stout pine boards. The fourth wall had thick bars of pine, socketed in the floor and ceiling, and secured by cross-pieces. Outside the bars was a passage, running the length of the cell, with a door at either end: one to the police offices; the other to the courtyard outside. A window, covered with steel mesh, admitted a little light when the doors were closed. Everything had been removed from my pockets during my search, but a blanket and two bowls were brought to me during the early morning. One of the floor boards was broken and so I reached through to the underside, found a stone, and began to sharpen two nails to cut my way out of the cell. It was going to be a long job—not only because the walls were thick and my tools were crude, but also because the sentries were unpredictable in their attentions.

The routine for men in solitary confinement was as follows. At dawn—sometimes half an hour before dawn—the sentry on duty roused the prisoners in the cells he watched, making use of his bayonet when prisoners were tardy in rising. Officially, one was supposed to sit up, with legs crossed, for the remainder of the day; prisoners were not permitted to use the wall as a back rest. In practice, I sat as I pleased and even took the liberty of standing up, now and again. If these sentries wanted to be able to creep up on me to surprise me sitting in a non-regulation position, they had to leave the outer passage door open. This gave me a view of the green hills and the blue sky; a small view but one I treasured. If they wanted to keep me in semi-darkness, to accentuate my solitude by cutting me off completely from the outside world, they had to close the door, the opening of which gave me ample warning that they were coming in to see what I was doing. In this matter, as with almost every other, the tenor of my life depended almost entirely on the character of the sentries, who changed every three hours, and the guard commanders, who changed every six hours. There were those who spent the entire time harrassing prisoners, and those who left us entirely alone. There were guard commanders who kept us short of food—kaoliang and hot water, slightly coloured to resemble cabbage soup—and declined to take us out for the two daily visits to the latrine permitted by the regulations. There were others who made sure that we had every one of the few amenities allowed. There was no question of washing, smoking, or even talking. Except during examination for one's offences, the requirement was the silence of a Trappist monk from dawn to dusk.

It is hardly surprising that a high proportion of the guards were unpleasant to us. Their peasant heads were filled with propaganda stories—often, fantastic or ludicrous—about the United Nations troops. One of these stories seemed a favourite, for we heard it again and again. While I was lodged in the police cell, it was told me once more in a novel form.

The guard commander, one afternoon, was a tall, young Chinese whom I called Noble: he wore, perpetually, such a noble expression. He had attended a missionary school for some time and spoke fair English. Poking his head round the door, he stared at me for several minutes. Then he said:

"You are American?"

I shook my head. "English," I said.

He seemed unwilling to accept this and pressed me again to identify myself. We tired of this after a minute or two and the cell fell silent again. At last he stirred, to make a fresh point:

"All Americans, all English, come to Korea to eat the red apples and ravish the women." He paused: In this sentence he had re-counted the favourite propaganda. But there was more to come. It was quite obvious that another question was forming inside his head and, at last, he got it out. His head stretched forward on his long neck, his eyes bulging with curiosity, he said:

"How many Korean women you have ravished?"

He was too disappointed with my reply to believe it.

After ten days, I was moved to another cell in a block which had been built originally by the Japanese for the accommodation of the families of the police—and so all my work towards escape came to naught. I was put into an old kitchen which had a damp mud floor and crumbling mud and wattle walls. What was even more disadvantageous was the fact that the door had a spyhole for the sentry, and the exit at the other end of the cell was blocked by a pile of aluminium aircraft fuel drop-tanks which rang at the slightest touch and contained plenty of gaps through which the sentry could maintain a watch. Yet, compensating to some extent for these drawbacks, I had companionship here, and, now and again, I was able to see the outside world The room on the southern side was occupied by the Camp Quartermaster's staff, the idlest group of soldiers I have ever seen. Most of the time they sat about, smoking, chattering, admiring one another's snapshots or their own faces in the mirror, or in singing.

To the north of me, the building divided into two rooms. The western room—really a woodshed—was occupied by a young American Air Force Corporal named Abbot who was a credit to his service. He and two American Air Force Officers—a black-bearded captain confined in the block opposite, and a young second-lieutenant at the extreme southern end of my block—were all accused of participating in Germ Warfare. They had all been in solitary confinement since April and had no hope of release since they had all resolutely refused to confess to participation in something which they knew nothing about.

From the Spring on, we had been subjected to endless propaganda on the subject of Germ Warfare which, latterly, had included signed "confessions" from members of various aircrews. Included in or accompanying these statements were paragraphs insisting that they had been made entirely voluntarily, that the writers could no longer bear the weight of their sins in this connection on their respective consciences after the kind and generous treatment accorded them by the Chinese People's Volunteers. At least two of these men had been in the village of Pyn-Chong-Ni, though never in our compound. Some time before their "confessions", they had been removed to Pyoktong. Another was known to the Marine Colonel who had expressed concern for the man's fate some time before his statement appeared. He had last seen him bound to a telegraph pole in shirt and cotton slacks on a bitter February night.

It was probably fortunate for Abbot and the other two that they were examined on Germ Warfare after statements had been obtained from airmen made captive earlier; and fortunate that none of them held ranks or appointments sufficiently important to cause the Chinese to persevere with them, as they did with more senior officers later. The story that Abbot told me in whispers through a hole in the wall confirmed opinions that we had already formed about the integrity of those "confessions" published on the use of germ weapons in Korea by the United Nations Command.

Abbot knew nothing about germ bombs; he had not even read

about the Japanese bacteriological warfare laboratories in World War II. When confronted with the subject by the Chinese, they had had to explain to him what they meant! He spent about a month living in a house with DP Wong and a number of other interpreters who passed each day with him, taking shifts so that he was never left alone. All day, every day, they talked of nothing else but the use of germ weapons by the American Air Force generally and by his own night medium-bomber unit in particular. They mentioned to him the names of officers still serving with the unit who were implicated, of others who had been executed since capture because they refused to confess to the crime, of others again who had confessed and so caused the Chinese to spare their lives. Never at any time throughout this period was he asked directly to make a statement or to "confess"; but by inference, through this skilful method of which the Chinese are masters, they called on him to do so.

At the end of this phase, since Abbot had not responded, DP Wong and his friends began to apply more direct methods. Without warning, he was awakened one night about half an hour after he had gone to sleep and was taken back into the room in which he normally spent the day. He was stood to attention for a long period while Wong and the others accused him outright of being an accomplice as his conscience had not compelled him to confess of his own accord. When Abbot again denied all knowledge of the whole affair he was kicked and beaten—DP Wong loved nothing better than this type of thing when he had plenty of support. Abbot was kept up until dawn, when he was permitted to return to his cell.

For three weeks, he had no real sleep, was tried and sentenced to death twice, and finally thrown into the dark woodshed he now occupied. Here, like the two others close by, and many more in the village, he remained in solitary confinement, deprived of washing facilities—often latrine facilities—and the opportunity to breathe fresh air and see the light of day. He had refused to give in on principle—not because he realized the appalling danger of giving way to his tormentors; he did not realize it fully even after I explained to him what had happened to the men with whom the

237

Chinese had persevered earlier. I was glad to have that young corporal from the State of New York in the next cell.

I have said that Abbot occupied the western cell of the two which joined the northern wall of my damp kitchen. To my surprise, shortly after entering my new cell, I heard the Padre's voice coming from the other one. He had been arrested some time after me: this was his second or third day in jail.

The floor of my cell was much lower than his and, without having to move from the position in which the guard commander had placed me, I could talk to the Padre by turning my head to speak through a small gap in the wall. He began to tell me what had happened; but of course, his troubles went back much further than this recent event.

I know of only two priests being captured in Korea. One was an American Roman Catholic chaplain, a splendid man who had died at Pyoktong of dysentery that was never treated because the Chinese did not want him to live. The other was our own Padre. In both cases, their presence was an embarrassment to our captors. They consistently reiterated that they permitted absolute freedom of religion, but they had not expected to be called upon to prove their words with deeds. The other camps, having no chaplain, were permitted to hold short services at Easter and Christmas and, later, in a very few camps, every Sunday. But the Padre felt strongly that he must continue his ministry and, consequently, made greater demands. He wanted to hold confirmation classes for those who desired it; to give instruction in theology; to hold services on special weekdays in the Christian year. To a lesser extent, the Roman Catholics wished to do the same thing under the leadership of the American officer that the Roman Catholic chaplain had instructed prior to his death. I know of no occasion when any religious activity of ours, in prospect or event, was directed against the authority of our captors: yet, at every turn, in every way, they frustrated our religious activities. "Religion," said Chen Chung Hwei, "shall be centralized on Sundays. There is no need for you to worship on any other day." In the early days, they sought to dissuade us from attending church services; but, seeing that this merely hardened us all the more against them, they turned to other means to thwart the Padre. Material was not available to make hymn or psalm sheets, a cross or candlesticks. We had to improvise for everything. All religious meetings—theological classes, confirmation groups—were absolutely forbidden. Permission for each Sunday service had to be obtained and the exact words to be used in prayers, psalms, hymns, as well as addresses, had to be submitted five or six days in advance, when the Padre would be subjected to a rigorous cross-examination as to the meaning of each phrase. If it was possible to impose a labour detail on the compound at service times, this was done. On other occasions, the loud-speaker system would broadcast gramophone records at the times appointed for service. At the end of each month, the Padre had to submit a report headed "Religious Activities for the month of. . . ."

These reports were used to harass him. The Chinese would fabricate evidence of clandestine meetings and then ask him why he had not reported the details of the meetings in his monthly report. Naturally he had no reply, and they would exploit their position to scorn and mock his Faith.

It hurt the Padre to hear words and phrases that were sacred to him discussed and sneered at by Chen, Tien, and others of the compound staff. They knew this, and hurt him in this way as often as possible. What they had failed to appreciate was that no effort of theirs would discourage him from performing his duty.

For many weeks, the choir had met regularly to practise in the Library for the service on the following Sunday; an event the Chinese had known of and permitted. In the second week in August, they suddenly pretended that it was a clandestine activity, a subtle plot against them organized by the Padre. They arrested him after giving him the opportunity to sign a "confession" to this effect, which they promised would save him from imprisonment—and, as he declined their offer, brought him over to the jail. When he was searched, Tien threw his Bible and devotional book to the floor and kicked them into a heap of filth in the corner. They were too stupid to realize that this merely strengthened the Padre's determination to resist them.

His companionship was a source of great comfort to me; at night, and in the daytime when the sentry was not paying us too much attention, we had whispered conversations through the wall. On the Sunday after his arrest, and the Sunday that followed, we were delighted to hear the distant sound of hymns being sung in the Library.

They released the Padre after about three weeks, having failed completely in their purpose: the church service continued under lay leadership and there was much hard feeling about his arrest. The attempt to obtain a "confession" concerning a plot with the choir was dropped; Tien saved face by getting the Padre to agree that he would hold choir practices on Sunday mornings only, before the service. I missed him a great deal when he left; but soon had another companion in Alan, formerly Spike's second-in-command, who had quarrelled with one of the Chinese administering his platoon.

Sometimes the days passed swiftly in meditation; sometimes they dragged intolerably. I would follow the sun's arc, its traverse of the sky, and its setting, by watching the movement of the few thin shafts of sunlight on the walls. I scratched off the days one after another on my calendar: August passed, then September. Another winter was coming and I had wasted a whole escape season.

In September I was informed by Chen that, in addition to the charges arising from organizing and attempting an escape, there were others. He produced an indifferent forgery of Spike's handwriting, accusing me of persuading him to stay in bed late in the mornings! Later, another obvious forgery was produced, ostensibly made by a British officer who had been in jail for a very long time and who, I was told, had decided to confess all his faults! At last, circumstances permitted me to tell the deception story we had planned. By good fortune, I managed to communicate secretly with Gallagher and Morton, so that we were ready to tell our story simultaneously. The Chinese released us to the compound within a few days of one another, which left Sam as the only one out of the original four still in prison. They had tried very hard to get us to incriminate Sam, against whom they had absolutely no evidence.

About this time they must have begun to suspect, rightly, that they had one of the most resolute officers in the British Army in their jail.

CHAPTER FOURTEEN

THERE had been more escape attempts in my absence: Walt, a young American fighter pilot, and Sergeant Brock had been the last to go, bringing the total number of men who had attempted it in the year to forty-one. Walt's departure had been executed so skilfully that old Yang, who administered our platoon, did not discover his absence for two days. I was very pleased to hear this story of a clean getaway at Yang's expense as he had been one of those principally concerned in arresting Sergeant-Major Gallagher by the stream. Poor Walt and Brock had already been brought back to the village after covering well over a hundred miles. They were lodged together in a foul, dark, rat-infested cellar almost opposite the North Korean police station.

Not long after my return, the Marine Colonel was arrested. Unquestionably, the Chinese had been preparing a case against him for a considerable time, knowing that he was the senior United Nations Officer in the compound and thus the officer whom we considered the commander. He was actually arrested on a minor charge of "stealing" his own boots from a store where all our own uniforms were kept impounded, and ordered to go down to answer this charge at Camp Headquarters. There, after a long spell in solitary confinement, he had other, more serious charges, brought again him.

The chief change in the routine life inside the compound that I noticed was that many of the British had taken up the American game of softball. We still played cricket twice a week on the square with our home-made gear, but the ranks of the cricket snobs were thinner. James and Sergeant-Major Ridlington had earned places in the top league of the three that were running. Paul captained a strong British team competing in the middle league. The Americans had made some marvellous equipment out of barbed wire, leather from old boots, and firewood, and the cries of players and spectators rang through Pyn-chong-ni when a game was in progress. The North Korean children would assemble on the hill above to watch whenever they got the chance.

I had just settled back into the routine of compound life when the Camp Headquarters made a change that constituted a major event in our lives. The prisoners in the compound were divided into two groups, and one group was withdrawn from the village.

Prior to my joining the Camp, a Chinese had said to me:

"You think you are going to a camp where there are watch-towers and high, barbed-wire fences. You are wrong. We do not send you to be a prisoner but to be a student at a sort of university. There are no fences to keep you in."

Though he was wrong about the university, he was right about the fences, generally speaking. Our camp was not surrounded by high fences until mid-1952. Before that, in Pyn-chong-ni, the compound was enclosed by a single barbed wire fence; but the Chinese principle of guarding their captives was entirely different from that adopted in western Europe or America. Instead of establishing compounds containing upwards of five hundred men, enclosed by the customary fences and watch-towers, they kept us in comparatively small groups, breaking these down, whenever possible, to as few as ten men. For, at the outset, their principle concern had been political subversion, and they realized speedily that this was proportionately more difficult as the numbers in each group increased. Later, when the indoctrination programme had failed, they feared plots against them and sought to prevent these by the same principles as before: small groups under close surveillance. Even as late as the summer of 1952, when they established an annexe to our Camp—Camp 2—they kept prisoners in several groups of eight and ten, and one larger group of about thirty, for many months. It was only the excessively heavy guard commitment that caused them to keep larger compounds—even in Pyn-chong-ni there was one soldier in the guard company for every two prisoners in the compound. We were never left completely alone. Though we secured the right to cook our own food, our doctors were not officially permitted to practice, for they were "bourgeois" trained, "un-Marxian", "undemocratic", "incapable of adopting a correct scientific attitude". Our labour details were supervised for many months by Chinese who demonstrated their ability to muddle even the simplest of tasks. Nor were we permitted to gather in groups for instruction in matters of general, non-political interest such as photography, architecture, motor or aircraft engineering. Carl tried for months to obtain permission to run a class in higher mathematics but was refused. Having failed to subvert us, our captors would not let us make our own regular diversions and entertainments. Even the bridge fours were inspected, when cards became available, by Chinese who wandered from room to room to see who was talking to whom, and what they were saying. Day and night, they roamed through the compound, watching us. Now, with the split into two compounds, there were less of us to watch in each.

Immediately after breakfast one morning at the end of October, the whole of our platoon was told to pack up for a move. We were given no details but merely told that we should leave nothing behind. I was packing my kit when Chang approached me to say:

"You are not going with the others. Pack your kit and go below to the schoolhouse."

One never knew what an order of this sort presaged. I said good-bye to my friends and descended the hill. The schoolhouse had been cleared and men were standing about on the square, falling out as their names were called and moving to join a growing body of men by the main gate. This was the remainder of No. 2 Company, of which my former platoon, already departed by another route, had formed a part. I was left with No 1 Company, who were now fitted back into the schoolhouse complete. The gate opening on the path to the hilltop where I had lived formerly was closed and locked.

Spike, Bill, Sergeant-Major Gallagher and I managed to find bed-spaces together in our new room. Sitting there, that first

243

evening, I was surprised to see Graham, our Mortar Officer, come in. He had been taken out of the compound immediately after the evening meal on the orders of Camp Headquarters.

"It isn't me they want," he said in answer to my query, "it's you."

He was right. One of the Chinese came in behind him to tell me to pack my belongings.

Chen Chung Hwei was waiting for me at Camp Headquarters.

"You were given a warning when you were released from jail that you should obey the regulations. You have not taken any notice of the warning. The Commander Ding has decided that you shall go to another place."

After waiting in a cold little room in the Headquarters for about two hours, I was collected by a non-commissioned officer and two men, all dressed for travelling, and carrying thin, individual sacks of rice. I had had experience of this before: it looked as if we were going at least one night's travel from Pyng-Chong-ni. I wondered if we were off to some penal institution or to the new annexe, and whether Sam would be coming with me.

The Camp truck was waiting in the courtyard by the police station, its engine idling. We climbed aboard, except for the non-commissioned officer. After waiting for more than half an hour in the cold night, one of those incidents occurred which almost every prisoner in Korea must have experienced if he made a journey by motor vehicle: the trip was cancelled. An orderly came running down the path from the Headquarters shouting something to the driver, who promptly turned off his engine, climbed out saying "Ta malega—" and began to pull the tarpaulin over the engine and driver's cab. By this time the orderly and the guard non-commissioned officer were engaged in speech, as the result of which I was told to get down and return to Camp Headquarters, where Chen was standing in the entrance to the courtyard. It was bad enough seeing him again; it was worse when he removed all my kit and locked me up for the night without any bedding. I spent a very cold night saying even ruder things about Chen than I had ever said before.

Seven days after the departure of my friends in No. 2 Company from the main compound, I was still in a room at Camp Headquarters, awaiting movement to whatever destination Ding had in mind. I had managed to get my kit back on the fourth day, when Chen informed me that there was a further delay in moving me. At dusk on the seventh day, I was taken down to his office and given another warning.

"The Commander Ding has decided to send you back to your company," said Chen. "You will not go away to Another Place; but I warn you that if you disobey the regulations in future, you will receive very severe punishment. We know everything that goes on in the Camp. You can never deceive the Chinese Volunteers!"

A guard and an orderly took me down the road that led to Pyoktong. About a mile west of the village, we turned off the road by another schoolhouse—still employed as such by the Koreans—and made our way up a long valley. On the eastern slope was a long building constructed in the Chinese style; the new No. 2 Company Headquarters. Inside, Chang and the company commander were waiting to receive me.

Chang was a short, plump individual, who, on his own statement, was a graduate of St. John's University, Shanghai. He had a fine ear for an accent and modified his English to suit his audience; to the Americans, he spoke with an American accent; to the British element, he spoke straightforward English. But more than this: at Pyoktong, where he had been stationed with captives in Camp No. 5, he had learned to assume a Cockney accent, and he tried this out on Sergeants-Major Morton and Strong—both Londoners—from time to time. He was very anxious to improve his English and spent a great deal of time studying and asking us to explain phrases that he did not understand. He was probably the only Chinese in North Korea who could recite the greater portion of Spenser's *Faërie Queen* and Fitzgerald's original translation of Omar's *Rubá'iyát*. But for all these accomplishments and a suave manner, Chang was the most dangerous man on the Chinese staff of the company—an unprincipled opportunist, who had readily lent himself to the beating-up of members of the escape party, including

245

the Australian pilots, Vance and Bruce, on their recapture in April 1952. Yet, strangely, Chang was the only Chinese in the Camp with sufficient intelligence to see that the best way to approach us as a group was with politeness, and amity. Though he was rebuffed again and again, he never gave up; and, unquestionably, he saved his masters a great deal of trouble by this policy, which, coupled with his considerable ability as an interpreter, made our relationship with the Company Headquarters less irksome than it might have been.

"So you've come to join us after all?" said Chang, in greeting. He interpreted the remarks of the company commander, a stocky Chinese we called Eleanor, who said that I must bear in mind all the rules and regulations and look after my health so that I could return to my dear ones, eventually. After a happy reunion with my friends, I found that I was allocated a bed on a raised kang (a sleeping platform heated on the hypocaust system) which was occupied by the Turks.

I was lucky to be billeted with the Turks: they were exceptionally polite as a group and very pleasant to live with. Of the eleven members of their squad, there was not one who was not a remarkable character—from Hamid, the senior Turkish officer, to Nafi, a private soldier who had been such a powerful influence amongst his compatriots in the Turkish soldiers' company at Pyoktong, that the Chinese had believed him to be an officer. Fortunately, they were still not sure about his rank; they had no efficient Turkish interpreter in Korea.

Although the nights were really cold, the day temperatures were still pleasant as we passed into November 1952; and this was fortunate because an inter-camp athletics meeting had been arranged which the Chinese styled the "Prisoner-of-War Command Olympics". We had already had a certain amount of propaganda about the International Olympic Games at Helsinki—the early Chinese reports insisted, for example, that America had tied with Russia for First Place. When the final scoresheets were published, however, it was seen that Russia was, in fact, placed below the United States, but this was explained without embarrassment as follows:

246

"Though the final points do not show an equal victory, actually Russia should be shown as First-equal because she would have won the necessary points at the Games but for biased judging against her in the following competitions . . ."!

Now the Olympic Games idea had been adopted as a super-propaganda stunt for the prison-camps and there was considerable doubt amongst us as to whether we should participate or not. The factor which really decided that we should take part as an officers' camp was that we would have an opportunity to communicate with men of our units held in other camps. The senior Air Force Lieutenant-Colonel was the leader of the party of participators and spectators, and Donald was the senior Briton. He returned on the eve of Thanksgiving Day with many cheering messages from our men in other camps and a most interesting account of all that had occurred.

Sensing the temper of their captives, the Chinese had made no attempt to hold "Fight-for-Peace" parades before the games, as they had done so often in the past. There was a review of the competitors by a Chinese General at the outset, which we had had to accept, but the many, inevitable speeches made only a few mild references to a hope for peace in Korea. The main snag was that a large number of photographers were present. Photographs were taken, not only of the events, but of the vastly improved food which was served at every meal—photographs that might well be presented to the outside world as an illustration of our normal daily meals at a time when we were living off cabbage and potato soup, the new winter diet. Certainly one of the Press representatives there must have welcomed the opportunity to exploit the situation for propaganda purposes. I refer to Alan Winnington, the London *Daily Worker* correspondent, who had assisted the North Koreans to interrogate United Nations' captives and consistently misrepresented our treatment to the advantage of our enemies and the detriment of his fellow-countrymen. When Donald approached him, he attempted a false joviality and said that he was hoping to come out to our camp to interview us. Donald asked him if he would care to interview him, personally, there and then; but Winnington regretted that he had other business and moved away, promising that he would come back to make an appointment. He avoided Donald for the rest of the meeting.

As we expected, in due course an illustrated book was produced concerning the Olympics, with captions that advised the reader of our happiness in the prison camps on the Yalu River. It made no reference to the many men undergoing solitary confinement, such as the Colonel (whose sentence had long since expired) or others, like Sam, who remained unsentenced, or others again who, held in lone huts in the mountains, were being tortured in order to obtain more "confessions" to waging Germ Warfare in Korea.

The peace talks were in abeyance when Thanksgiving Day came round again but, fortunately for us, the Chinese were now trying to convince the outside world that they were treating their prisoners with generosity; and that the United Nations Command was consistently maltreating the prisoners they held. As a result, we had extra food once again for Thanksgiving Day and, later, for Christmas and the New Year. But we paid for our feasting by reverting to a steady diet of cabbages, potatoes, and, at intervals, beans, immediately the feast-day had passed. Undoubtedly, conditions of living had improved; but almost all we had to cook our vegetables with was salt and water and there were times when it was difficult to face the same meal morning and evening, day after day.

Another improvement in our camp life as the year waned was the introduction of non-political fiction into the new Library. There had been a small consignment of books in the summer which contained one or two works by Leo Tolstoy and two by Dickens. Now, further additions appeared, stamped with the mark of the French Bookshop in Tientsin. This confirmed the statement by Camp Headquarters that considerably more money had been allotted for our welfare. Our supply of newspapers and magazines was supplemented, too, but these were all devoted to the Marxist cause. The London *Daily Worker* appeared with fair regularity, three months in arrears, and continued to provide us with good sports news and a heavily biased picture of life in the world in general and the United Kingdom in particular. One day, whilst I was reading the *Daily Worker*, James told me that he had seen a picture of an American prisoner published under the caption

"Not much ill-treatment here" or something of the sort. The picture showed an officer shaving while a comrade looked on, smiling. The prisoner was evidently healthy: the picture was taken only a fortnight after his capture. *But it was actually published in the London* Daily Worker *nine months after the man had died of untreated dysentry.* A death certificate had been signed by an American doctor who was with James at the time.

As the Padre had remained with No. 1 Company, James had taken over the job of Protestant Chaplain for our compound—a task he performed with reverence and dignity. Jumbo had assumed the leadership of the Roman Catholics since the split and, between them, these two kept our Christian worship going. Duke, an American Infantry Major, and Theo, our Machine-Gun Officer set about making a new set of altar furniture for the services, carving candlesticks from firewood, and a cross, lectern, and *prie-dieu* from some pine trunks we had been given for seats in the Library. The Padre was allowed to visit us on Christmas Day to celebrate Holy Communion and was delighted to see all that had been done. It was less of a pleasure to see Chen Chung Hwei, who accompanied him and tip-toed about wishing people a "Merry Christmas". I felt less angry at this when I heard that Sam had at least been released back to No. 1 Company. We now began to hope for the release of our Colonel, the Marine Colonel, and Denis.

Christmas Day 1952 was a memorable day—particularly the evening. An inter-denominational carol service was held about seven o'clock in a Library gaily decorated with paintings, streamers, and pine branches, the work of Guy, Recce, and the Sergeants-Major, led by Sergant-Major Baker of our Support Company. Our thoughts were very naturally all of home and we were not in the best mood to receive an address from Ding, the Camp Commander, which Chang was to read to us at nine o'clock.

Chang sensed our mood. He knew that we should not be receptive to his good wishes after what he had to read out, so he extended them beforehand. It was principally an American audience, and Chang spoke with an American accent.

"Say, I've got a Christmas message from Commander Ding for

all of you and, in a few minutes, I'm going to read it out. But before I do, I want to say 'Happy Christmas' everyone. I hope that next year you'll all be back home with your families. Now here is the message from the Camp Commander."

He began to read from a page of typescript in his hand, and his appreciation of our reactions had been accurate. It was in the worst possible taste; for, after starting mildly, Ding had been unable to restrain his fanaticism for the Communist cause. He quoted—or rather, misquoted—the Scriptures, particularly the teachings of Christ. We heard the beloved Christmas words, for instance, rendered as follows: "Peace on earth to men of good will"; and the only men of good will, it seemed, were those who followed the policies of the Cominform group of governments. As Chang read on, the silence seemed to intensify. When he had finished, no one spoke; but I have neither felt nor seen before such profound disgust expressed silently by a body of men.

"That's all," said Chang. He was not sorry for what had been said; only sorry that he had been the one who had had to say it, and so lose popularity.

The new compound, which had been occupied since late October, was roughly U-shaped. The main living-block was the base running along a platform cut in the eastern slope of the valley; the kitchen and a small living-room formed the left arm; the Library formed the right; within the arms and base was a parade-ground— a "square" of mud we had dug out ourselves. A promenade ran the length of the main living quarters, shorter and narrower than that before the schoolhouse in Pyn-Chong-ni.

At two minutes to midnight on 31st of December 1952, Sid and I stood on the promenade, looking up at the bright stars shining through the clear, cold night. Suddenly there was a cheer from the Library, and we heard them singing "Auld Lang Syne." We looked at one another for a moment and then shook hands.

"Happy New Year!" we said. The same wish was in both our hearts.

CHAPTER FIFTEEN

HITHERTO, we had ruled out escape in mid-winter; for in the two earlier winters of the war, prisoners had been too weak to survive exposure in an open boat or the rigours of a prolonged cross-country journey. We now had a plan which dispensed with the latter; and the doctors felt that some of us were sufficiently fit to risk the former. The plan was to escape in February along the frozen surface of the Yalu River to the sea. It was certainly feasible in white clothing on the snow-covered ice for any small party of men determined to succeed. The first two pairs amongst the British began to prepare: Peter, a young subaltern of the Rifles, and Tom, who had commanded a platoon in our D Company, Sid and I. At the same time, Guy heard through his liaison with the Americans that the Air Force Colonel Mac and Harry, an infantry major, were planning to go about the same time. It was agreed that we should all try to make our escape from the compound on the same night; for if one party went several nights ahead of another, the guards, who did not expect a break in this bitter weather, would be alerted and a second escape would thus be far more difficult. We all had to escape with fairly large loads because we needed food more than ever in these low temperatures, and escaping from this compound with such a bundle would be exceptionally difficult if the sentries were alert and at full strength.

There were many anxious moments. Mr. Hobbs had procured us beans from the cook-house previously, and Donald—now a cook—had supplemented these with other items. Sergeant-Major Askew, of Frank's Mortar Troop, had stolen meat for us. Sid was parching the dried beans over a kang fire behind the huts one morning when one of the Chinese compound staff appeared—an unpleasant man we called Clem. Something had gone wrong with the warning system and I saw the blood ebb from Sid's face as he threw the beans far into the back of the fire and pretended to be heating up some potato soup saved from breakfast. Clem was looking in all the fire boxes as he came along; he paused and looked in the one where Sid was sitting. I thought he was never going on but, at last, he seemed satisfied and walked away. The days passed as we slowly assembled the various items of kit that we needed. Duggie, the 8th Hussars Doctor, and Bob, checked on the food value of each item we intended to carry in our rations and warned us that we should be existing on an absolute minimum diet.

Colonel Mac very kindly offered us the first place in the order of escape. Tom drew cards with me to see who should go out first: he won. That night we dressed in our kit and prepared to break out as soon as possible after dark. But, to our annoyance, the guards seemed unusually alert, and the compound staff were inside the compound in strength, shining their torches around the square whilst the sentries did likewise behind the buildings. We decided that it would be better to postpone the attempt for twenty-four hours, expecting that the state of alertness would diminish.

On the following night, the first two pairs got dressed again; Colonel Mac and Harry got ready to pull their kit out of hiding as soon as they had the signal that Tom and Peter had gone and we were in process of going. But we got no further than that. Two members of the compound staff came straight up to Peter and picked him up with all his kit on him, arresting Tom in the same way a few minutes later while he was actually in his room. Then they began looking about for more of us. I had barely stripped myself of my foodpack and handed it to Sergeant-Major Strong for disposal before Yang came up to me and shone his torch all over my clothing. Plainly I had no pack or bundle on me and he went off unhappily, muttering rude Chinese words, looking for Sid, who had just managed to get rid of his kit also.

We had just recently started to have gramophone concerts of classical music—another result of the increased allowance for prisoners. That particular night in late February, one of these concerts was in progress. Sergeant-Major Strong and Anthony sat listening to Tchaikowsky in apparent rapture as they dispersed the contents of a large pack of concentrated food. Fortunately, we were able to warn Colonel Mac and Harry in time to stop them from getting out their kit from its hiding-place.

As we went to bed that night, heavy-hearted at our failure and at the arrest of Tom and Peter, one thing became abundantly clear. Someone in the compound was acting as informer for the enemy— a suspicion we had formed long ago. Only a fellow-captive could have told the Chinese who was taking part in the escape, and when. Either through fear or malice, someone had told them what he knew, and they had thus been able to come straight into the compound, pick up Peter and Tom, and check the remaining four. Someone had signalled to our enemies that two men had got dressed for an escape while Sid and I were actually in the process of dressing. We retired to our kangs with bitter hearts.

Nothing happened for four days. Peter and Tom, who had been held in arrest near the Company Headquarters for the first night, were removed to the village. On the fourth day after their arrest, Chen Chung Hwei arrived at the Company Headquarters and sent for me. He informed me that he had positive information that I was one of those responsible for putting Peter and Tom up to an escape—they had actually planned it themselves—and that I had plans to escape myself. If I confessed now, I would save myself a great deal of bother and retain my freedom within the compound. If not. . . . He cannot have been very sure of his ground for, after haranguing me for half an hour, during which I declined to speak, he gave me twenty-four hours to think the alternative over, reminding me that I had received a warning twice before about breaking the regulations, and that I had already served a jail sentence for escaping. I thanked Heaven that their records were so bad that they knew nothing about my other escapes, and went back to the compound. I had an uneasy feeling that he was not bluffing; and I disposed of the more precious articles of my kit with Mr. Hobbs and Sergeant-Major Baker.

Twenty-four hours passed and I remained in possession of my limited liberty. On the following evening, Yang came down to my room after supper and told me to pack my kit. It was the 1st of March and the day had been bright and comparatively warm. However, the evening sky was filled with thick, grey clouds, and the temperature seemed to be dropping. As I left my room, carrying my bedding, eating bowls and spare clothing, an American major called out:

"Never mind! It's better to go to jail when the winter's over. You've managed to stay loose until the spring."

I was to remember his words later on that night.

After eight hours examination during the night, I was allowed to leave my examiners to get some rest—I thought. Chen had left us after two or three hours, handing over to a tall Chinese with an irritable face and spectacles in yellow-tinted frames. His name was Kung.

Kung followed me out on to the road and passed a remark to the guard commander who had joined us as soon as I left the house. We went back to the newly prepared cell-block (now on the south side of the road) and I expected to be put into the cell where I had stowed my kit on coming back into Pyn-Chong-ni, but I was mistaken. I was taken to an outhouse at the end of the cell block, stripped of my padded jacket, pushed inside, and locked in. I was uncomfortably aware that it had been snowing for several hours and that the temperature was well below freezing point. The outhouse was filled with old pieces of timber and a few agricultural implements but it had nothing to keep me warm. I took a certain amount of exercise but dared not sweat too much in case the moisture froze. If that happened, I should have frostbite before morning. I spent an extremely uncomfortable night, being unable to sleep because of the cold; my whole body ached with it. When the dawn came, I saw with dismay that it was still snowing.

I was not given breakfast that morning—but that might have been as much due to administrative inefficiency as malice on the part of Kung; I had been forgotten before in this way whilst in prison. An evening meal arrived just before dusk. Shortly after, Kung arrived to ask me if I had changed my mind about making a confession. I had not, and he went away without further comment. My second night was even more miserable than the first: I could not stop shivering; at times, my whole body shook uncontrollably. In the light of morning, I discovered that my fingers were blue and badly swollen: my numbed feet were in an even worse condition. I realized that I was already in the throes of cold shock.

In order to draw some attention to my condition, I refused breakfast when it came; and I refused the evening meal. Evidently the guard commander reported this, for Kung appeared again at dusk, to ask what was the matter with me. I showed him my fingers. He grunted, said nothing, and went away. The sentry on duty closed the door and my heart sank: I feared that I had not been successful. At this stage of our captivity, with our names released as prisoners, I had been sure that they would not carry the cold-treatment to such extremes as the loss of limbs from frostbite. I had believed that they would stop when the danger point was reached. I had become finally convinced of my error when the door was reopened and a medical orderly came in—a decent little chap whom Tony and Sid had named "Dolly". He took my temperature, examined my fingers and one of my feet by torchlight, and then went out again. Ten minutes later, he returned with a vile-tasting draught of medicine and instructions to move me elsewhere.

One never knew what to expect from the Chinese. I was placed in a room with a heated floor, so hot that I had to place most of my clothes underneath me in order to lie down in reasonable comfort. On the following morning, I wakened from a sound sleep to find that my shirt had a huge scorch mark on it!

My new circumstances were vastly improved. Firstly, Kung did not reappear—he had evidently had to report failure of his measures and did not want to lose more face. Secondly, some items of my kit were returned to me. Though I was not permitted tobacco, of course, I was given my pencil, but no paper of any sort. The fire was kept going under the floor for several days while the extreme cold lasted and, for two days, I continued to receive my draughts of medicine twice daily. My two daily meals were served to me regularly and, generally, fairly hot. Although they were Chinese-cooked and very monotonous, they kept my strength up. I did physical training exercises daily when the sentry was not watching.

One morning after I had been in jail a week, I went out rather earlier than usual to the latrine. To my surprise and pleasure, the first person I saw, walking up and down nearby, was Denis, who appeared to have reasonable liberty within the limits of the court-yard of the house in which he was kept. He was taking exercise, one end of his beat bringing him close to the crazy-walled latrine I was visiting. As the sentry was standing some yards away, throwing stones into the stream below us, I risked giving Denis a quiet hail which, by good fortune, he heard. In this way, we established first contact—later devising means of communicating more fully with one another, though we came near to discovery on several occasions. Denis was able to come outside whenever he wished, during daylight, but my visits to the latrine were at uncertain times—sometimes only once, sometimes not at all in a day, according to the whim of the guard.

Gradually, I pieced together what had happened to him. At the end of his six months sentence, he was visited by an unknown Chinese who reminded him that his sentence had expired, declaring:

"Although you have not fully recognised your errors, the Camp Headquarters believes that, inwardly, you are sorry for your mistake. As a result, your sentence in prison is over."

Denis began to think of getting his belongings together to move back to the compound.

"Fine," he said. "When shall I be leaving?"

"Your sentence is over," said the Chinese visitor. "You stay here."

So the same prison life had continued for Denis for another five months in exactly the same way except that, just before Christmas 1952, he had been moved here from the lonely hut he had occupied on a hillside just above the village containing the annexe to the Camp.

Now, it seemed, he was receiving visits from Big Chu who was trying to persuade him to sign a document that he would "co-operate" with the Camp Headquarters if they returned him to one or other of the compounds—by which they meant him act as informer for them on activities in the Camp. How they had underestimated Denis! It was a great comfort to have him close by.

I spent considerable time in observing the world through a hole in the wall. Whenever the sentry was otherwise occupied, I watched the Chinese as they passed each day, noticing changes in various appointments and routines, changes in accommodation, since I was last in solitary confinement.

Three things remained exactly as before: the morning and afternoon lessons when the soldiers of the guard company continued their reading and writing exercises: the daily hour of military training which was so badly done that I almost broke out on several occasions to show them how the instruction should be put over; and the daily "hate-and-love" meeting—always timed for the last hour of daylight. All the soldiers would assemble in the courtyard opposite to sing their Marxist songs—"The East shines Red", perhaps, or "The Chinese Volunteers cross the Yalu River"—or to practise a new one just arrived from General Headquarters. In between, there would be lectures in which one could distinguish the words "Mao-Tse-Tung", "Stalin", "Chou En-Lai", "Lenin", and other Communist leaders. The bright boys in the audience would clap loudly whenever these names were mentioned, sometimes rising to their feet and indicating to their fellows that they should do likewise. But other speeches would contain the names "Mi-goor", "Li-gee-way" (Ridgeway), Too-loo man (Truman). The love was changed to hate, cartoons of the hated faces might be displayed, fists would be shaken by the leaders and the soldiers would be pressed to imitate this action. The meeting often ended with a song about the international brotherhood of men.

If the Chinese were consistent in nothing else, they were in their attempts to maintain order within the compounds. By the early spring of 1953, a clear procedural pattern had emerged; a pattern that bore strong resemblance to the procedure used in disposing of political offenders in the countries behind the Iron Curtain.

When any individual or group within a compound had too great an influence; or when they were suspected of being involved in some breach of the regulations, those concerned were placed in solitary confinement. Two main factors influenced the speed and measures adopted to settle these cases: the importance of the case, and how full the cells were at the time! If there was plenty of room, and it was merely desired to keep the individual from the compound for a long period, he might not be examined for weeks or even months. If the case was really important and a "confession" desired for some special use, the examination would be set in hand without delay. If "confessions" were not obtained by stratagem—as with our Colonel—or by pressure, after a reasonable time, again the prisoner would almost certainly languish for many weeks, often months, without any attempt being made to arrange a trial. For the principle in all cases was the same: a prisoner was never released from the jail until he had made a confession of one sort or another; a trial was never held, sentence was never imposed, unless a plea of guilty to some charge—any charge—had been submitted. In this way, the Camp Headquarters could always justify their arrest.

My case was not exceptionally serious. The Chinese suspected that I had been engaged in escape activities; indeed, they had a certain amount of evidence that this was so, but it was evidence of a very limited nature and they could not reveal the source. Having failed to extract a confession from me, I was left for several weeks without further examination as a punishment for my lack of co-operation. When my case was taken up again, sufficient time had elapsed for them to try a different angle without losing face.

It was Chen Chung Hwei who finally came to see me, wearing an oily smile and avoiding any mention of my offences or of my confinement in the outhouse. As soon as he spoke, I knew that he had been sent to obtain some sort of confession. I waited to see if he was about to offer a bargain that I could accept.

"You are a very foolish man," said Chen Chung Hwei, as if chiding me for betting on the last horse in the race. "I think you are tired of being separated from your friends."

I agreed that I would like to see my friends again. Chen nodded.

"Now, I think you have broken the Camp regulations on several occasions?"

I made no comment, waiting for the proposal.

"For instance, you have appeared late on the morning roll-call four times. And you have sometimes been on the roll-call improperly dressed—not wearing your hat."

This was the bargain: I was ready to come to terms for my freedom. On the following day, I signed a statement that I had broken the regulations relating to roll-call and that I would try not to break them again. With a smile, Chen pocketed the documents.

"I will ask the Camp Commander to refer your case to your Company Headquarters for punishment," he said. "I think you may be released now that you have recognized your mistakes."

I was released on Easter Saturday. On Sunday, with great joy, I saw Denis walking down the path into the compound. It was a truly Happy Easter!

The first thing I noticed on my return was that a stout fence had been put round the compound. The first thing I heard was that agreement had been reached to exchange seriously sick and wounded prisoners and that the truce talks were expected to begin again. I began to wonder if this was why Denis and I had been released a good deal sooner than we had expected—Big Chu had been hinting for some time that Denis would soon be released but we had not really expected it in view of his refusal to sign the "co-operation" certificate. I soon observed that, since the date of the agreement by the Chinese to reopen truce negotiations, amenities in the compound had been greatly improved. The food was infinitely better; new washbowls were brought in, and there were many more of them. Tobacco rations were increased; razors were issued; three boxes of matches were given monthly to each prisoner. But there was more to come.

Unknown to us, Camp Headquarters controlled yet another compound in addition to Nos. 1 and 2 Companies and the annexe, (No. 4 Company). There was a No. 3 Company, containing those captives from the other rank camps who had proved so dangerous to the Chinese that they had required special confinement. Now, with the prospect of the outside world hearing first-hand details about our living conditions from the sick and wounded going out, the wretched lives of these men were suddenly improved a hundred-fold, and a number were permitted to visit us to engage in sports contests: softball, basketball, volley-ball, and British soccer. The visitors were accommodated in Pyn-Chong-ni village and thus saw No. 1 Company first. On the following day, the Sunday after Easter, they paid a morning visit to us and, later, some of us were allowed to visit No. 1 Company for the remainder of the matches on the ground in front of the schoolhouse.

I had often been told by the Chinese and North Koreans how bitterly our men hated their officers; how we despised them. This was always a remark which hurt, but I had never foreseen an opportunity to refute it such as occurred when we saw the men who were comrades from our own units.

Riflemen McNab and Agnew could not stop shaking hands with James. And from my Battalion there were Nugent and English of Sam's Support Company Headquarters, Sergeant Smith of C Company, and Corporal Bailey of the Anti-Tank Platoon. There were two gunners, and two Royal Marines from the Commando besides. We stood on our square after prolonged handshakes, quite unable to express fully our great joy at meeting again. Several minutes passed before we could even begin to exchange news.

The story that these men had to tell appalled us. Their rations throughout the previous autumn and winter had been the same as those given to men from Nos. 1 and 2 Companies in solitary confinement. Many of their numbers were still held separately after savage treatment during jail sentences, but there was hope that these sentences would be terminated now that general conditions were improving. Like us, they had been subjected to the minor punishments of standing to attention for long periods, beatings, and prolonged examinations. But the experiences of some of the men had been even worse. Godwin, Corporals Upjohn and Hartigan, Privates Flynn, Haines, and Lance-Corporal Matthews amongst others had been manacled and confined in boxes, six by three by three feet, for periods up to six months. Corporal Walters, my operator, had suffered such confinement for a lesser period; but had also been compelled to stand to attention for over forty hours on one occasion, until he collapsed. Fusilier Kinne, with whom I had been kept in the south during the late spring of 1951, had been kicked so savagely during a beating-up in jail that he had sustained a double-rupture and now, on his release, was no longer able to walk properly. Yet all these men had stood out against the demands of their captors and refused to "co-operate" on release from these torments. The notes our visitors had brought contained amplification of the accounts they had given us; and we could only hope that, at last, their sufferings were almost at an end.

The final agreement to exchange seriously sick and wounded captives led us to hope that at least four of those in our compound would be included—possibly more. There was a major who could not be cured of his beri-beri, in spite of the recent improvements in our diet; Sergeant Shahir, a Turk, who had suffered a terrible wound in his right thigh and buttock which was still incompletely healed; an American infantry lieutenant whose heart was weak; and Tom, whose loss of a leg surely entitled him to repatriation. There were others, of course: Anthony, with a wounded leg that regularly became inflamed and gave him a high fever, and Hector, the South African pilot, whose wounds required considerable attention on an operating table, were such cases. The lieutenant and the major left us, with all our good wishes. Tom was taken out amidst the smiles of the Chinese and a cheer from us. Sergeant Shahir was not even considered, though our doctors all tried hard to persuade the Company Chinese medical attendant—an ill-trained medical orderly, inadequately disguised as a doctor—of the seriousness of his condition.

We were now permitted to hear the radio news in English from Peking, daily, except when there was news of importance that our captors did not want us to hear. On these occasions something went wrong with the master radio at Camp Headquarters and no news came through. We did, however, hear the news of the exchange of the major and the lieutenant—but Tom was not mentioned. The names of the last men to be exchanged were broadcast and his was not amongst them. Our anger was intensified when we managed to obtain the news by chance that he was still in the village, having refused to sign a paper expressing gratitude to the Chinese for the good treatment he had received.

Undoubtedly, many of those who had been returned to the United Nations' side of the line were seriously sick or wounded men. But one could not help wondering if it was entirely a coincidence that a not inconsiderable number of them were men who had written "peace-fighting" articles praising their captors, and who now contributed articles to the London *Daily Worker*. For instance, one soldier—another prominent member of a self-styled "peace-committee"—was returned because he was suffering from a cracked rib, sustained whilst playing football for Camp No. 5, two weeks before the exchange.

To our delight, the truce talks were resumed with every sign of making progress. As the prospect of peace drew nearer, so our conditions improved.

In the second half of May, an inter-company sports contest was held in Camp 2—though the members of the annexe (No. 4 Company, where Joe and all the new officer prisoners were held) were not allowed to send down a team. However, No. 3 Company sent across representatives and they spent almost a week with us as a result. Fortunately, the Chinese permitted us to run the meeting ourselves and thus there were none of those setbacks which characterised the activities they supervised. MacT, a very able American captain, was an overall authority. Through him, the compound had expressed its determination that there should be no political flavour of any kind in the speeches or decorations provided by the Chinese. Niu, who was the co-ordinator for Camp Head-quarters in this instance, said that he was most hurt. Looking round the meeting, attended by the committee we had formed amongst ourselves, he said reproachfully:

"You demand that we shall not bring in politics! You demand that there shall be no movie-cameras to take propaganda pictures! I do not understand why you should adopt this attitude; why you should anticipate that we should be guilty of such behaviour. This is a sports meeting and a means of improving your daily life. Such improvements have been our aim consistently. We do not try to force you to accept our political views!"

He said it, without a smile, to men who, less than two years before, had been told that entertainments, including sports events, could only be arranged if they had a cultural motif—such as the exposure of America's aggression throughout the world.

Times had certainly changed.

From the extra rations given to us over the period of the sports meeting, we saved a certain amount for Coronation Day, the proximity of which we knew of from letters. No. 1 Company had prepared a considerable amount of rice and potato wine in secret vats; we had kept back saki. Denis and I were both warned on the evening of June 1st that any attempt to celebrate Coronation Day would result in severe punishment. No warning was given in No. 1 Company, but Sam was arrested early in the morning of June 1st, an event we connected with their preparations for the day.

Largely owing to Chang's anxiety not to have trouble at a time when the truce looked to be near, the Chinese staff remained out of the way while we had our Coronation meal on the evening of June 2nd. Our festivities went off without incident, though the Chinese looked in through the window at the outset to see what was happening. We were all ready for trouble, for we had put up the Queen's picture—hidden safely for just this moment—and a crown that Arthur made. The singing of the National Anthem, too, went off without incident for the first time in our captivity.

In No. 1 Company, however, Sun, supported by others, came in to the party given by the British under Paul—the next senior to Sam—and tried to snatch the cake made in secret from materials laboriously collected. All he actually got was the plate! So menacing was his reception by this time that he and the other Chinese leapt through the window and turned out the guard. After a good deal of confusion in the darkness—the lights were turned out at the main by Sulky Tien—the party dispersed, well-satisfied with their contribution to Her Majesty's celebrations.

The Marine Colonel had been returned to the compound after Easter, having suffered considerably during his eight months in solitary confinement. He had been stripped to the waist on a January night outside Ding's house. He had been beaten up. There had been demands for "confessions", and demands for certificates stating that he would "co-operate" on his return. Now, with the renewed prospect of peace, he came into the new compound for the first time. His release led us to hope, once again, for the release of our Colonel.

In the absence of the Marine Colonel, Denis had discussed with the next senior American Officer certain draft orders regarding the behaviour of the United Nations' captives in the event of a truce and the exchange of prisoners-of-war. It was felt that these were necessary in order that we should maintain a correct attitude towards the Chinese in all camps; that there should be neither fraternisation, nor acts of violence by hot-heads. An order was written and copies issued secretly. These were eventually circulated, unknown to the Chinese, to all camps except those holding recently captured prisoners in staging areas south of the Taedong River. In No. 1 Company, this order had been read out by Sam—the senior officer in the compound. In our compound, it was read out by the compound leader, the major of the United States Marines, sentenced at the same time as Denis in early 1952.

The Chinese got to know of both these incidents, though there were no Chinese present during the reading. Perhaps because they knew that we still retained control within the compounds, Camp Headquarters became particularly watchful and nervous. In late June, I was re-arrested.

On this occasion, I occupied the room formerly used by Denis in February-March. Four nights of examination followed, at which Chen presided until, to my delight, he was forced to retire when an abscess burst in his mouth. Moaning, spitting blood and pus, he hurried away and I was left with two Chinese I had never seen before. The fourth night's interrogation was the longest: I was questioned and harangued until dawn, when it seemed to me that my inquisitors were as exhausted as I was. Later, after I had slept for a time, and when I was quite alone, I tried to puzzle out what they were getting at.

The questions had referred to the Coronation, to the orders issued about our behaviour in the event of a truce, and to escape activities—concerning which they were evidently guessing. But none of these points had been pressed. I had been told to confess to my crime—yet nothing specific seemed to have been mentioned. I could not understand it.

Perhaps, in all the world, there is no race as accomplished as the Chinese at auto-suggestion. In retrospect, as the days passed without further visits from the interrogators, I felt that they had been trying to suggest something to me; and that this period of respite was to serve as one in which I could dwell on their words and realize what it was that I should confess to. After coming to this conclusion, I reached another: they believed me to be in possession of knowledge I did not possess. I began to feel as if I was reaching the end of a mystery story, the plot of which I had failed to follow in detail. Thus the words of the detective just prior to the denouement made no sense to me as they dealt with matters I knew nothing about.

On July 19th, I had the good fortune to find out what it was all about.

Visiting the latrine that day, I managed to make a brief contact with Guido, who had come down to the village on a labour detail in the hope that he would see me. He told me of an attempt to assassinate the Camp Commander.

"What's happened in the truce talks?" I asked him. "Are they coming together again after the release of the prisoners by Syngman Rhee?"

"Well," said Guido, "General Nam Il says——"

But I was not to learn what he said. At this crucial moment, an interrogator appeared and almost tore us apart in his fury. To my dismay, Guido was marched away and I was returned to my room. From that hour on, a Chinese orderly lived with me night and day, except during interrogation. I had no opportunity to make any further contacts with the compounds.

However, Guido's words had served to enlighten me on the question of my guilt.

A few days before my arrest, Guido and Walt, the American fighter-pilot, whilst on a detail chasing pigs that had escaped from the sty, managed to slip away. The two had stayed out several hours, making a general reconnaissance of the area in case the need to escape arose, returning of their own accord to the compound. Evidently the Camp Headquarters had been perplexed by this. To them, it seemed that these two had gone off for one of two reasons: either to escape—which they had not done; or to make contact with secret agents in the hills. It was a constant bogy of theirs that every boulder, every tree hid a secret agent—the Oriental

265

mind has been so busy with secret plots for centuries past that it has a congenital plot-complex. But though they were wrong about Guido's activities on this occasion, they had not been wrong, apparently, about the agent. On the day following my arrest—an arrest aimed at finding out who Guido had contacted, supposedly on Denis's and my orders—a Korean had walked up to Ding, as he left his house, and discharged a revolver at him. Unfortunately, he missed! The only injury Ding had sustained was a graze from stumbling in his flight from the would-be assassin—who had been killed by guards a few seconds later.

Having no evidence against me, but convinced by their imagination, the Chinese were now hoping that I would confess that we had sent Guido and Walt out to identify Ding, by means of a photograph, to the man who had been sent as executioner.

It began to look as if I was in a very difficult position. I could only hope that the proximity of a truce would continue to save me extreme pressure in interrogation as, very probably, it had saved me until then. How I wished I had heard what General Nam Il said!

When Big Chu visited me, I knew that something important was going to happen. After two hours' conversation one afternoon, he went away. At a quarter past eight that evening, I was taken before Ding and formally charged with being an accomplice before the fact in the attempt on his life. I had never seen Ding more angry; nor more frightened. He smoked incessantly and his hands trembled. He was a changed man from the Ding who had lectured to us so confidently early in 1952 and, before my arrival, threatened those who were "the people's enemies" with life imprisonment in labour camps.

Though Ding spoke for over an hour, what he actually said was this: a truce was near but I would not benefit from it as he had every right to hold me prisoner for committing an offence against international law. If I confessed to Denis's part, I would be released, having acted under his orders. But failure to confess would be interpreted as a hostile act, clearly demonstrating that I was in sympathy with the crime. It was up to me.

I returned to my cell with my escort, where I remained for several days without receiving further visits. Then, on the morning of July 27th a Chinese whom I had never seen before came into my cell carrying a long paper rolled up in his hand.

"Read that," he said.

I took it from him and unrolled it, expecting to see a sentence of imprisonment. It was a formal notice signed by General Wang Yang-Kung stating that the Truce would come into effect that morning at eleven o'clock. I asked the time and he showed me his wrist-watch. It was a quarter to eleven.

That night, Big Chu returned. He read a confession by the American Colonel who had signed the order on our conduct in the camps after the Truce came into effect. He added that the Colonel, the senior Major in No. 1 Company, and Sam had been given prison sentences—a year each for Sam and the Colonel, six months for the major. I asked to see Sam's confession.

"He has not confessed," said Big Chu. "He is a very stubborn man who refuses to admit his mistakes."

The whole point of showing me these confessions and sentences was to impress on me that they could keep captives under sentence after the others had gone home. I said nothing further and he left me.

I had one more interview with Ding; one final opportunity to confess, he said. Our Colonel, Denis, Sam and I—together with many others—were hoping for rewards when we returned home. This and not political conviction had led us to resist the truth our captors had put before us. We had sold ourselves; we were the proven enemies of the people. But even if we were returned home, let us not think that we had escaped from the power of the mighty Chinese people. They could punish us anywhere: they would follow us to the ends of the earth.

Ding's snake eyes smouldered, the nostrils on his thin nose dilated. I suddenly realized what it meant to him to find his captives slipping away from him still unconverted to Communism. All the pain and suffering he and his staff had inflicted on prisoners in the Camp had been to no purpose. We were going and there was nothing he could do to stop it.

267

On August 5th, the day the first prisoners started for home, I was released—the last member but one of the prisoners kept in isolation in the village. Ding had released me without a confession. He knew perfectly well that he had no right to keep me, though there had been times when I wondered how far he would take his bluff! Back at the Company Headquarters, I found that a new company commander had arrived—a man with tinted spectacles, nicknamed "Tints". He spoke to me through one of the interpreters.

"No trouble from you," he said. "Now there is peace in Korea. Soon you will go home to your dear ones to lead a peaceful life. No trouble from you and you will be all right."

I walked back down the path into the compound.

CHAPTER SIXTEEN

THE whole atmosphere in the compound had changed. Our attitude was one of impatience to depart, mingled with doubts that our captors would fulfil their part of the bargain. They had tricked us so often in the past, and we had looked forward to this day so much, that, now it had arrived, we could not bring ourselves to believe absolutely that it was all coming true. But day by day the Peking Radio news gave details of the exchanges at Panmunjon, describing the affecting scenes when their own men returned from the cruel United Nations Command—and the reluctance with which United Nations' captives left Communist custody to return once more to the harsh capitalist world!

One of the popular subjects for discussion was the expected visit of the Red Cross representatives—a subject which interested the Chinese as much as us, apparently. Big Chu made several visits to the Company Headquarters to ask individuals and small groups, called up from the compound, what their views were on this matter.

"What will happen when the Red Cross people come?" asked Chu. "What will you say to them?"

These questions were put to us by Chang and other interpreters, also. It was plain that they did not want to lose face by having to listen to reports about the days when it had been of no concern whether a prisoner lived or died; and the days, not so far back, when the fate of a prisoner removed from the compound was very uncertain.

Big Chu had more to say on the Red Cross.

"You must admit to them that we have done everything to improve your living standards. Why, only recently, the General Commanding all Prisoners-of-War held a conference in Pyoktong to examine your demands for improvements in your daily life—you sent two representatives from each company."

His listeners reminded him that such a conference was, indeed, "only recently". Memories went back further than May 1953.

"And if the Red Cross should come—and we are not frightened of showing the Red Cross how we have treated you—what could they do for you?"

The question of Red Cross comforts was raised.

"Cigarettes? Candy?" asked Chu. "But the Chinese Peoples' Volunteers can give you all you need of these things."

Sure enough, not long after my return to the compound, cigarettes and other comforts were issued in quantity. We had been accustomed to receiving one packet of cigarettes at feast times, such as Thanksgiving and Christmas. On the signing of the Truce Agreement, two hundred cigarettes had been given to each man. Now we had five hundred apiece; and with the cigarettes, many other good things. Two days later, Chang said, very casually, to our compound leader:

"By the way, there are some Red Cross gifts for you to collect. You can send a detail down for them if you want them."

The detail brought back American cigarettes by the crate, shaving gear, soap, matches, towels—many, many items, the familiar names of which suddenly brought home really near to us.

On August 17th we left our compound forever. A convoy of trucks arrived in the morning rain; we climbed aboard and drove down along the rough track to the road, passing for the last time the few houses near the compound fence, and the schoolhouse where the track joined the road.

Outside the main gate of No. 1 Company Compound, the trucks stopped; we were told to dismount and go inside. The square was flooded after two days of rainfall and we waded round it to ascend the steps at the western end of the promenade. The first person I met inside the schoolhouse door was Sandy, the Rifles doctor.

"The Colonel's back," he said. "Came back last night—he's over there."

I pushed my way through the crowds in the old library, squeezing between little knots of excited people who were exchanging the news of the two compounds. Near the end of the room, I stopped for a second to look at the Colonel, before taking my place in a queue of men who were anxious to shake his hand. He was very thin; his face was drawn and his eyes tired. Seeing him there, I really began to believe for the first time that the Chinese intended to release us.

He had been in solitary confinement for nineteen months.

Our departure was delayed for two days by the heavy summer rains. Sections of the road eastward to Manpo-Jin—the entraining point—had been washed away.

On the night before we left, Ron—the Australian pilot with whom I had escaped at Pyongyang—came back from Pyoktong. He had been to see the Red Cross with an American from the compound and he had a most interesting story to tell.

Apparently, the Red Cross had been scheduled to visit our Camp in a few days time. They had now been told that the repatriation programme had been accelerated and that we were due to move to the staging point at Kaesong over a week before the date originally notified, thus making it impossible for them to come to see us. Having no immediate inspection on hand, the team volunteered to come at once; but the Chinese had regretted that this was impossible: the road from Pyoktong had been washed away, they said. It was so impassable that they had taken Ron and the American along it to visit the Red Cross Headquarters—and sent them back the same way by truck. In spite of Big Chu's assertion, our opinion that the Chinese did not want the Red Cross to visit us was being steadily strengthened.

The two representatives from our Camp had been given a very limited opportunity to talk to the Red Cross team. Whenever a question was asked concerning conditions before the New Year 1953, the Chinese Red Cross representative insisted that the question was irrelevant, or that they had no time to conduct a long inquiry. It was plain that the characters of our captors had not changed in any way.

It now remained to be seen whether there had been a general acceleration in repatriation, or whether we were merely being moved south towards Kaesong to keep us away from the Red Cross.

On the morning of August 19th, the motor column moved out of Pyn-Chong-ni to the east.

It was an uneventful journey. The Korean people waved to us, apparently knowing that we were going home. No enmity was shown, except where this had been organized. In a few villages, small groups of youths had been assembled to shake their fists at us and throw stones as we passed. In the late afternoon we reached the rail centre of Manpo-Jin and, by dusk, a train was drawing us south.

On the platform at Manpo-Jin, where we entrained in box-cars, we saw Sam and others under sentence. Kept separately, they were put aboard the train under the arrangements of the Public Prosecutor, Chen Chung Hwei.

By the following evening we had reached Pyongyang, where we changed to another train. Next morning, we passed through the country across which I had escaped to the coast in the late summer of 1951—I noted the point at which I had crossed the railway line. In the afternoon, we drew up in Kaesong station, which I had not seen since I detrained there with my Battalion in November 1950, just prior to the advance north through Pyongyang.

Clear of the town, we passed between the green rice paddy and looked eagerly towards the south. There, unmistakable in the afternoon sunlight, was the huge, jagged range that lies between Kaesong and Seoul; a range that lies south of the Imjin River.

We were looking at territory held by our own side.

The staging area consisted of a series of tented camps south-east of Kaesong, set on the sides of the small, rolling hills that lie between the jagged peaks round the town and the river-shore. After one night in the first camp we entered, we were moved to another over the hill, but left the sergeants behind. In the new camp, Sam and the others, hitherto held apart, joined us. At last, we were all together.

The standard of the food deteriorated as the days passed, and it did not increase our happiness to discover that we had been brought south merely to mark time within sight of our own lines. The stratagem to keep the Red Cross from seeing us had worked. Our only advantage lay in the fact that we were near enough to have a better chance of escape if something went wrong.

After eight days, repatriation began from our camp. Every night, about ten of our number would go out; a proportion being taken from each nationality represented. Every day one hoped that one might be lucky that night, and after each disappointment, there was always the hope that to-morrow might bring better luck.

The Colonel was taken out one afternoon. We awaited his return anxiously, discussing what action we should take if, at the last moment, they tried to hold him back. He returned after about an hour and a half, however, to tell us that he had been taken over the hill to the sergeants' camp for an interview with Wilfred Burchett, correspondent of the newspaper *L'Humanite*, who had reported from the Communist side of the line for some considerable time. The interview had been designed to obtain the Colonel's views on his captivity—in particular his solitary confinement. The Colonel had given him a very concise reply:

"The food was rotten, and I was damned bored!"

That was not the story, however, which the Communist Press printed. Nor did they describe Burchett's reception by the sergeants. He had been booed from the moment of his entry through the gate just as he had been booed by our soldiers when he attempted to lecture them many months previously in Camp 1 on the Yalu River. On that occasion, they had had prior notice of his arrival

and had prepared miniature hangman's nooses, which they swung
to and fro as they sat on the ground beneath the platform from
which he spoke.

The Padre held a Church Service for the Protestants each Sunday
in the mat and timber structure which served us as a dining-hall.
On the second Sunday, we read Psalm 126:

> "When the Lord turned again the captivity of Sion"
> "Then were we like unto them that dream"
> "Then was our mouth filled with laughter"
> "And our tongue with joy. . . ."

I looked south to the hills beyond the Imjin River, and felt that
I ought to remember the words; and to remember all my many
prayers that had been answered during my captivity. Returning
to the increased tempo of life which awaited me once I crossed into
Sion, it would be so easy to forget.

It was Randle of the 8th Hussars who told me the news one
evening. He came running up from the dining-hall as I came down
the path from the hill above.

"They're calling the names," he said, "and they've called yours!
They're sending out a really big bunch to-night and you're in
it."

I was with the Colonel and Denis; Sam was just ahead of us; Sid
was coming back from the crowd in the dining-hall, who were
listening to Chang reading out the names.

"I'm down for repatriation, Sid," I said. "I can hardly believe
it."

"Neither can I," said Sid. "I'm coming with you!"

We collected our belongings and said our farewells. A truck
took us into Kaesong, where we were accommodated for the night
in an old temple. Many of our sergeants were already there, and
some of our men. I thought that I should find it difficult to rest but
I fell asleep almost as soon as I had pulled my blanket over me.

We rose at dawn and, by seven-thirty, were ready on a square outside the temple walls to embus in the convoy of trucks drawn up nearby. Before they were brought forward from the park to collect us, however, we had to have a final speech, reminding us of our good treatment, of our close bond of friendship with the Chinese Peoples' Volunteers, and our debt to them in being returned home safe and sound.

The trucks were called forward, drawing up a few feet from us. Steps were brought forward to save us the effort of clambering over the back. Chang got into a truck with Carl and me; he was very affable on the surface, and gave us the information that we were due to be handed over at nine o'clock exactly. Beneath his affability, I could see that he was very nervous. I have an idea that he feared that we might do him violence on the last lap of the journey.

The convoy drove through Kaesong and out on to the road that leads to Panmunjon. At a quarter to nine we stopped at a last check-post, run jointly by the Chinese and North Koreans. A Chinese inquired in a honeyed voice if we would care to refresh ourselves with some hot water. We declined. The truck moved on and entered a one-way circuit.

We passed the huge building in which the Truce Agreement had been signed; passed the area where, for over two years, the negotiators had discussed the terms of the Truce. Chang began to point out other places of interest, but my eyes did not follow his directions. Some little way ahead, and growing nearer every second, I saw an area into which helicopters were descending. The truck halted for a moment before turning right on to the main Panmunjon road, littered with good American boots and clothing which the returning Chinese and North Korean prisoners had cast off as they returned to their own side. Now I could see tents and the unmistakable white hats of American military police. Before I could realize it, we had pulled up near the tents, Chang had jumped off, and a pair of steps had been put against the back of the truck. An American began to call out our names as he and a Chinese checked them against a list.

I did not need my bundle of belongings any more. It remained by the seat on which I had been sitting. I suddenly realized that it was a very hot morning as I came down the steps into the sunlight to be clapped on the back by an American soldier who led me towards a wooden arch marked:

"Welcome to Freedom."

I passed underneath.

It was nine o'clock on the 31st of August 1953.

THE END